THE FANDOM FIFTY

Edited By
Diane Lee Baron

Firebringer Press
Baltimore, Maryland

The Fandom Fifty

Edited by Diane Lee Baron

Additional Editing by Phil Giunta & Steven Howell Wilson

Proofreading by Paul Balzé

Cover and Book design by Ethan H. Wilson

Cover Art by Todd Brugmans

ISBN: 978-1-948178-02-0

Published by Firebringer Press

Copyright © 2019 by Diane Lee Baron

CONTENTS

The Artists

Todd Brugmans

Suzanne Elmore

Laura Inglis

The Authors

Keith DeCandido

Michael Jan Friedman

Phil Giunta

Robert Greenberger

Susan Staneslaw Olesen

Don Sakers

Howard Weinstein

The Committees

Inge Heyer

Miriam Winder Kelly

Martha Sayre

Melissa James

Sharon Van Blarcom

Renee Wilson

Steven H. Wilson

Cindy Woods

Sandy Zier-Teitler

The Stage Crew

Robert Ahrens

Lewis G. Aide

George Laurence

The Entertainers

David Keefer

Cheralyn Lambeth

Dean Rogers

John Scheeler

Kathleen Scrimger

Weston Scrimger

Cynthia & Richard Siebigteroth

Lance Woods

The Klingons

Marc Okrand

Cheryl Koblinsky

The Masqueraders

Thomas Atkinson

Stephen Lesnik

Brian Sarcinelli

Cindy Shockey

Sarah Yaworsky

The SuperFans

Diane Lee Baron

T.A. Chafin

Daniel Corcoran (Renfield) & June Swords

Pat Duff

Phil Duff

Lisa Sponaugle

Patrick Sponaugle

Ariel Vitali

Martha Sayre

The Inheritors

Thalia Eigen, Grace DeWitte & Nellie Vinograd

Llyssa Holmgren

Ethan Wilson, Christian Wilson & Jessica Headlee

FOREWARD

The Fandom Fifty introduces some of the most diverse individuals inhabiting this end of the galaxy. These are true fans, people who were placed under the spell of science fiction and who wanted to make that magical feeling last. Most of the fans were initiated into fandom via *Star Trek's* original, Sixties incarnation, while others were mesmerized by the first *Star Wars* movie. But no matter their awakening into SF, they all ended up in the same place—the science fiction conventions of Maryland.

These conventions, or *cons*, are the repositories of the genius and creativity that has been cultivated by science fiction TV shows, movies and books. Admittedly, we who are profiled in this book are *nerds*. We are fascinated with the milieu and minutiae of science fiction universes. If we were given our choice, we might even want to live in those fantastic places and times. But, since we can't, we go to cons. We socialize, mix, and mingle with others who are like-minded and who give our our own brands of weirdness a pass. And it's fun. We get to spend long weekends talking and playing in our sandbox, and everyone is welcome to join us.

As if it weren't enough that we have lovely hotels in which to congregate, costume competitions (also called masquerades), "Ten-Forward" dances, and singers, including a favorite Maryland act called the Boogie Knights. There are panels about star systems, favorite tv shows, writing and costuming ("Cosplay" to more newly minted fans.).

Science fiction writers wander the hallways by the dozens and are treated as the royalty they should be. Fans dress as their favorite characters, either from popular culture, or from places that only exist in their imaginations. Stars from favorite shows and movies entertain with finesse. And fans socialize, meeting up with old friends or making new ones with only a smile and a hello.

It takes a lot to put on a convention. I put on a one-day convention in the Eighties in Connecticut. It drained my will to live, so I know hard work when I see it. Many of the people in this book are the behind-the-scenes folks who do the dirty work: registration, program book, security, technical assistance, programming, masquerade, art show, live events and on and on. And these people do it for free. They do it because it gives them pleasure to put on an event that others love to attend. In Maryland, Shore Leave has passed its 40th anniversary while Farpoint has passed its 25th. That's dedication.

My purpose in writing *The Fandom Fifty* was to honor people who have participated in the Maryland conventions, each in their own unique way. Some folks are in the book just because they are such enthusiastic fans. Many of the people interviewed could have easily fallen into two or more of the categories listed. The conventions have become a way of life for many, including me, and it seems impossible to imagine a world without cons. Lifelong friendships have formed, business associations have been created and creative ideas have been born at the Maryland cons. They are villages in a magical land. Enter with an open heart and an inquisitive mind.

Diane Lee Baron

September, 2018

ACKNOWLEDGEMENTS

It takes quite a team to assemble an interview book such as this one, and I'd like to recognize the following individuals:

Lewis G. Aide-for his hard work with all the photographs, and his technical assistance as well.

Paul Balze-for his work as Proofreader of this book.

Todd Brugmans-for the stylish retro cover of this book.

Stephen Lesnik- for the use of his photograph of Sarah Yaworsky.

Ethan Wilson-for his work as the Book Designer.

Steven H. Wilson & Phil Giunta-for editing and publishing this book under the Firebringer Press banner. Their dedication to providing a place for beginning writers to be published has afforded me the joy of seeing this book become a reality.

DEDICATION

This book is dedicated to my mother, Lois Gertrude Baron, who believed in me and understood me like no one else ever could.

This book is also a nod to all of my convention friends, who make me feel loved and valued whenever we are together.

Lastly, this book is a thank-you to Marilyn Mann, Sharon Van Blarcom and the Wilson family, who have always welcomed my contributions to their conventions and promoted me in my efforts.

THE ARTISTS

Todd Brugmans

On His Real-Life Job:

I am a Brokerage Entry Writer for a company who reports to U.S. Customs what contents are being imported into the country. I am responsible for correctly identifying and reporting the tariffs and fees associated with bringing goods to the United States.

On His Personal History:

I had a mostly positive upbringing, though I have had my share of health issues over the years. I've had some great successes in my life, attaining Eagle Scout, and serving as a leader in the junior Masons (DeMolay). And of course, I have my love of all things science fiction.

I hold a Bachelor's Degree in Fine Arts: Multimedia Discipline from Kean University in New Jersey. My skills range from drawing to basic video editing, sculpture, and photography to creative writing. There is still so much to learn.

Many of the celebrity caricatures I've drawn have some element of humor to them. When I share the artwork with others, I get a real kick when they "get" the joke. I started with just a pen and some scratch paper, worked my way through many sets of colored pencils, and now I've developed a sense of style using computer software.

My second attempt at being married has been my most rewarding experience to date. A few years ago, I suffered a stroke and a heart attack. That was my most terrifying experience to date! I credit some of my closest friends and my wife with the fact I'm still here and still producing fan art.

Through my art, I have helped charities with their fund-raising efforts by offering celebrity-autographed original artwork.

On His Introduction to Fandom:

I was roughly ten years old when I discovered fandom. My older cousin was starting college at Rutgers, and the two of us went to an exhibit of science fiction costuming in New Brunswick, NJ. We saw two of the space suits used in *2001*, a couple of *Star Trek* uniforms, a few outfits from *Planet of the Apes*, and a Sandman's uniform from *Logan's Run*. While we were there, we picked a flyer for a local *Star Trek* club, U.S.S. *Avenger*, part of Starfleet International.

On His Introduction to Conventions:

My first of the full-blown media conventions was a Creation Events show I attended when I was 15. I remember being initially overwhelmed by just how many people I met and talked with. It wasn't until after I could drive that I started truly embracing the sci-fi convention bug. I recall there was a show in Atlantic City, NJ, where I heard of a new series being presented on a fledgling network, and executive producers Doug Netter and John Copeland were guests at the convention. The first footage we saw was a test model of a fighter operation in outer space. The Series: *Babylon 5*.

On His Years in Fandom:

Officially? 38 years. I really didn't start making a name for myself in the con-circuit until 1998 or so. I had been drawing cartoons inspired by chat groups and making them available online in the early days of social media. I made a habit of drawing caricatures of the actors and asking them to sign those, so I'd have something wholly unique. I often got very positive feedback from the actors and encouragement to continue what I was doing.

On Influential Media:

One of the greatest inspirations I can hold up is the original *Muppet Show*. Jim Henson had a showcase where humor was mixed with some of the most creative acts of the mid-to-late Seventies and into the Eighties. There were musicians, artists, puppets... It was magical.

Star Trek, Babylon 5, Doctor Who and *Star Wars* helped to solidify and diversify my fanhood experience, as well as a Japanese cartoon called (in America) *Star Blazers*. I later learned it was called *Space Battleship Yamato*, but it had real-life issues, with characters struggling with alien technology that didn't always work out, and there were characters who died (unheard-of in most American cartoons). It was through watching shows like these I came to appreciate a really good story.

On Becoming a Convention Artist:

I got started by submitting my artwork through contests being run by the conventions. The contests were looking for a new logo, a mascot, or just some side filler art for the program. I wasn't always successful, but I kept at it, and continued to develop my illustration skills so I could produce the desired results. I have a reputation for getting work done quickly, and that has helped with being able to deliver to the organizers of these events, who are operating with tight deadlines. [Editor's Note - Todd created the Farpoint Convention mascot "Farp" via one of these contests.]

On Creating Program Covers:

The process for doing program cover art relies largely on what the convention would like to see. In these cases, I work to build on the theme for that year. There are some conventions which offer me free rein. I did a series of covers which covered the sub-genres of science fiction. One year was all about aliens, another year it was about robots. I did an epic space battle and mad scientists. In each of these covers I worked in some degree of humor, which I enjoy mixing into science fiction. When the covers call for a more serious work of art, I'll step up to the plate.

On Book Covers:

I start with the author's vision of how they would like their work to be represented. I haven't had the luxury of reading the work I'm doing the cover art for, and that helps me remain objective with my initial drafts.

Sometimes I'll take chances with the design details; some work better than others. In the end, I'm not satisfied until the author is. After all, it's their work of art, I'm just supplying the window-dressing. I have done covers for two books: *Heroic Park* by Lance Woods, and *Gal Wonder* by Diane Lee Baron.

On His Renaissance Fair Comic Book:

My friend Dan Kostelec is a performer at several Renaissance fairs, performing in the guise of "Willy Shakespeare" for his half hour "interpretations" of the Bard's plays, usually with a bizarre twist. The shows require audience participation; he will feed lines to an unsuspecting person, and hilarity ensues. Over the past few years, I had been drawing t-shirt designs inspired by his unique versions of the plays. One day, Dan came to me and said, "Let's do something more ambitious." The end result was the book version of Dan's *Julius Caesar: Beware the Ides of March of the Penguins.* I illustrated it cover to cover. The comic book features likenesses of William Shatner, Peter Capaldi, Leonard Nimoy, and Marty Feldman, to name a few. It was self-published at a local Staples, and, though our first attempt, it was a successful first effort. We're working on developing a second comic in the near future: *Macbeth: Death by Fluffy Kittens.*

On Starfleet:

I have been a member of Starfleet, off-and-on, for easily 25 years. I have held active positions on three chapters, U.S.S. *Highlander*, which used to be based in Frederick, MD, U.S.S. *Avenger*, based in North Brunswick, NJ, and U.S.S. *Challenger,* based in Seaside Heights, NJ. Over the years I have held many leadership positions, ranging from the chapter level to a position on Starfleet's executive committee for a year.

I was second in command on the *Avenger* for several years. These days I'm content with being a chief bottle-washer and P.I.T.A. (Pain in the A$$) officer aboard the *Challenger.* I'm currently in charge of the Operations Department, which basically includes creative ways to promote the chapter to the world at large and assisting with membership recruiting and retention. I hold the fictional rank of Rear Admiral. That and a glass of water will still leave you with something to drink.

On His Favorite Con Activities:

A lot of it is reuniting with friends I don't often get the opportunity to hang around with. Some of it is my never-ending quest to meet the actors who have fueled my imagination, collect their autographs, and come away with a story to tell. I am fascinated by their behind-the-scenes glimpses into how these shows get produced.

For the Maryland conventions, there is a special restaurant trip my wife and I make without fail, and we've always got some friends in tow. It's an Italian restaurant called Liberatore's in Timonium. If you have never been, I *highly* recommend it. If you have, I may see you there.

I love the Masquerade, and I enjoy getting to meet the authors. The vendors are ever enticing me to part with my money. And I enjoy sitting in on the charity auctions, especially when I have contributed something to auction off for a good cause.

On His Favorite Con Story:

My first story is from when I was attending the Voice of the Resistance Convention in California. It was a showcase for *Babylon 5* fans, and the majority of the cast was in attendance. This was the largest gathering of the chat-group community for *Babylon 5* as well. The chatters assembled for dinner one night outside the convention restaurant on the patio. While we were there, I launched into a comedy routine inspired by one of the characters. Someone had a tape recorder handy and caught the entire shtick. We glanced into the restaurant and saw several members of the cast sitting down to have supper. Andreas Katsulas came outside for a cigarette break, and we seized upon the opportunity to play the recording for him. After finishing his cigarette, he took the young lady with the tape player by the hand, saying "Peter (Jurasik) has to hear this," and whisked her inside to the table where Peter Jurasik, Bill Mumy, Wortham Crimmer, and Andreas were seated. Peter listened to the recording, which initially he thought to be something he'd said (I can imitate Peter's character fairly well), then he realized it wasn't him, but some idiot out on the patio. He got up, and we had a memorable moment. He came outside to our patio table, he and I traded pleasantries, and he told me when I'm imitating his character, I just had to slow my delivery just a little bit, and I'd have it EXACTLY. It was truly a once-in-a-lifetime moment.

The other story is more recent. At Shore Leave 39, we had the pleasure of having Kevin Sussman (Stuart from *The Big Bang Theory*) as a guest. I had been contracted to do a mock comic book inspired by his character. It was auctioned to benefit the Julian Fleming Memorial Fund, which assists with the rising cost of healthcare for terminally ill children. I watched as the bidding rose to record numbers for Shore Leave. My heart was overjoyed to see a record-breaking $1400.00 bid for the artwork, which Kevin was gracious enough to autograph. That I had a part in helping raise funds for a cause near and dear to my heart is a memory I will forever cherish.

On His Favorite Con Guest:

Do I have to narrow it down? I've had so many great experiences over the years. Picking one would seem hardly fair. Some of the guests have been very insightful, some downright friendly, and others have been so outrageous that they make memories everywhere they go. I've met Ray Harryhausen, the master of stop-motion animation. I've met film-icons like Ernest Borgnine and Leslie Nielsen. There was John Barrowman, and several of the actors who've played *Doctor Who*. I've met Torri Higginson of *Stargate: Atlantis* fame, Jewel Staite of *Firefly* fame, and Michael Hogan from *Battlestar Galactica*… the list defies narrowing down.

On His Reason for Attending Cons:

Initially, it was the convenience of having some fantastic fan-run shows within a few hours' drive of my home. These days, I feel I'm part of something more, having shared my artwork with the conventions. I have made so many friends among the true heroes: the convention staffers. Their tireless efforts to put on great shows is nothing shy of miraculous, and I get to play in their world.

On Something Others May Not Know About Him:

I present myself to friends and strangers alike as an open book. I have a wicked-sarcastic side, and sometimes I will push the boundaries of good taste. That being said, I really don't like Mexican food. Tex-Mex I can handle to a certain degree, but Mexican cuisine, I'll pass, thanks.

Jean Suzanne Elmore

On Her Real Life:

I am retired. I worked as a Credit Investigator and was employed by WFBR Radio. I also worked as a Dividend Clerk, a Substitute Teacher, Receptionist, Secretary, and finally Billing Clerk before I retired. I loved exploring opportunities and learned from each job and the people I worked beside.

I grew up near where I live now in Baltimore County, Maryland. I was joyously married for 31 years, two months to Michael W. Elmore, who passed on from this world in July 2003. My husband was a Trooper with the Maryland State Police for over 35 years. I have been privileged to live with a number of kitties and currently reside with Cali, who is a sweet companion and sometimes irritant.

On Her Introduction to Fandom:

My introduction to fandom was reading about it in several publications, including newspapers, *Starlog* and *TV Guide*.

On Her Introduction to Conventions:

Starbase Baltimore was my first convention. I enjoyed most of it, but it was not what I expected. Fortunately, less than two months later, I attended Shore Leave II and found fandom, friendships in the *Contact* group and so many new avenues to explore. I have been part of fandom for over 39 years.

On Her Current Connection to Fandom:

I currently am on staff at Farpoint, and I attend and often volunteer for Shore Leave.

On Influential Media:

My interest in *Star Trek*, where a diverse team of individuals worked in concert for a common goal, brought me into a new group of people where I learned new skills, used skills I had developed in new venues, and in general had my universe extended beyond what I had been living. I made lasting friendships and found support in times of need.

On Convention Jobs:

I've worked with Security, Costume Call (Masquerade), Publicity, Art Show, and Registration. I was the assistant to Lew Aide of Conventional Magic on Saturday nights for over seven years. I worked on panels, special events and on the program books. I even worked as a runner. I enjoyed those I worked with, and, for most of the time, I enjoyed the job I was doing, but I especially loved Masquerade. I began as a spotter for Masquerade and did most jobs from security to backstage then co-chaired and finally chaired Masquerade for years. I have seen huge changes in how the conventions are presented and run. It's been a joy and privilege to participate.

On Art Shows:

I began by entering small etchings on glass in the Art Show around Shore Leave III or IV. I have also entered colored pencil drawings. I painted on glass for years and finally have entered fascinators and jewelry I design and construct. I loved painting on glass, notably the designing and final product. I painted many dragons, starships, and *Star Trek*-inspired pieces, but I was very proud of "Lady Glenna," a piece featuring a knight, lady and dragon that eventually sold at Pendragon Gallery in Annapolis. I like designing and then creating something original.

On Acting:

I participated in many showcases and skits in the early years including *The Best Little Pon Farr Palace on Vulcan* and *Star Trek IV: The Voyage the Hell Home*. Eventually I created Con Artists, who presented a number of skits or one-act plays for several years. We began as the entertainment at Costume Call at Shore Leave with *Triumph*, a one-act *Star Wars* piece with Luke, Leia and Han. My husband, Mike, did the props. We added to the group each year and thus did more ambitious works with Mike creating larger and more ambitious props. When we transported the props to the conventions, Mike called our car "the Clampett Mobile" saying we looked like *The Beverly Hillbillies* going down the road. I loved my group and the rehearsals as much as the actual presentations. Our group included Tom Atkinson, Gerry Sylvester, David Gordon (the original players), Cindy Lewis Woods, Betsy Childs, Tori Holmgren, Bill Holmgren, Laura Bolling, Bram Crocker and Chuck Coates.

On Favorite Con Activities:

Saturday night Masquerade and Ten Forward are the highlights for me. But each convention has special activities to anticipate and enjoy.

On a Favorite Con Recollection:

I loved working on Masquerade but especially standing in the wings, sending the contestants onto the stage. Some were terrified but determined, some excited and proud of their work, some filled with joy and anticipation. They had imagined, designed, created and now were displaying their work—this was so exciting for me. My favorite was at an OctoberTrek entry—Number 21, Debra Mischke in "His Mother's Green Coat." After the death of Jim Henson, Debra came to us with this tribute. She took the stage in darkness, and when the spotlight hit her, Debra was standing in a full-length, hooded green cloak. She stood with her back to the audience. When she turned around, the hood was down revealing a green and yellow cap (reminiscent of Big Bird); the cloak held open revealed a mural of all of Henson's popular characters. The announcer said, "In keeping with the tradition of Jim Henson, most of the materials used in making these murals were leftover scraps found around the house." The entire audience came to its feet and erupted in applause in praise and support of this loving effort. That memory can still bring me to tears-

Thank you, Debra, and all the wonderful participants who entertained us with their heartfelt endeavors, like the Seven Dancing Raisins, the frightening Alien, the ladies who recreated our lovely heroines, and so many more.

On Attending Maryland Conventions:

I look forward to Shore Leave where I began in fandom. I enjoy the hotel, and there is lots of parking. I have many friends there to visit, and I know I will enjoy the programming each year. I attend Farpoint, where I am still on staff, and everyone feels like family. I always anticipate that something exciting is waiting to happen, even if we are snowed-in.

On Inspirational People:

The people who inspired me were Nancy Kippax, Bev Volker and Terri Sylvester, who encouraged my efforts in art and writing, and Marion McChesney, who changed my outlook on my life. There are many more friends who have changed my life by being a part of it—that's what fandom is really about.

On Things Unknown About Her:

That's a secret!

Laura Inglis

On Her Real Life Job:

I'm an underwriter.

On Her Personal History:

I live in western Maryland. My hobbies are trading cards, art, sports, hiking, and conventions.

On Her Introduction to Fandom:

It was Starfleet, I think. They were the only group of fans in my area. Fandom wasn't like it is now, where there are organized fans everywhere.

On Her Introduction to Conventions:

During college I attended a Creation Convention in NYC. *Next Gen* had just started airing, and the guests were Marina Sirtis and Sylvester McCoy. I had never heard of *Doctor Who*, but I thought this guy who played the spoons was very entertaining.

On Her Years in Fandom:

20+

On Her Connection to Cons:

I run the dealers' room for Farpoint and the Mid-Atlantic Nostalgia Convention.

On Working the Dealers' Room:

I don't think attendees realize how long it takes some vendors to set up. There are vendors who need at least eight hours to set their display. Keep in mind that doesn't include the time it takes to load up your vehicle to begin with. I have always had a fairly simple display, but I'll help some of my dealer friends when I can just because it is a lot of work; and, if you sell comic books, it's lifting a lot of heavy boxes.

As the person in charge, I make sure that I get there before all the vendors to ensure the tables are where they should be and the tables are labeled with everyone's name.

On Her Artwork:

I use mostly markers and colored pencils, but I also paint every once in a while and do some digital work. My favorite subjects include robots, spaceships, monsters and sports.

Firebringer Press has used my art for the covers to *By Your Side* and *Testing the Prisoner*. I've created licensed artwork for over 50 trading card sets including *Batman*, *Space 1999*, *Thunderbirds*, *Doctor Who*, *Transformers* and *Star Trek*.

On Convention Art Shows:

I put pieces in the Farpoint art show once in a while, but I like having a table with my art, so I can talk to people about it. Having it in an art show seems very disconnected to me.

On Influential Media:

Star Wars is a huge influence, and cartoons in general.

On Her Favorite Con Activities:

Unless there's a panel I really want to see (rare these days), I like staying on the exhibit floor, especially at bigger shows like San Diego Comic-Con, or Awesome Con where there are so many great artists and fan groups to walk around and chat with. Even the *Star Wars* community is really stepping up their game at shows like Awesome Con with such a great variety of characters, droids and props (the landspeeder and the *Millennium Falcon* cockpit) to get photos with. Of course, I make sure I allow time for shopping, too.

On Her Favorite Con Story:

We were set up next to Majel Barrett-Roddenberry at a show. My dog Buster was just a puppy. Majel loved him and insisted he sit with her for a while. She even tried putting a sharpie in his paws and getting him to sign autographs. One night we were coming back from a walk and went past the bar, where Majel was holding court. She saw us and called us over. She had saved some of her steak dinner for Buster and sent her assistant up to the room to get it.

On Con Guests:

It's hard to pick just one favorite as I've met so many over the years. I like people involved in the animation industry, either as voice actors, artists or producers. I enjoy hearing the stories of how things are done, and the voice actors are always a lot of fun. I especially enjoy people like Jim Cummings and Rob Paulsen, who have voiced just about every character there is and can change voices in the middle of a conversation.

On the Reason She Attend Maryland Cons:

They are local, it's nice to not to have to travel very far once in a while.

The Authors

Keith R.A. DeCandido

On His Real Life Job:

Freelance writer, freelance editor, martial arts teacher.

On a Brief Personal History:

Brief, huh? I'll try... I was born in 1969, my parents—who were SF/fantasy fans—fed me a steady diet of Tolkien, Le Guin, Heinlein, and Wodehouse when I was too young to know better. I was doomed. I started writing when I was six, but they didn't start paying me for it until I was 20, when I was much better at it. I started attending conventions here and there in high school and college, and started seriously attending them in my 20s, when I was part of a public-access talk show called *The Chronic Rift* that ran in New York from 1990-1994. (In 2008, we revived the *Rift* as a podcast.) In 1993, I became an associate editor of SF/F at a book packager. In 1994 I sold my first short story, and in 1998 I sold my first two novels. Since then, I've been a prolific fiction writer, editor, nonfiction writer, and more. My work has been nominated for awards, and even won one once, and hit a best-seller list or two. I attend an average of 15-20 conventions a year. In addition, in 2004, I realized I needed to do battle against the aging process when I turned 35 and started taking up martial arts. I'm now a third-degree black belt in karate, and in addition to writing and editing, I also teach karate to kids in various locations around New York City.

On His Introduction to Fandom:

I kinda stumbled into it. My parents were huge fans but never part of capital-F Fandom. I hit a few cons when I was a teenager out of curiosity, then got aggressively into it by way of helping promote the TV show. Once I started working in the field, getting involved in fandom became kind of important, both on a personal *and* professional level.

On His Involvement in Fandom:

Mostly attending conventions, not to mention writing fiction in the worlds of things that I and others are big fans of. My bibliography includes fiction based on worlds that have huge fan bases, from *Star Trek* to *Supernatural* to *Firefly/Serenity* to *The X-Files* to *World of Warcraft* to *Sleepy Hollow* to *Orphan Black*.

On Attending Maryland Cons:

When we were looking for cons to do to promote the *Rift* in the 1990s, we looked at ones we could drive to from New York. One year, I went to Balticon, and another year we went to Shore Leave. In 2000, I had sold my first *Star Trek* fiction, so I thought it would be good to attend both Farpoint and Shore Leave; and Balticon has continued to be an important part of my con-going. Also a few years ago, (Re)Generation Who started up, and they've been kind enough to have me as a guest each year so far.

Honestly, at this point, the four main ones I go to—Farpoint, (Re)Generation Who, Balticon, Shore Leave—have become homes away from home. Going to each one of them is like a family reunion. I have a lot of fans at all of them, plus I get to meet cool people. Balticon in particular is one I'm fond of and never miss because it's at Balticon in 2009 that I met the woman I married in 2017...

On His Years at Maryland Cons:

Since the early-to-mid-1990s, so around 25 years or so.

On Becoming a Boogie Knight:

I've been a percussionist since college. In the past I've played with a few bands, most notably the Don't Quit Your Day Job Players from 1993-2000. In 2005 at Dragon Con I was watching the Boogie Knights perform, and I thought that they could use a percussionist, so I offered. They accepted, and I made my debut with them at Farpoint in February 2006. Performing on stage is always wonderful, whether I'm doing it as a writer, musician, panelist, whatever. Our songs are also very silly and fun, and we always have a blast up there.

On His Favorite BK song:

Probably "House on Pooh Corner," a parody of "House of the Rising Sun" taking place in the Hundred Acre Wood.

On a Funny Moment While Performing:

With the Knights? Probably Claudia Christian, who was on after us, joining us on the tambourine during "Arthurian Pie."

On Favorite Con Activities:

I enjoy the panels, workshops, and performances that I do. I love talking about things I'm passionate about, and I love hearing from other people about them.

On Science Fiction Writers and Writing:

Two of my closest, dearest friends are fellow genre writers—in fact, both stood by me and Wrenn at our wedding: Laura Anne Gilman and David Mack. Plus, there's the four I mentioned above, Ursula K. Le Guin, Robert A. Heinlein, J.R.R. Tolkien, and P.G. Wodehouse. Others would include Harlan Ellison, Mary Shelley, Alfred Bester, George Pelecanos, David Simon, and also comics writers Chris Claremont, J.M. DeMatteis, Ann Nocenti, and Walt Simonson. As for specific books, I'd have to single out *Frankenstein, or the Modern Prometheus* by Shelley as my favorite novel and *Dancing on the Edge of the World* by Le Guin as my favorite nonfiction book.

On a Book He Recommends:

Frankenstein, because it started the whole thing.

On Influential TV Shows:

Well, the biggest kinda has to be *Star Trek*, since a) I've been watching it since birth and am still a huge fan of the franchise and b) between fiction and nonfiction, I've written more about *Trek* than any other single subject, I think. Two others would have to be *Doctor Who* and *Farscape*, the former out of sheer fangooberishness (though I do have a tiny number of professional *Who* credits) and the latter because not only was I a huge fan of it, but I got to script the "season five" comics series in collaboration with series creator Rockne S. O'Bannon.

On His Favorite Con Recollections:

How do I narrow it down? Talking politics in the midst of the 2008 presidential election with George Takei, Walter Koenig, Mike Baron, and Peter David? Moderating a panel on the Fifth Doctor's first season with Peter Davison, Matthew Waterhouse, Sarah Sutton, and the magnificent Janet Fielding? Being George Takei's backup singer (along with Peter David and Robert Greenberger)? Being on a panel with Samuel R. Delany at San Diego Comic-Con and impressing him with what I said? Moderating the official *Farscape* tenth anniversary at San Diego with Ben Browder, Claudia Black, Rockne S. O'Bannon, and Brian Henson? Being put on a panel with Harlan Ellison, Peter David, and Scott Edelman, which was just Harlan carrying on while Peter, Scott, and I sat there letting him go? Being at a room party when Jo Walton dumped an entire drink on David Brin's head? Being at the infamous final Disclave when the hotel was flooded? Managing the Byron Preiss booth at San Diego when we had all kinds of luminaries appearing at the booth, most notably Stan Lee his own self? Debuting the Don't Quit Your Day Job Players' first CD at Philcon 1996? Craig Shaw Gardner at NECON in 90-degree heat outdoors seeing Neil Gaiman in his leather jacket and shouting, "HEY! NEIL! WE'LL STIPULATE THAT YOU'RE COOL! TAKE OFF THE FUCKING JACKET!"? Doing a Boogie Knights concert with both Robert Asprin and Peter David in the audience? Doing a panel on research with Terry Pratchett at WorldCon? Ultimately, I think the winner has to be when I was the subject/victim of a comedy roast by my fellow *Trek* scribes at Shore Leave in 2009.

On Favorite Con Guests:

Nathan Fillion, because he stood up at several conventions and sang the praises of my novelization of *Serenity*. He was also an absolute sweetheart when we met at the Big Damned Flanvention in 2005. Close second would be two married couples: John Billingsley and Bonita Friedericy, and Armin Shimerman and Kitty Swink, who are four of the finest humans extant.

On Con People Who Impacted Him:

Oh, that's easy: Wrenn Simms and Meredith Peruzzi. They're two of the most important people in my life, and I met them both at cons.

On Something People May Not Know About Him:

I appeared in four Gilbert & Sullivan plays in grade school: *The Mikado, HMS Pinafore, The Pirates of Penzance,* and *The Gondoliers.* In *Penzance,* I played Major-General Stanley, and yes, little eight-year-old me performed "Model of a Modern Major-General" half a dozen times on stage in front of people.

Michael Jan Friedman

On His Real Life Job:

I teach in the NYC school system.

On His Personal Life:

I grew up in Queens, NY and currently live in lovely Port Washington, NY, on the north shore of Long Island. I have a wife and two adult sons. My hobbies are running, kayaking, and single-wall handball.

On His Introduction to Conventions:

As a writer, I gradually received some invitations. I think Bob Greenberger engineered the first one to a Maryland con.

On His Current Connection to Fandom:

I write books, comics, and occasionally for the screen—almost always science fiction or fantasy. Half of my 76 books have the name *Star Trek* on them.

On Becoming a Writer:

I'd always aspired to be one. When Isaac Asimov came to speak at my college and said he was a full-time writer, I knew I had a chance—like one in a million, if I was lucky, but still a chance. I wrote in college and then on weekends and vacations after I got a job, and finally finished a book back in '81—an heroic fantasy called *The Hammer and The Horn*. Warner Books was just launching their Questar imprint and they needed titles, so they bought it. Boom—I was a writer!

On Influential People and Media:

Edgar Rice Burroughs, Ray Bradbury, Poul Anderson. *Lord of the Rings. The Once and Future King. Star Trek. Twilight Zone.* Comics like Green Lantern, Thor, Avengers, X-Men.

On Years in Fandom:

About thirty.

On Activities Outside of Maryland Conventions:

Plenty of other cons around the country, including the San Diego and New York Comic-Cons. Book store appearances.

On Favorite Con Activities:

Meeting fans across an autograph table. Mystery Trekkie Theater 3000 for 25 years at Shore Leave. Panels in general.

On His Favorite Con Recollection:

I'd brought my younger son Drew to a Shore Leave. He was only four at the time. We were in the dealers' room checking out some toy spaceships when a towering Klingon in full regalia—a guy who was close to seven feet tall with his Klingon boots on—came and stood next to my son. Drew didn't notice for a while. Then he glanced to his right, saw the guy's bat'leth, and started looking higher and higher until he was craning his neck to see the Klingon's face—which must have been frightening as hell for a four-year-old. Just as I was about to intervene, to tell Drew that it was okay, the Klingon wasn't real, the Klingon noticed that Drew was looking at him—whereupon he grinned, bent down, and said in the friendliest of voices: "Hey, little dude!" Drew smiled, and the crisis was averted.

On Favorite Guest Stars:

Jimmy Doohan. I was sitting in the green room when he arrived and started giving out refrigerator magnets with a Scotty cartoon on them. He was down-to-earth, always entertaining, and full of young-actor-in-New York stories. Marina Sirtis is among the most entertaining guests. I love her sass.

On Reasons for Attending Cons:

As a writer, I attend them to sell books and alert readers to what I'm working on. But the Maryland cons in particular have become more like family gatherings for me, enabling me to see many of my favorite people in a short time. One of my favorite times of year is when I come off the ramp from 83 and pull in front of the Hunt Valley Inn; I just feel like I'm home.

On His Secret Past:

I was a Division One athlete in college (yeah, that was a long time ago).

On Maryland Cons:

When I look at my Facebook friends list, it has a drastically disproportionate Maryland flavor. I feel fortunate to have had the chance to make so many good friends at the Maryland cons.

Phil Giunta

On His Job in Real Life:

I always say that I have two jobs. One pays the bills, but the other is far more gratifying. We'll start with the former. For the past twenty-five years, I've worked in the IT industry, starting as a help desk and desktop support technician and working my way up to my current role as an Infrastructure Engineer where I get to play with servers, networks, and virtual environments.

In my college days, I began writing fan fiction in such universes as *Star Trek, Star Wars, Indiana Jones,* and others. That went on until 2003 when I felt confident enough in my writing ability to outline my first original novel—a paranormal mystery called *Testing the Prisoner*—that was published in 2009 by Firebringer Press. Since then, I managed to publish a second novel in the same genre called *By Your Side* along with about a dozen short stories in speculative fiction with various publishers.

As of now, I have a paranormal mystery novella and several more short stories on the way and a science fiction novel in progress. Writing certainly hasn't started paying the bills yet, but there's nothing more rewarding than seeing your work published and earning solid reviews from readers.

On His Personal History:

Though originally from Philadelphia, I now reside a bit farther north in the Lehigh Valley with my wife, Evon.

Fishing has been my primary hobby for the past thirty-odd years. I enjoy being outdoors as much as possible in the warmer months. If

I'm fishing alone, I'll often bring my current writing project with me and once fishing is over for the day, I'll pack up the gear and write by the water for a few hours.

There was a time when I was an avid builder of plastic model kits, mostly science fiction ships and vehicles. I still have most of the finished pieces on display at home, but since I began writing and publishing, I haven't been able to make much time for that. Perhaps someday when I retire, I can get back to it. That's about the only way it will happen at this rate.

By necessity, home improvements have become a hobby that keeps me busy year around. I also enjoy working out about three or four times per week, especially since both of my jobs are sedentary.

On His Introduction to Conventions and Fandom:

I started attending Creation *Star Trek* conventions in Valley Forge, PA in the late '80s and into the mid-'90s. In 1993, I joined a Philadelphia-based chapter of Starfleet, the USS Thagard (named after NASA astronaut and scientist Norman Thagard). Through that group, I was introduced to the Maryland SF conventions—Farpoint, Shore Leave, and Vulkon—as well as NovaCon in Virginia. This was also the time when I was writing fan fiction and publishing in various fanzines, including the *Norman*, an annual fanzine published by the USS Thagard.

On His Current Fame and Connections to Conventions:

Whatever modicum of fame I've achieved in fandom was earned simply by attending SF conventions for nearly 30 years and then becoming an author guest at Farpoint and Shore Leave beginning in 2010 just after my first novel was published. I've also been an author guest at the Great Philadelphia Comic Con, Balticon, and Philcon.

Until recently, I also attended Chiller Theatre and Monster Mania in New Jersey on a regular basis, but not as a guest, just as a fanboy and autograph collector.

On Becoming a Writer:

First, I've been an insatiable reader since I was a kid, mostly mysteries, science fiction, paranormal, and fantasy. I list out specific authors in my response to your question about who influenced me.

In the late '80s, I started writing *Star Trek* fan fiction. I wasn't shy about it. I gave every story to friends for critique and the feedback was overwhelmingly effusive, so I kept writing, learning, honing my style, and expanded to other titles that inspired me—*Star Wars, Indiana Jones, Blade Runner, MacGyver, The Avengers* (Steed and Peel, that is), and others. I published most of these stories in various fanzines until 2003 when I decided that I learned enough about character development, story structure, plot, and pacing to write a completely original story and <gasp> become a published author!

I outlined a paranormal novel about child abuse, forgiveness, and redemption called *Testing the Prisoner*. Truth be told, writing was a slow effort in the beginning, mostly because the process of finding an agent intimidated me, so I did not make writing a priority at first. So even as I worked on the first draft, I thought, *where am I going to take this?*

In 2006, I learned that Steve Wilson had self-published his first SF novel, *Taken Liberty*. I asked him if he was willing to publish other writers through his imprint, Firebringer Press. He was familiar with the quality of my writing, so he agreed to read my manuscript. That was enough to kick my ass into gear and finish it. If memory serves, I submitted the third draft of *Testing the Prisoner* the following year, and, after several rounds of edits, it was published in 2009. Since then, I've published three other books through Firebringer Press with two more on the way.

I've since published numerous short stories with other small presses such as Crazy 8 Press, Cat & Mouse Press, Greater Lehigh Valley Publishing Group, and Smart Rhino Publications.

On Influential Media:

In no particular order, some of the writers who have influenced and inspired me include Edgar Allan Poe, Harlan Ellison, Arthur Conan Doyle, Peter David, Ray Bradbury, Carl Sagan, Alan Dean Foster, Arthur C. Clarke, Rod Serling, and several others.

Actors who have done the same for me include Cary Grant, Humphrey Bogart, Orson Welles, Audrey Hepburn, Katherine Hepburn, Christopher Reeve, Harrison Ford, Richard Dean Anderson, William Shatner, Leonard Nimoy, and others.

TV shows and films include *Star Trek*, *Twilight Zone*, *Outer Limits*, *MacGyver*, *Quantum Leap*, *X-Files*, *The Pretender*, *Monk*, *Psych*, *Eureka*, *Warehouse 13*, *Star Wars* (episodes IV through VI), *Blade Runner*, *JAWS*, *Superman I & II* (Christopher Reeve), *Close Encounters of the Third Kind*, *Dead Again* (Kenneth Branagh and Emma Thompson), *Identity* (John Cusack and Ray Liotta), *Moon* (Sam Rockwell) and others.

On His Years in Fandom:

Nearly 30.

On His Favorite Con Activities:

I still enjoy meeting the celebrities, sitting in on their Q&A sessions, getting their autographs, but as the years pass, spending time with the many friends I've made over the years has taken precedence. As an author guest, I enjoy participating or in discussion panels even when I think I have little to contribute compared to the more senior and experienced writers, but at that point, it becomes a learning opportunity.

On His Favorite Con Recollection:

In 1995, I wrote a short story called "The Convention," about a young man who dies in a car accident and goes to the Great SF Convention in the Sky. At the time, the USS *Thagard* had a drama group led by member Matt Black. Matt suggested that we turn the story into a short film. I wrote a script and the project was retitled *ForeverCon*. Part of the film was shot at Shore Leave 18 and then the finished work was screened during the masquerade the following year at Shore Leave 19. It was well-received and the USS *Thagard* sold quite a number of VHS copies for charity at that Shore Leave.

I played the lead role in the film and members Angel Avery, Peter Butler, Vince Maiocco all had major parts. Other members played extras and worked as crew. It was a wonderful time.

On Meeting Authors:

Generally speaking, I would have to say that when I first attended the Maryland conventions, I was excited to meet all of the *Star Trek* novelists and comic book writers whose work I'd been reading for years. People like Howard Weinstein, Michael Jan Friedman, Peter David, Bob Greenberger, Steven H. Wilson, Brad Ferguson, and Carmen Carter. With regard to Steve, Bob, Howard, and Michael, I managed to cultivate friendships that last to this day.

In fact, Steve Wilson has not only become a close friend and writing mentor, but as I mentioned earlier, he is also my publisher at Firebringer Press, and in 2012, Bob Greenberger invited me to contribute stories to the *ReDeus* mythology series that he co-created with Aaron Rosenberg and Paul Kupperberg. I credit fandom and conventions for helping to jumpstart my professional writing career, something for which for I'm deeply grateful.

Beyond the writers, beyond the celebrity guests, I've been blessed to immerse myself in a supportive and talented community. Yes, it's as dysfunctional as any other family at times, but being part of fandom and attending the conventions has enriched my life in ways I never imagined when I walked into my first convention three decades ago.

On His Favorite Guest Stars:

My favorite celebrity guest was Richard Dean Anderson, who was the headliner at Shore Leave 36 back in 2014. I've been a fan of his ever since *MacGyver*. I started carrying a Swiss Army Knife as a teenager because of *MacGyver* and my wife and I are both fans of *Stargate SG-1* as well as *Legend*, his short-lived Western series that aired between *MacGyver* and *Stargate*.

It's challenging to narrow down my favorite author guest to one, but I'd have to say that Harlan Ellison was the most memorable. I drove up to I-CON in 1998 (or 1999?) specifically to meet Harlan, as I consider him one of my inspirations to become a writer. I was well aware of his cantankerous reputation, which I always found entertaining especially during his segments on Sci-Fi Buzz on the early days of the Sci-Fi Channel.

At I-CON, I was not disappointed.

I brought a stack of his books with me to be autographed, including one called *Doomsman*. As Harlan was signing my books, he stopped at that book and said, "I'll buy this from you." Now, at the time, I had no idea why he made that offer. What's more, I had not read the book yet so I said "No."

You don't say "No" to Harlan Ellison.

In response, he flung the book across the table. "Then I'm not signing the fuckin' thing!" I cannot tell you how excited I was to be cussed out by Harlan Ellison! It was like earning a badge of honor. In the end, I traded *Doomsman* for a copy of *Ellison Wonderland*—which he signed—but not before snatching up *Doomsman* and waving it excitedly above his head. I also managed to get my photo taken with Harlan in which he unmistakably expressed his sentiments about our encounter.

It was not until Farpoint 2011, or thereabouts, when Ann Crispin happened to mention her friendship with Harlan. She said that Harlan is a great guy, except when anyone mentions *Doomsman*. Given my experience, I was compelled to ask for details. Apparently, the publisher had someone else rewrite most of the story, which infuriated Harlan and launched him on a crusade to collect as many copies as possible and either tear them up in front of fans or take them home to be burned.

A few years later, I managed to score another copy of *Doomsman* from a used book dealer at Balticon. That one is staying on my shelf.

On Attending Conventions:

I began attending conventions as a way of meeting the celebrities I'd grown up watching on TV and in movies. While that's still a part of the experience, it not as much of a priority, especially at conventions like Farpoint and Shore Leave where I enjoy reuniting with friends I see only a few times per year. Social media is no substitute for this.

I also enjoy the author discussion panels, regardless of which side of the table I'm on. Participating in the panels is fun and a great way to share whatever value I bring to the topic, but I also hope to learn from other panelists and take something away that might improve my own writing.

On What People Don't Know About Him:

Thanks to social media, there is little that we *don't* know about one another! Honestly, there is nothing I can think of. My life is fairly mundane. Over the past five years, I've opened up publicly about my struggle with depression and anxiety, something I'd previously kept hidden. As I reached middle age, I no longer felt the need to conceal that. It's part of who and what I am and I do my best to manage it.

Robert Greenberger

On His Real Life Job:

When not writing, editing, or making convention appearances, I actually work fulltime as an English teacher at St. Vincent Pallotti High School in Laurel. We moved to Maryland from Connecticut in 2013 to be closer to our daughter Kate.

On His Introduction to Conventions and Science Fiction:

I was born in Brooklyn and raised on Long Island, which is where I was introduced to comics and science fiction, thanks to my parents, who were both readers. Around 1971, at the tender age of 13, my best friend and I heard about comic book conventions in New York City through fanzines, which we had learned about from comic book letter columns, so we took the train to the famed Statler Hilton Hotel, home to Phil Seuling's legendary New York Comic Art Conventions.

From that introduction to comics fandom, we discovered comics-related fanzines but didn't really see the *Trek* zines until much later. Another new friend was publishing his own zine, and I covered the 1975 *Star Trek* con for it. He went on to publish the one and only issue of *Hemogoblin*, the zine my friend Jeff and I conceived.

I was a gofer at the very first Creation convention, after befriending co-organizer Adam Malin as I slowly got sucked into New York fandom. In January, 1972, I was there for the very first *Star Trek* convention and wound up working for them their final two years.

All of the above not only solidified my interest in comics and science fiction, but convinced me my fascination with Clark Kent and journalism was my path. I intended to get into publishing, newspapers or magazines. It never occurred to me that I would be in comics, although I had many NYC fandom friends make that transition.

On Working for *Starlog* Magazine:

I attended SUNY Binghamton, working on the school paper and meeting my future wife. As I neared graduation, I applied to some 40 outfits, netting a single interview which happened to be with Starlog Press. I had been a regular reader since *Starlog* debuted in 1976, so I included them in my blanket search as a lark. Well, Kerry O'Quinn was taken with my samples and knowledge. He offered me a job as *Fangoria*'s managing editor, but the job wouldn't start until September. Thankfully, a fandom pal, Paul Levitz, had taken a job at DC Comics and rapidly risen through the ranks, and he threw me a lifeline of summer work at DC.

While there, I made some friends (along with more than few rookie mistakes) and then went to *Fangoria*. While working on that and *Starlog*, I conceived of *Comics Scene*, which debuted in November 1981 as the first nationally distributed newsstand magazine to cover comic books, comic strips, and animation. I was its first Editor and got to know people across the industry. As a result, when the publishers canceled it with issue #11 (despite rising sales), I was assigned work on their boxing and wrestling magazines. I sought an exit strategy.

On Working for DC Comics:

During this period, DC was gearing up for their 50th anniversary and had two major projects in development, and it was decided someone had to work with the editors. That became me, and I joined them in January 1980. Over the next sixteen years, I rose from Assistant Editor to Manager-Editorial Operations. During that stretch, I edited quite a few comics, including an eight-year run with the *Star Trek* and *Star Trek: The Next Generation* titles and the introductory issues of *Suicide Squad*.

While working on *Trek*, I befriended David Stern, who was editing the *Trek* novels for Pocket Books. I was keeping careful track of stardates as well as their forthcoming novels to avoid duplicating storylines or guest characters. Dave then started to invite me to the cocktail parties he threw for the many local Trek authors. I struck up friendships with several, including Mike Friedman, who had just published his first novel with them. Peter David, who I first met when he wrote for *Comics Scene*, was also writing for them and became my regular *Trek* writer.

On Writing Star Trek Fiction:

In publishing at the time, shared universes such as Robert Asprin's *Thieves World* were a sales success, so talk turned to several authors joining together on a collaborative novel. I had been beginning to think about writing fiction, so I volunteered to join in, figuring whatever deficiencies I had as a tyro would be glossed over by the others. This resulted in Peter, Mike, Carmen Carter, and me writing *Doomsday World*. I had begun consulting on the continuity with Dave Stern, leading me to working with him behind the scenes on the *Lost Years* novels and even trying my hand at a first novel, which only proved I wasn't ready.

But I was ready for more fiction and collaborated with Mike and Peter on two more novels before flying solo on 1990's *The Romulan Stratagem*. Since then, I have written numerous media tie-in novels and short stories, delighting in playing in so many fun sandboxes. More recently, I've concentrated on original fiction, which has been really gratifying. As for a favorite, it could be my first full novel, since it was a major accomplishment for me and has garnered very good reviews.

On Mystery Trekkie Theater:

Mike, Peter, and I became very close friends as a result of our work at DC Comics and Pocket Books. We're always there for one another and enjoy the fruits of our fevered collaborations. That bond allowed us to strut our stuff with the *After Earth* franchise, which had incredible potential. We always enjoy one another's company, so once they began working on *Trek* stuff, I had them invited to Shore Leave as guests. There they, too, have become fixtures. To ensure that, Peter conceived of *Mystery Trekkie Theater*, using the *Mystery Science Theater 3000* template but devoted to skewering *Star Trek* episodes. Peter always wrote the opening skits and when he needed a Klingon puppet, he asked Kathleen O'Shea to use her skills. That began a romance which endures. Anyway, for 25 years, we would pick an episode, screen it separately, then get together about a month prior to the con to compare notes and draft a final script. At Shore Leave, we'd carve out time for a final run-through, and then perform it. The audience always seemed to have a good time, and the opening skits grew increasingly elaborate. Often, we'd get the celebrity guests to play along with us, from George Takei to Andrea Thompson, and they were incredibly good sports about it. Yet, all good things must come to an end, and, after my relocation to Maryland, getting together for that first rehearsal became increasingly difficult. Plus, we'd done it for so long and our lives were getting busier. In 2017, we had one final blowout and called it a career.

On Being a Con Guest:

Overlapping my entry into the professional publishing world, I transitioned from fan to guest at conventions, which was a fun thing. I love cons and meeting fans, promoting things I am passionate about, and traveling to new places. This includes being invited to join Howard Weinstein at Shore Leave III in 1981. I have been a regular there ever since. Along the way, my familiarity with a wide variety of genre material led to my being invited to judge masquerades (and co-host one of the famed San Diego Comic-Con masquerades).

On Masquerades:

It's fun seeing the detail, imagination, and attention to character that people bring to their costumes and presentations. My eye has grown sharper and more exacting with time and experience, and my wife, Deb, has trained me to examine the costume as a whole, from head to toe, from makeup to accessories. It's always a little odd when people I know compete, and, when my kids competed, I always excused myself.

On Influential Media:

Throughout the years, I have been a sponge, absorbing bits and pieces from the people I have worked with. I find things creeping into the way I speak or act or write. Obviously, *Superman* and *Star Trek* have been hugely influential in my life, each giving me opportunities I could never have imagined. Certainly, I learned a lot from the veteran DC editors I trained under; people like Len Wein, Marv Wolfman, and Dick Giordano. While I've always appreciated the various fiction editors I have worked with, I have never found the *one*, my Maxwell Perkins, which I feel has kept me from reaching my full prose potential.

On the Conventions:

I love interacting with fans. Promoting stuff for DC or Marvel meant being cemented in the booth for long stretches, so chatting with them and hearing what's on their minds is always fun. When I am at an SF show, it's about getting together with colleagues whom I don't see otherwise, sitting with them on stimulating panel discussions or going out for a meal. Over the last few years, I've evolved into an emcee for Shore Leave, introducing the various guests, and keeping things running. For the Baltimore Comic-Con, I have also had the pleasure of interviewing celebrity guests on stage.

On Celebrity Guests:

In the early days of shows like San Diego or Shore Leave, it was a lot easier to hang out with the various celebrity guests. I spent one memorable afternoon in a corner, talking comics with Mark Hamill. I got to enjoy dinner out with Howie and George Takei, away from distractions. These days, such happy encounters are challenging if not impossible to arrange—we all have too many obligations at the con.

On Working with William Shatner:

My years in fandom have made me comfortable dealing with all manner of celebrities, but I still get a fan's thrill meeting someone I truly admire. In 2013, I made certain I got be the one to introduce William Shatner at his first Shore Leave. Recently, when Shatner was touring with a screening of *Star Trek II: The Wrath of Khan*, Inge Heyer, chair of Shore Leave, recommended me to the Lyric Theater as moderator for his post-screening interview. I over-prepared for the discussion, uncertain of what would happen. It turned out that fans had been invited to submit written questions in advance, and the tour manager had me help sort and screen the questions. Afterwards, I was taken to the green room where Bill Shatner and I had half an hour or so to ourselves, getting to know one another. That was perhaps cooler than being on stage with him. Still, all those years before large crowds kept the butterflies at bay and our on-stage talk was smooth. He was "on" and in fine form, using me more as a foil than a moderator, and I just rolled with it. The hour-plus flew by and he warmly thanked me afterwards. So he was pleased, meaning I had done my job.

On Maryland Conventions:

Having been a part of the Maryland convention scene for the last thirty-plus years, I can say that the various shows continue to put the fans first. Shore Leave and Farpoint (and, before Farpoint, Clippercon and OktoberTrek) all have their own flavor, but they are run by and for fans, not looking to get rich but to put on a three-day party with friends. As they have grown and endured, the additions of kids', science, author, and other tracks of programming means there is most certainly something for everyone. Balticon continues to emphasize the power of the written word, eschewing Hollywood celebrities. Baltimore Comic-Con has a few big, genre-related names to help goose attendance, but it's always about comic books.

Susan Staneslow Olesen

On Her Real Life Job:

I've been a licensed foster parent for almost 30 years, specializing in special needs foster care. I have two permanent guys—my husband and I have been working with one for 35 years—but we've also had temporary children to give other people a break. In addition, we took in a homeless-then teen about seven years ago, gained a baby and an older kid, giving us a total of three biologicals and five additionals.

In addition, I was the media tech assistant for my public library for more than ten years, responsible for processing and upkeep of all the DVDs, music, and audiobooks. Unfortunately, I had to revert to clerking last year due to childcare issues. I write for the library's public blog and run the library's writers' workshop program. In the past, I was a special education teacher. We also spent three years doing kitten foster care for an animal shelter, raising 50 kittens and cats in three years.

On Her Personal History:

I grew up in a small town in Connecticut, where I still live. Everything was quiet and forested, surrounded by an empty dirt road, a gas pipeline, and a school, so we had acres and acres of uninhabited land to explore. Check out the atrocious cover of my book *Best Efforts*—that's one of my hangouts, which I wrote into a scene in the book. I was gifted with the chance to go to a private prep school for high school. From there I went to Wells College, AP-ing English and Sociology, graduating with a major in Developmental Psychology and minor in Russian Studies. I did win the Senior Library Prize for Special Collection—for my *Star Trek* books! From there my life was pretty straightforward—I started work at a residential school for severely disabled children, met my husband, got married, had my kids, and pretty much carried on in a style that was half *The Waltons* and half *National Lampoon's Family Vacation*. It's really very dull. If you drop by, it's much more of a reality show, or a cross between Norman Lear and *Laverne and Shirley*, with kids walking in and out almost on cue.

On Her Introduction to Fandom and Conventions:

My dad was an elementary school science teacher and a science fiction/fantasy fan from days of yore, so I would have to say I was born to it. These were the days of our great moon explorations; my family and I lived science fiction. I have faint memories of watching *Star Trek* in its original run, though I was four when it went off the air. I can remember being six or so and raiding my mother's dresser for her book on *Baby and Child Care*, desperate for an author photo of Dr. Spock and his pointed ears. So, it was always there. When I was eight or nine Dad introduced me to the *White Mountains* series. So, science and science fiction were *always* part of my world.

When I was eleven, *Star Trek* came into syndication on our local channels, and I was done. I welcomed it like an old friend, and it became my religion. Seriously. There weren't a lot of *Trek* books out then, and I think I read every one of them. We memorized everything. In the days before videotape, we recorded the episodes on audiotape to listen to. When I wrote a major college term paper on *The Wrath of Khan* (another distinction for writing I received), I recorded it onto a reel-to-reel player to get my quotes. By 1980, my best friends and I had started our own fan club (The United Trekkist Association) and published our own bimonthly fanzine/newsletter. Yes, we were running a fan club and magazine at fifteen, with a readership of 40. It was a game to us then, but boy did we learn future skills! First on typewriters, then later on those early Tandy computers with 16K—my dad was teaching computers by then and could take them home for the weekend.

In Stephen King's *On Writing*, he talks about printing his own newspaper when he was a kid, and I laughed when I read that. We were writing and printing our own fanzine, so I knew writing was sort of preordained for me (both my dad and my grandfather have publishing credits).

On Influential Media:

Star Trek, above and beyond. Everything I am, everything I do, everything I believe, has been directly influenced by *Star Trek. Lost in Space* was my other earliest memory. Between *Star Trek* airings, I was an *Emergency!* fiend. Having come from a family of doctors meant medicine was second-nature to me—we had all my grandfather's surgical tools and books just lying about, so, up until the end of high school, I had thoroughly planned a career in medicine. I read every *Star Trek* novel as it came out—a book a day at times; I actually have a report card that says I'd do better in school if I didn't read so much. My friends and I devoured *Alien, Raiders of the Lost* Ark, and of course *Star Wars,* and then the *Star Trek* films – it was a wonderful time to be a teen! I skipped school to watch the maiden voyage of the *Enterprise* shuttle. I was home on a snow day, student teaching a birth-to-three classroom, watching the *Challenger* launch when it exploded. In college, a friend got me into *Doctor Who* just in time for Baker to become Davison. I dragged a poster of Tom Baker to the mall, matched yarns as closely as possible, and knitted my very first scarf from the official BBC pattern. Years later I became a rabid fan of *Torchwood,* along with *Firefly, Babylon 5, The Prisoner,* and *Twilight Zone.* My husband was a huge *Stargate* fan, so I absorbed a lot of that just from being in the room. My two tattoos are for *Star Trek* and *Firefly.* And how can you not love at least some aspect of *Harry Potter*?

While I devoured *The Making of Star Trek,* and David Gerrold's book *The Trouble with Tribbles,* I suppose *Star Trek Lives!* had a bigger impact, since it told me all about those huge *Star Trek* conventions in New York, so close yet so far away. I would have killed to go to one of those! My mother thought 20 miles was the end of the Earth. Shatner once spoke at UConn around '77 or '78, and I begged to see him, but even though it was in-state, it was I'mnotdrivingallthewayoutthere.

Outside of *Star Trek,* my favorite novel was *Alas, Babylon* by Pat Frank. Yeah, it's idealistic, yeah, it's outdated, but I still love it— survival after nuclear war. I don't know how many times I've read it. When 9/11 hit, I sent a two-word email to my best friend, who was in

L.A. at the time: *Alas, Babylon.* He remembered the chilling words. And then I high-tailed it to the store and laid in the supplies the book had taught me, Just In Case.

The Girl With All the Gifts by M.R. Carey was amazing. *The Martian. Retribution Falls* by Chris Wooding is my all-time favorite novel of the last decade. Read it as a *Firefly* novel; it's superb. I know people want me to say the classics, and I've read many of them—Asimov, *Ringworld, A Canticle for Liebowitz, A Clockwork Orange, Planet of the Apes, Chronicles of Amber,* etc, but they haven't made my brain leap as some of these others have done. Loved *Day of the Triffids,* and *Something Wicked This Way Comes,* and *All Summer in a Day*—I love Bradbury. People are begging me to read *Handmaid's Tale,* but I won't. I know it will make me supremely angry, and my blood pressure doesn't need that. I want stories to make me forget reality; not make me feel hopeless. *Earth Abides* was one of the worst books I've ever read.

On Discovering Maryland Cons:

My first *Star Trek* event was January or February of 1977 which was a sort of mini-convention run at an auditorium in the town my Dad taught in. My friends and I were dumbstruck. There were speakers, maybe a dozen tables of stills and merchandise, episodes on 16-mm film, and more. We were eleven. This was Heaven. From there, we learned of a guy who did *Star Trek* programs in libraries. We followed him everywhere like groupies—this town, that town, then a little local convention, for about ten years. Then, in 1983, Creation held a convention in Hartford—*an actual* Star Trek *convention!* We could not get there fast enough. Walter Koenig was the main guest. I was 17 and a Chekov groupie. I could have died. Of anyone, *it was Chekov!* As I was walking toward the auditorium, and the crowd parted, and there coming toward me, three feet away, was Walter... Holy Dilithium! I managed to mumble *"Zdravstvoytye,"* at him, and he smiled and gave a nod and said *"Zdravstvy,"* back, and that was it. That is the absolute closest I have ever come to fainting in my life.

About a year later there was a little con just fifteen minutes away up the highway—Conn Mini Con. The only speaker I remember was

Bill Hickey, who was an extra in the rec deck scene in *Star Trek: The Motion Picture*. Didn't care. *Everyone* was interesting back then. My friends and I were stuck on one trivia question for the trivia contest, but we'd seen this girl with a *Star Trek Concordance*, so we tracked her down and asked if we could look something up. That was Dawn, and we've been best friends since. She joined our fan club, and we met members of the Boston Star Trek Association that ran the BASH convention. So, they joined our fan club, and we joined theirs, and actually worked on committees for the 1986 Platinum Anniversary Convention.

In the BSTA, Dawn learned of August Party in Maryland, and went down there in 1985. [Editor's Note: August Party was held at the University of Maryland's College Park campus, at the Adele H. Stamp Union, beginning in 1975. The 1985 reunion was held in Tyson's Corner, VA.] At August Party, Dawn learned of Shore Leave, and we decided to make a trek—so to speak—down in 1986. The Omni's elevators couldn't begin to keep up with the demand, and some waits for an elevator were 20-30 minutes. [Editor's Other Note: The 1986 Shore Leave was was held at the Omni International—the one-and-only time that the convention was not held at the Hunt Valley Inn, after it moved there in 1979.] But it was the best damned convention I'd ever been to, from Boogie Knights to Temple of Trek to a wedding to my first-ever screening of *Rocky Horror*—we were amazed. Thus began our endless trips up and down the coast. Shore Leave, Farpoint, OktoberTrek, Fan-Out, Clippercon, and more. I missed 1993 because I'd been on maternity leave, and I missed 1997 because I had a high-risk pregnancy, so we took a little trip to Boston instead. My kids bitched and moaned so bad about it not being "their" hotel, we said never again, and I haven't missed one since.

So, in short, I go the Maryland conventions because we recognized a long-haired girl in a parking lot at Conn Mini Con.

On Becoming a Science Fiction Writer:

Always, always, I was making up stories and playing them out. I think that's the life of a lonely kid. Didn't matter the TV series—

Emergency, S.W.A.T., Barnaby Jones, Lost in Space (I was a *huge* Will Robinson fan) —I'd create a character for myself and insert me into a story. *Star Trek* was just the next step in the line. At nine or so, I read a short story in the back of one of my grandmother's magazines about a family of kids who get abandoned and fend for themselves until social services finds them, etc., and it kicked my brain into high gear. I created a brother and sister who were alone in the woods, but then realized they couldn't survive, so I created an older brother to help them, then an even older teen brother who would be able to earn money. Every night I would go over the story in my head, but eventually it got so long and involved that I started writing it down. When *Star Trek* sent my brain into overdrive, the story was very easy to slip into that universe. I never wrote it that way—there are some parallels I never intended but I was unable to eliminate some similarities no matter how I tried and rewrote. That formula was so deep in my head I couldn't ditch it. I've gotten past that point now, but in those early years, *everything* I wrote started out in a *Star Trek* universe, and eventually I got things published in fanzines.

I find writing out of time period much more interesting. Space flight, alien life, xenoarchaeology, chemistry, magic—so much to think about, so much to learn, so many possibilities! Why limit myself? I had created six or seven different characters as a teen—Sarah, Serena (who became a *ST:TNG* story in a fanzine), Theo (a novella that got me my distinction in Creative Writing in college), Rio (whose story has never found its way yet), Aila (*Prisoner of the Mins* series), and one more I don't remember. My brain twists and turns too much to be a straight writer. It soars with what-if and what-could-be, and I have no choice but to follow it down the rabbit hole.

On Her Published Books:

I could talk about them all day. What to say?

The *Best Intentions* series is about Sarah Kirushenko, one of thirteen siblings with a father who's a brilliant but alcoholic galactic archeologist who stumbles upon the find of a lifetime, only to be unable to handle the fame it brings. When her mother dies, all hell breaks loose, trapping the children on a hostile alien planet as Sarah begins to lose her mind from the stress. It's a family drama set in the future. It's a story about love, loss, longing, loyalty, and reconciliation. My kids still haven't forgiven me for part of it. I've always said *Best Intentions* was my Ph.D for psychology.

I tried for years to write the *Best Intentions* series, but I never got anywhere with it. It was too ambitious for squeezing into one novel, and by the time I was done asking myself, *but why*? the main original story was actually book three, I had a four-volume series I'd never anticipated, and enough leftover written material to make a prequel. *BI* was my learning curve. I spent years refining it, learning grammar and layout and storyline and character development and mostly editing. I went to every talk and panel I could on writing and publishing, every workshop—Ann Crispin ripped my innocence so bad on book three I cried for three days and didn't touch the manuscript for almost a year, and in the end I decided not to give it to a publisher. I'd heard that once a publisher bought your characters, you lost control over them. If they didn't want to publish the rest of the series, you couldn't just write more on them and publish elsewhere; they were frozen in time. I couldn't do that to those characters; they were as real to me as family. So, when a co-worker discussed how she self-published her novels, I jumped on the self-publishing bandwagon just to keep the rights to those characters.

My second series was different. *Prisoner of the Mind* began in college, the story of a 13-14 year old, average girl, who is accidentally kidnapped by her world's worst enemy, the Kerasi Coalition, and forced against her will to become a diplomat, brokering peace between the two worlds. She wants no part of it. She's in mortal danger every moment she's with them, but plucky Aila manages to take things into her hands and do it her way.

I had a sixth book brewing for *Best Intentions*, but I refused to let myself work on it until I beat *Prisoner* into shape. Because it was a single volume, I wanted to try traditional publishing. I paid for an editor and increased the quality. I went to a writers' workshop, met with a NY agent who loved the book, had lunch with me over it, wanted to see the entire thing, and I sent it to him immediately. And I *Never. Heard. Back.* I sent follow-ups. Nothing. It was a reputable agency, he was a reputable agent, but I never heard from him again. I was crushed. I sent out more queries. It was a YA book, about a fourteen-year-old girl. Those things were hot sellers in the days of Katniss and Triss. The final straw was a rejection letter telling me my heroine was too young for a YA novel. That is the *key* age for a YA novel!! And that's when I said "Screw the publishers," and relegated it to self-publishing. I sent it out to a second editor, and I didn't care for the changes he recommended. While pondering that, not only did I find the change it needed, my head exploded with new ideas and a sequel formed, and while I wrote an outline for that, a third novel formed, and then a fourth, and I pretty much wrote two, three, and four simultaneously. Unfortunately, I wasn't able to pull everything together by the end of four, so it spilled over into a fifth and final volume, which I'm writing right now.

I was in a writing group for ten years; I didn't realize how much I wrote for it. *Brain Splatter* was my first anthology, for the way my ideas splatter onto paper. It was never meant to be published; people kept asking me for reprints of things, and my dad could never find his copies, so for Christmas I stuck them together with a couple of my longer fanzine stories and ran off a dozen copies to give to people, and then yanked it. But other people wanted copies, so I swapped out the fanzine stories, edited things, and put it out. Some of it is good, some is mediocre, but they're there. Currently I have a companion anthology of 20 short stories for *Prisoner of the Mind* called *Kerasi: Foundations* coming soon, two short stories coming out in *Writer's Unite!* anthologies, and several essays in various on-line publications. And the conclusion to *Prisoner* due in 2020. *Then* maybe I can get to some other works I've been dying to write.

On Introducing Her Children to Fandom:

My children were pretty much born to it. They thought it was *normal*. They thought *all* hotels had costume contests. I tried hard not to be the psycho con-mom: although they did costume contests, the rule was, you're here to have fun, not win a prize. If you win a prize, that's great. If you don't, you still had fun. Sometimes they won, sometimes they didn't, but they accepted the rule. If it wasn't fun anymore, they didn't have to do it. Eventually they started designing their own costumes, and Mom was out of the picture. They designed their own crafts and art for the art show. They volunteered and worked behind the scenes, and that was fantastic. They made friends with other con kids and maintain those friendships today. They go to conventions for the people and the hanging out, not the actual Con.

Because fandom attracts such a wide variety of people, they've had exposure to so many unique people that they're very accepting of everyone. To some degree, they know how spoiled they are. When someone mentions a star, my daughter whips out her phone and shows a photo of herself with that star. "Oh yeah. I met them years ago." My son is still rocked by having drinks in the bar with LeVar Burton, an icon of *his* childhood. Although they still have their fan moments (my older daughter did not—did not—speak for hours after meeting John Rhys-Davies), the star quality is diminished, and they see the stars for the people they are, not the character they were. I think they'd all say they've loved growing up in fandom.

On Her Favorite Con Activities:

Nothing, absolutely nothing beats Big E Con. The aircraft carrier *Enterprise* was in drydock in Norfolk, Virginia, and by attending we could get a tour of the ship. I can say I have actually stood on the bridge of the real *Enterprise.*

Guests, certainly, are my favorite part of conventions. Sure, I love seeing my favorites—I sat in line for three hours at a Comic-Con for the cast of *Firefly*—but it doesn't matter who the guest is, they're almost always interesting, even if you have no idea who they are or what they do. Michael Ansara was fascinating, because he did one episode of *Star Trek*—but *so* much else. Sometimes the guest is a bit player—but he's worked with a hundred bigger-named stars and has *so* many stories to tell.

After guests, I suppose panels and workshops. I went to a choreography workshop at Buffalo Who Fest with the choreographer from *Doctor Who*. I did a voice acting workshop at Farpoint with Kathy Garver. I've done Kath David's Puppet Workshop. Perhaps the most useful workshop I attended was a three-hour seminar at WorldCon on Artificial Languages. We learned about them for two hours, then broke into groups and had to create several words for our creature. Our group was assigned Aardvark, taking into account the type of animal, what it did, possible mouth movements, and what would be the most important words for it to develop first. It was fascinating, and now I wind up creating pages and pages of alien languages. You know you've gone absolutely batty when you're trying to come up with a word in a language you've made up, then realize you already know the probable prefix and a suitable root word. Sometimes accuracy is a sickness.

Panels would come next—I adore the hard-science panels where I can learn something. Loved the guy who used to come to Farpoint and talk about autism, or the flu, or whatever was new that year. [Editor's note: This was most likely Dr. John Cmar.] The chances to learn are endless.

On Writer's Panels:

I've only been on panels for a few years, but 2018's Continuity v. Canon was just the right/wrong combination of people and was a total hoot. A panel of male vs. female writers came off strongly. And I always love listening to—and doing—readings, though public reading is an art form, and not all authors have the gift. Without digging in the files, I can't think of more than those.

I'm a bit divided on panels. There are two kinds of writing panels—those specific to genres (panels on comic characters, or novels, or anime) or panels for the beginning writer, like traditional vs. self-published, or writing for beginners; and after a time you get tired of sloshing the same stuff around. Is it helpful for the newcomer who's never sat there before? Of course. But I'd love to see panels go a little deeper for the not-so-newbie—Editing to make your editor weep with joy; Avoiding clichés in writing; Winning first paragraphs; Everyone's a beginner; let's take them a step further.

On Con Recollections:

So many memories. Sharing a hot tub with Jason Carter didn't suck.

One time, Peter Jurasik was auctioning off some personal items to raise money for a neighbor's child who needed open heart surgery or something, and people just started pouring out money—like $1,000 for something that was probably only worth $100. And he just started crying on stage because of the unexpected generosity. Half the audience was crying at that point. Having drinks with Majel [Barrett Roddenberry] at the Platinum Anniversary Convention was something special, sitting at the feet of the Queen while she smoked like a chimney, hanging on to her every word. I can't imagine—especially at my age then—any deeper hero worship.

The Platinum Anniversary Convention is probably the Crown. The Boston Star Trek Association held a private banquet for the guests and the members, so we got to dress up formal and be in a room with Gene [Roddenberry], Majel, George [Takei], Robin Curtis, and a few lesser guests. I had dinner with Gene and Majel. They were at another table, yes, but I was in the room! And when you're barely 20, 21, that's pretty damned awesome. And Gene—and I know the man was not a saint by any means, but he did put his money where his mouth was. Gene was on stage, and they were auctioning off merchandise, and Gene was signing some of the items and someone in the audience won/acquired the item, but the person was in a wheelchair, and certainly could not come up on the stage. And The Great Bird himself came down from the stage and knelt by that person, spoke with them, and signed the item. And that left me with such a profound love of the man, despite his faults.

At Buffalo Who Fest, the guest of honor was Jon Pertwee. Such a sweet man. They were showing an episode of his series *Worzel Gummidge*, and who walks in as it starts but Pertwee. *And he sat next to me.* I dared not move, I don't think I breathed, caught between the geekiness of "Holy *crap*! Please don't let me seem like a dork!" and *"Holy crap! look who's sitting next to me!!!!!"* So I spent more than half an hour sitting next to Jon Pertwee, scared stiff I'd look like an idiot if I said a word.

On Con Guests:

Bill Campbell was always a delight. Eve Miles was so damned funny I had tears pouring down my face. I saw part of Henry Winkler's talk at Philly Comic-Con, and that was like a dream—so was LeVar Burton, for that matter. Mark Lenard was always the nicest man, kind, quiet, charming, and very fan-friendly. De Kelley was a delight, very polite and kind. But if I had to pick just one, I would have to say John Barrowman. I've seen him twice, and he is absolutely zany and crazy and wild and funny beyond reason, and then will turn around and do or say something nice, or tell a story, and have you in tears for a different reason. He is just amazing in person—the kind of person you never want to leave the stage. Just being in the room with him is a party.

On Those People Who Made Lasting Impressions:

I'd have to go back to that story about Roddenberry. He's the man who started it all. George Takei remains a remarkable man, having lived through so much history. He told a story about filming in Eastern Europe, and how his taxi driver suddenly sped up and tried his damnedest to run down someone walking on the side of the road. The driver explained it was a Romani, a gypsy as we call them, and the racial hatred was so extreme they basically aimed to kill them on sight, and it was not only horrifying to hear, but to see how shaken George was by it.

When my husband still came to conventions, we used to bring L., and L. has cognitive issues and is more like a 2-3 year old. The guest at Shore Leave that year I think was Torri Higginson of *Stargate*. So, Mike stood in the autograph line to get L. an autograph. Torri was exceptionally patient and talked with L., and you could almost see the light suddenly click on—the person on the TV was right there in front of him. TV really existed. It doesn't sound like much to you or me, but truly, it was a *monumental* cognitive leap for him, and he has not stopped talking about her since.

So many, many people over the years, so many acts of kindness that you witness at conventions—people who are so accepting of others with differing abilities and fandoms and styles and orientations and whatever. People eager to help in any given situation. I suppose it's the kindnesses that really leave the lasting impressions. There are bozos and jerks in every crowd, but, overall, I want to say it's the kindness of people, both guests and fans, that stands out most.

The Boston Star Trek Association would have a picnic every summer at Shirley Maiewski's house—Grandma Trek, who had been in on Bjo Trimble's original campaign to save the series, and wrote the short story "The Mind Sifter." She had an entire room of *Star Trek*—a *Star Trek* museum for 1985 or so—and it was a wonder to behold. Who didn't want to be just like her?

On What Cons Have Given Her:

Conventions have given me everything—my friends, my dreams, my reality. Here were 1,000 people just like me, who didn't mind talking on esoteric subjects for hours. Friendship, goals, learning, the chance to meet celebrities—I mean really, in the end, conventions not only created my dreams, but made so many of them come true. I sat in the Captain's chair when they had built the bridge at a display in D.C. I stood on the bridge of the Aircraft Carrier *Enterprise*. I've traveled many places. I've met the original crew, every one of them. I've learned writing and illustrating and effects makeup and so much more. From a fifteen-year-old kid cranking out episode reviews and learning layout and deadlines and proofreading for fun, to someone who cranks out novels and wears a guest badge on their shirt—that's a dream come true. Almost all of my friends today, ones I've had sometimes for decades, have all been people I've met through fandom or at conventions. Conventions are a dream-factory of possibilities.

On Things People Don't Know About Her:

What can I say that I won't regret saying?

We got a write-up in *Starlog* magazine, December of 1985, for our Barbarian Banquets—costumed medieval dinners in the woods.

My first "published" work was in a *Remington Steele* fanzine!

I have a species of Hosta planted around my yard with the trademarked name of Captain Kirk.

My great-great grandfather is a folk hero in Lithuania—the kind who has parades and schools and museums in his honor. I was recently featured in three Lithuanian newspapers, talking about him for their 100th-year-of-independence celebrations.

I almost never call anyone on the phone. I've lost out on many things because I won't do it. It can take me days to build up to it. Anyone can call me, but good luck waiting for me to call you.

Don Sakers

On His Real Life Job:

For 42 years I was on the payroll of the Anne Arundel County Public Library. In high school and college, I was a part-time Page; upon graduation in 1980 I was hired as a full-time Librarian. I worked on the information desk at various library branches until 2016; just after my 58th birthday, I retired. Today I'm a full-time starving writer, living on a meager pension.

On His Personal History:

I was born a U.S. Navy brat in Yokosuka, Japan in 1958. In my childhood the family moved at the Navy's whim; we lived in Scotland, California, and Hawaii before settling in the ancestral homeland of Baltimore, Maryland.

I attended Loyola College in Baltimore, a small liberal arts college run by the Jesuits—the same folks who brought us the Spanish Inquisition. I graduated in 1980 with a Bachelor of Arts in Math and an inadvertent minor in English Literature.

In 1983, I met the man of my dreams, Thomas Atkinson, at a Balticon. We moved in together in 1987 (after Worldcon), bought a house together in 1994 (right before Technicon) were united in Civil Union in Vermont in 2001 (the weekend before Boskone), married at the Toronto Worldcon in 2003, and had our marriage recognized by Maryland in 2013 (and renewed our vows at DarkoverCon that year).

I wrote science fiction from grade school. I published my first short stories in 1981 and my first science fiction novel in 1988. Currently I have 32 published books. In 2009, I took on the position of book reviewer for *Analog Science Fiction* magazine.

On Being Introduced to Cons and Fandom:

My first con was DisCon II, the 1974 Worldcon. I had no idea what to expect. I've been in fandom for 44 years (over three centuries in dog years).

On Balticon:

At the 1974 Worldcon, I found flyers for local cons, including Balticon. My first Balticon, the following year, was Balticon 9. I attended Balticon regularly thereafter, with a hiatus in the mid-1990s. It's hard to narrow down specific events and people.

There was Balticon 1983, in the Inner Harbor, where I met a young costumer named Thomas Atkinson...eventually he would become my husband. So, yay Balticon!

I remember another downtown Balticon, sometime in the 1980s, when I was able to fulfill one of Esther Friesner's life goals by having a group of half-naked slave boys (one of them green) carry her around the con in a sedan char.

There was a Hunt Valley Inn Balticon, sometime in the late 70s, where Anne McCaffrey was the Guest of Honor—it was probably the first time I'd seen the great lady, and the whole weekend was suffused with her grace and intelligence.

On Being a Writer:

I've always wanted to be a writer; I started my first "novel," handwritten in a school copybook, when I was twelve and a half years old. In the next few years I started submitting short stories to the magazines...the first was published in 1980.

In 1988 I turned one of those stories into my first published sf novel, *The Leaves of October*. Unfortunately, the editor who bought the book departed the publisher before it came out, leaving no one who had read the book. *The Leaves of October* was not so much released as it *escaped*. Promotion was nil, and the book dropped out of sight without a ripple.

My writing career didn't advance much further until 2002, when developments in print-on-demand and e-books made self-publishing more viable. Since then I've released a bunch of books in both print and e-book formats.

Curse of the Zwilling (2003) is a dark fantasy set at Patapsco University, an imaginary liberal arts college in Maryland. The book centers around a grad student and four undergrads in the so-called Department of Comparative Religion, i.e. Magical Studies. When an ancient malevolent evil reappears, the five students must use all their abilities to fight it.

Meat and Machine (2014) is career retrospective of my LGBT stories, essays, and other short pieces. *Elevenses* (2016) collects 11 of my most popular short stories, along with food and drink suggestions for each. *A Cosmos of Many Mansions: Varieties of Science Fiction* (2017) is based on my first 50 book review columns for *Analog*.

Many of my science fiction books are part of a larger universe that I call the Scattered Worlds Mosaic. While each book is self-contained, and they can be read in any order, they share a common background and fit together into a coherent narrative (hence "mosaic"). My Scattered Worlds titles (so far) are *Dance for the Ivory Madonna, All Roads Lead to Terra, Weaving the Web of Days, A Voice in Every Wind, The Eighth Succession, Children of the Eighth Day*, and *The Leaves of October*.

On Influential Media:

Where to start? Asimov, Heinlein, and McCaffrey. Blish, Bradley, Butler, Clarke, Clementinal, Delany, LeGuin, Moorcock, Norton, Silverberg, two Smiths (Doc and Cordwainer), Zelazny. *The Twilight Zone. Star Trek. Star Wars. Babylon 5. Max Headroom. The Big Bang Theory. Killjoys. Doctor Who. Forbidden Planet. 2001. Buckaroo Banzai. Fullmetal Alchemist. Galaxy Quest.* As for comics or magazines, I have one of each: *The Legion of Super-Heroes* and *Analog*.

On Costuming:

My husband, Thomas, is a costumer, and we're both involved in the fannish costuming community. We're long-time members of the

Greater Columbia Fantasy Costumers Guild. Thomas is director of the Shore Leave Masquerade, and I'm one of his chief assistants. I've also been emcee for the Philcon Masquerade.

I've been in enough costume presentations, many of them award-winning, to earn the rank of Master Costumer in the International Costumers Guild. The most successful of these were "The 1001st Night" at the 1998 Worldcon in Baltimore (I was a genie); "Death's Defeat" at the 2004 Worldcon in Boston (I was Anubis); "CostumeCon 1889 Masquerade" at the 2009 CostumeCon in Baltimore (I was one of several Snow Queens); and our *Twilight Zone* tribute "Fridays at Ten," which won Best in Show at the 2001 Worldcon in Philadelphia.

While I can make costumes (fabric paint and beading are my skills), I'm much better at creating and executing the presentation part of masquerade costumes.

On Convention Panels:

I enjoy most panels at cons. Exploring an issue through the viewpoints of multiple people is invariably interesting and thought-provoking. I've sat on many panels—certainly well over a hundred—and been in the audience for many more. I've also made something of a name for myself as an effective moderator, especially at cons in the Mid-Atlantic region.

Some of these many panels stand out in my memory, even though I don't always remember the year or specific con. One con (Albacon, maybe?) did an annual "Alien Artifacts" panel that was great fun: Each panelist brought an object and passed it down the table; and the others acted as anthropologists explaining their theories about this artifact from an alien culture.

In a related vein, for a while Thomas and I did a traveling panel we called "Report of an Anthropological Expedition to Mundania," in which we shared our observations and theories of the non-fannish world. That was a hoot.

Recently, I've twice been a panelist (at Farpoint and Balticon) on a panel titled "Fandom Trolls and How to Vanquish Them," the brainchild of Jessica Moran. Other panelists included Keith R.A. DeCandido and Jennifer Povey. Both times, the panel led to profound and heartfelt discussions among panelists and audience; both times, it could have easily been a two-hour (or longer) event.

At a recent Balticon, I moderated a panel of military SF writers titled "Is it Torture if it's the Good Guys?" with Mark Van Name, Charles Gannon, S.M. Stirling, Christiana Ellis, and Griffin Barber. There was a standing-room-only audience. After a brief introduction, in which I reminded the audience that we were all fans and I wanted to keep discussions respectful, I asked the panelists something like "When is it okay to go beyond the boundaries?"

The panelists each gave reasoned answers that showed they'd given the issues a considerable amount of thought. But they all sounded like well-rehearsed, stock answers—so I took a big chance. I said, "Those were fine answers, but I sense that there are some powerful experiences behind them. Would anyone be willing to share?"

Well. The writers rose to the occasion, and what followed was a raw, intense, and sometimes-painful hour in which these writers talked about their own experiences and relationships with violence. The packed room was completely silent; the stories were deeply personal, powerful, and morally nuanced. All were moved.

Sometimes panels go off the rails in one way or another. I was on a panel at a Gaylaxicon with other panelists who apparently had some sort of personal grudge against me—they attacked and contradicted everything I said, until finally I said that it was obvious they didn't think I was qualified to be on the panel, so I was going to go sit in the audience—which I did.

At an Albacon long ago, I was on a panel with Larry Niven and no fewer than *seven* others, a number that virtually guarantees disaster. The moderator asked panelists to introduce themselves; by the time the third person had spoken, others started jumping in to address the panel topic, and it became a free-for-all. The moderator was virtually ineffective; after 40 minutes of this, he finally said, "Mr. Niven, you haven't said anything yet." Niven responded, chillingly, "I have been politely waiting for my turn…as has the gentleman next to me." (I was that gentleman.) I sputtered something, Niven made some coherent comments on the topic, and the rest has faded from memory.

The 2004 Worldcon in Boston took place in an enormous convention center with hundreds of rooms and a dozen levels. I was scheduled for a panel called "Us vs. Them" in a certain room. When the time came to start, all the panelists were there…but there was no audience other than my husband. We waited the requisite ten minutes, then shrugged and dispersed. I hung back, conferring with Thomas about what to do next. When we left the room a few minutes later, we saw a huge group heading in our direction.

They were our audience. Turns out the room had been switched at the last minute—but only the panelists knew. The audience showed up at the old room, and it took some time to get everything straightened out, at which point they trooped *en masse* to the correct room, to find only one panelist left.

I shrugged and said, "We don't need writers for this. Who's willing to come up here and be part of the panel?" Several people volunteered, and we wound up having a great panel completely on topic.

Which reminds me of a game we played at some of the early Darkover Grand Councils after the con moved to Maryland. Panels ended at midnight; about 1 a.m. about a dozen of us were roaming the halls, and we saw an open panel room. So we went in. Some of us took the role of panelists, others played audience. We started with the topic "How Do You Like Those Shoes?" To our surprise, other passersby strolled in and fell into the audience role, even asking questions and debating points. By the end of the hour we had a respectable crowd of night owls. When we left, another group took the front table and started another panel.

We continued impromptu panels in the wee hours for a few years.

On two occasions I managed to make the best of panels going off the rails.

The first was a late-night panel featuring the legendary Hal Clement, me, and two other writers. When the other two didn't show up, I gave the audience two options, "We can either try to address the topic at hand with just the two of us, or I can sit back and shut up, and we'll turn this into the Hal Clement Hour." The Hal Clement Hour it was: Mr. Clement spoke and answered questions, and it was marvelously successful.

At the 2006 Worldcon in Los Angeles, I was scheduled to moderate a "Global Warming" panel with Jerry Pournelle and two other writers. I was a little nervous—Doctor Pournelle was a forceful speaker not unaccustomed to controversy, and I knew his opinions on the topic were…a bit unorthodox. Even though I knew he was a consummate gentleman, I worried that I might not be up to the moderator's task of making sure everyone gets heard.

I needn't have worried. The other panelists bailed on me.

I took the same tack as I had with Hal Clement. "Folks, you didn't come here to listen to *me*; with your permission, I'm going to turn the floor over to Doctor Pournelle." I sat back and listened, except for occasionally prompting him or picking a questioner from the audience. Again, a great success.

I can't let this topic pass without mentioning the Panel from Hell. It's a popular theme for panels—writers regale the audience with tales of panels gone wrong. This particular one was arranged by Priscilla Olson at a Boskone, and I was one of the participants.

It started easily enough. Two writers who were not scheduled on the panel stepped up to insert themselves, which brought the number up to (I believe) seven. A couple of panelists built elaborate fortresses out of their own display books, blocking other panelists. Then one panelist launched into a lengthy, incoherent ramble…

In the audience, someone's cell phone rang, and they started carrying on a loud conversation. Another audience member rose to start his own pointless oration. Then the wall telephone in the room rang; Priscilla answered it, then announced that due to a schedule mix-up, we had to move the panel to another room down the hall. A smaller room.

By this time, the audience had caught on that all these distractions were previously arranged. The rest of the hour progressed with one contretemps after another, and by the end everyone was laughing so hard we were all gasping for breath.

On the Fans:

The primary thing I've learned is that the vast majority of fans are intelligent, articulate, and respectful. They're creative, compassionate, and always willing to consider alternate viewpoints and opinions. They're among the most appreciative, participative, and rewarding audiences in the world. Even the few bad apples are not just tolerated but accepted and even cherished.

I've also learned that there is no subject so technical, so obscure, or so inconsequential that you won't find at least two or three fans qualified and eager to discuss it intelligently.

On Con Activities:

In terms of formal activities, it's the panels that I find most rewarding. It's a rare con where I can't find half a dozen interesting subjects, along with any number of intelligent, creative people to discuss them. The concentrated intellectual ferment of con panels is hard to find elsewhere.

I'm always happy to spend some time in the dealer's room, where I'm usually looking for books. I enjoy masquerades and try to make time to make a turn through the art show. When I can, I love to spend time with filksingers, especially in a bardic circle arrangement where I can hear lots of different filkers. Although the group is formally split up, I'll make extraordinary effort to see Clam Chowder perform.

But the formal program is just one part of a con. Informally, I like spending time with friends both old and new. I'll generally visit a few room parties, though my nights of starting on the top floor and party-crawling all the way down have dwindled with age.

What I like best of all at cons is the informal, open-ended, come-and-go conversations that spring up from time to time in the bar or other communal space. These are the kind of sprawling conversations in which people drift in and out, topics range across the entire universe, and things are still going strong after six or seven hours. These conversations don't happen at every con, and they're completely unpredictable—but when they do happen, you'll see me sitting there engrossed.

On Favorite Con Recollections:

That would have to be the story of how Technicon was invaded by exploding mutant blind albino cave cows.

Technicon was a small, friendly con in Blacksburg, VA, and, in the early 1990s, half a dozen of us from the Baltimore area drove there each year. Along the way down the Shenandoah Valley, we would usually stop to visit one of the many caverns in the area. On one of those trips, we began talking about cave cows.

Many generations ago, we postulated, some bovines fell into a cavern and couldn't get out. Various unspecified mutations helped their descendants to survive, though of course in the lightless caves they gradually lost their coloration and sense of sight.

Much later, when scientists discovered them and brought some up to the surface to study, no one allowed for the difference in pressure—like deep-sea fish., the cows had a tendency to explode in the rarefied air of the surface.

We arrived at Technicon and spread news of these cows, adding details about the strange subterranean civilizations they'd built up (and also adding liberal amounts of alcohol). Everyone we talked to became incoherent with laughter. (To be fair, from the start, we were pretty incoherent ourselves). For all I know, legends of mutant blind albino exploding cave cows are still being spread in the region.

On Anne McCaffrey:

I've been fortunate enough to attend several cons with the late Anne McCaffrey as Guest of Honor. She was always gracious, intelligent, and good-humored. She told fascinating stories, and she was so brilliant in so many different directions that it was always a pleasure to spend time with her.

On Influential Con People:

I have an embarrassment of riches here. I'd say at least half of the most influential people in my life are folks I met at cons.

I've already talked about my husband Thomas, whom I met, courted, and married at various cons. So I guess I'll choose spouses Lisa A. Barnett & Melissa Scott. I met Lisa and Melissa at the Boston Worldcon in 1980, and over time they both became like sisters to me. We had so much in common: we were all LGBT activists and SF/fantasy writers, and our outlooks on life were very much in tune.

It's a friendship that lasted. Lisa passed away in 2006; Melissa and I remain part of each other's family.

On the Magic of Cons:

When I walked into my first con, the 1974 Worldcon in Washington, DC, my first thought was "I'm surrounded by people like me." I suppose most of us have had similar reactions upon our first exposure to fandom.

I was (and am) a gay, autistic, non-theist science fiction fan. I'm an intellectual with an IQ score north of 160, a Navy brat who grew up in exotic locales and went to a sheltered parochial elementary school.

I'm not just on a different wavelength than the mainstream world—I'm in a totally different *universe*. When I'm dealing with the mundane world, I always have to watch myself, ride herd on the weirdness as it were. I have to make a constant effort to stay on their level.

At cons, I can be myself…and feel appreciated for it.

On Something Others May Not Know:

In 44 years of living in and around convention fandom—quite a bit of it on panels and other public venues—I don't suppose there's much that my fannish friends don't know about me. In fact, it's more likely that there are things they wish I'd shut up about. Still, let me make an honest try here:

For many years in my library career, I did bedtime storytime for preschoolers while wearing blue flannel, one-piece, footie pajamas, complete with a trapdoor in the back. (I wore these over a tee shirt and running shorts, I hasten to add.) The pajamas, of course, were made by my costumer husband. I also had a tiger playsuit for special occasions.

Howard Weinstein

On His Real Life Job:

I'm a freelance writer and self-employed dog trainer, juggling both for the past 20 years. While neither has made me rich, I'm grateful to have found two jobs I really love doing. But I'm considering reducing dog training so I can focus more on writing. I just wish each day had ten extra hours in it, so I could do both more and better.

On a Brief Personal History:

Born in Ja-maica, mon—that's Jamaica, Queens, NYC. I still consider myself a transplanted New Yorker, even after almost 30 years in Howard County, Maryland (sure, yeah, they named the county after me...) Married, no kids—just Corgis. Hobbies: I don't really have hobby time any more (see above), but I have enjoyed building (and writing magazine articles about) scale models.

On His Introduction to Fandom and Conventions:

My first convention was the very first *Star Trek* convention, in Manhattan, back in January 1972. I was an enthusiastic *Star Trek* fan, already dreaming of being a *Star Trek* writer, and the convention happened to fall during my college winter-break vacation. My friends had all gone back to school by then, and I didn't want to miss this special event – I figured there might never be another one (though I was wrong about that!). So, I went by myself. It was quite an experience seeing talks by Isaac Asimov and Gene Roddenberry, the then-new *Star Trek* blooper reels, the NASA displays... and then wandering through the very crowded dealers' room.

The following year, the convention committee changed their dates to Presidents' Day weekend (thus becoming known as FebCon), which no longer coincided with my college vacation. So, I wasn't able to attend the ever-growing cons in '73, '74, or '75. Little did I know that by 1976, I'd be a professional *Star Trek* writer and making my first convention appearance as a guest.

On His Current Fame at Cons:

The word "fame" is way too strong, but once I sold my script for "The Pirates of Orion" episode to the animated *Star Trek* series in 1974, the *Star Trek* universe opened up to me. Following my rookie guest stint at Febcon '76, I started making appearances at other *Trek* cons in the New York area and elsewhere, plus speaking engagements at libraries, schools and colleges.

Then I started writing *Star Trek* novels for Simon & Schuster, which in turn led to my being one of a bunch of writers and scientists called in for one-on-one brainstorming sessions to help Leonard Nimoy shape the story for what would become *Star Trek IV: The Voyage Home*. Meeting and spending a few hours with Nimoy—a creative force I greatly admired—was one of the thrills of my life. I'll never know what exact role I played in the inclusion of whales as a key part of *Star Trek IV*, but my small involvement enabled me to visit the sets during shooting in the Spring of 1986, and got me a teeny-tiny "Producers Thanks" credit on the movie (still my favorite *Star Trek* film).

While I haven't written any *Star Trek* or science fiction in a while (I'm now focused on historical fiction), and don't do many conventions these days, I'm grateful that two Maryland cons I've been with since pretty much their inception (Shore Leave and Farpoint) still invite me to be a guest each year. They give me the opportunity to talk about my own new writing projects, engage fans in spirited discussions of new *Star Trek* and other genre films and TV shows, and pass along what I've learned from 44 years as a professional writer to up-and-coming writers.

On How He Became a Writer:

Stupidity! I was too young and dumb at 19 to accept the reality that unknown East Coast kids can't sell TV scripts to Hollywood-based shows. But reading the classic behind-the-scenes book *The Making of Star Trek* in 1968 or '69 lit my creative spark: I wanted to be a TV writer, and I wanted to write for *Star Trek*.

That I actually achieved that goal in 1974 (before I turned 20) is mostly due to miraculous luck and timing. But "The Pirates of Orion" gave me the credit and credibility to open the door to all the *Star Trek* writing I would do over the next 35 years.

On Influential People and Media:

Obviously, my stumbling into fandom is all *Star Trek*'s fault! But *Star Trek* introduced me to the work of such talented writers as Harlan Ellison, Theodore Sturgeon, and David Gerrold, and put me in a unique position to meet and spend some personal time with many writers, producers, and actors I admired—among them, Gene Roddenberry, Leonard Nimoy, George Takei, Walter Koenig, and Harve Bennett, to name a few.

I'm glad I got the chance to chat with Harve at what was apparently his very first convention appearance, decades after he'd produced *Star Trek II, III, and IV*. [Editor's Note - Farpoint 2009 was not Harve Bennett's first convention appearance, but it was his first since exiting the Trek franchise in 1989.] Before I introduced him at his first talk, I told him I always thought of him as the guy who saved *Star Trek*, rescuing the series from the bog that was *Star Trek: The Motion Picture*, and leading to all the *Star Trek* permutations that followed those well-done 1980s movies. He appreciated the compliment—and, no surprise, he deservedly thought of himself the same way!

On His Years in Fandom:

Well, actually, since before I knew "fandom" was a thing, since I'm one of the first generation of *Star Trek* fans who watched the show in its first run from 1966-69 on NBC—and wrote "Save *Star Trek*" letters to the network when the show teetered on the edge of the cancellation abyss. Then I discovered the larger world of fandom at that inaugural 1972 *Star Trek* convention.

On Fandom Activities:

Over these many years, I've appeared at conventions in New York, New England, Pennsylvania, Cleveland, Chicago, New Jersey, even Texas. And I've written articles for the late, great *Starlog* and more recently for the official *Star Trek Magazine*. Some of those articles are available for reading at my website, www.howardweinsteinbooks.com – just click on the "Interviews & Articles" section.

On His Favorite Con Activities:

Leading writing workshops with some of my author colleagues, where we try to help new writers improve their skills; appearing on varied panels; doing the relaxed Bob & Howie Show with my longtime pal Bob Greenberger, wherein we chat with audience members who care to wander into the ballroom at 10 AM on Sunday mornings about what we're working on, and current developments in the science fiction media world. We love answering questions and moderating spirited exchanges of opinion—and we try to avoid spoilers.

On His Favorite Con Recollection:

Before I lived in Maryland, I used to bring my charming little Welsh Corgi named Mail Order Annie with me to cons in the Baltimore area. Annie would go on stage with me, pose for pictures and petting—and also join me for a little charity auction item we called "Ice Cream with Howie & Annie." I'd then treat the highest bidder to ice cream from the hotel snack bar, and some private time with me and Annie to talk about whatever and have Annie show off her extensive repertoire of cute tricks.

One time, as Annie and I walked down the hotel hallway, a little girl asked if my dog was "child-friendly." I assured her Annie loved kids, and Annie made a new friend, one of many.

On His Favorite Person to Meet at a Con:

A famous person? As in actors, writers, etc.? Wow, I've been fortunate enough to meet so many, I couldn't choose one. So, I'm going to go with favorite people—and not the celebrities, but all the kindred spirits I've met, some of whom I only knew briefly, others who became longtime friends.

Although, now that I think of it, I would like to name two actors who demonstrated class and kindness. At my rookie con as a guest, FebCon '76 in New York, I was a very shy 21-year-old kid, with a shaky claim to "fame." At this last of the fabled FebCons, the actually-famous guests and the folks running the con kind of knew each other. As the newest kid on the block, when I hung out in the hospitality con suite (the long-gone Commodore Hotel's Presidential Suite), I mostly sat and listened.

The con suite, for those who may not know, was set up as a refuge where the guests and con staff (mostly high-school and college kids) could relax, grab drinks, snacks or breakfast, and just avoid the crowds. One morning, I had breakfast at the big dining room table with several con helpers and DeForest Kelley—Dr. McCoy himself!

When De got up to leave with the helpers assigned to him, I trailed behind, and someone near the door asked if they could take a picture with De. Ever the true Southern gentleman, De said OK, stopped and smiled for the camera. I mumbled something about getting myself out of the picture; De invited me to stay, and when I said, "I'm just one of the little writer guests," he replied in his soft Georgian drawl: "Well, without you writers, we actors would have nothin' much to say."

Decades later, when I was a convention veteran, and had met many actors and writers I admired, I found myself in a moment of deja-vu. It was at Shore Leave in 2008, and I'd invited a 13-year-old email-penpal and super-fan named Kalliope Dalto to attend her very first convention with her Dad. The formidable Malcolm McDowell was one of the big-name guests—and he happened to be one of my young friend's favorite actors. I think Kalliope would've sold a kidney to meet him.

Since I'd be introducing Malcolm at his first talk, I went into the ballroom's "green-room" corner where he sat relaxing quietly about

15 minutes before he'd be going on stage and introduced myself to him first. Since he'd long played so many characters notable for their dangerous intensity, I had no idea what he might be like. Turned out he was a pussycat. I briefly told him about my friend Kalliope and asked if he'd mind if I brought her back to say hello.

Malcolm graciously said yes, and he did much more than give my star-struck young friend a quick, polite greeting—he gestured for her to sit down in the armchair next to his. When I mentioned that she wanted to be a writer, and had just had her first short story published in a Johns Hopkins University young-writers journal, Malcolm said to Kalliope almost exactly what De Kelley had said to me 32 years earlier: "Without writers, we actors would have nothing to say."

On His Favorite Con Guests:

Impossible to name just one. But I loved when conventions invited some of the old-time character actors to appear as guests, especially because so many of them are gone now. These actors may only have appeared in one or two *Star Trek* or *Twilight Zone* episodes, but they were also ubiquitous as TV guest stars for decades. One of the most delightfully-charming pairings I had the pleasure of seeing were William Schallert (Patty Duke's TV-sitcom dad and Nilz Baris of "The Trouble with Tribbles") and Antoinette Bower (Sylvia from *Star Trek*'s "Catspaw" episode) at Shore Leave.

I don't know how well they knew each other, or whether they'd ever worked with each other. But they were gently, humorously magical onstage together, sharing show-biz stories and answering questions like a couple of dear old friends—or an old married couple. I did get the chance to mention to them later that they'd be perfect playing the parts made famous by Katherine Hepburn and Henry Fonda in the movie version of the play *On Golden Pond*.

On Why He Attends Cons:

I'd have to say my reasons have changed over all these years. Initially, I attended that very first New York *Star Trek* convention because I loved *Star Trek*. I had no idea there were so many other fans who felt the same way. Conventions gave us a shared experience.

Then I went back as professional writer because I was invited to be a guest speaker, with pretty much no idea what that entailed or what doors might open. What I discovered was a world inhabited by kindred spirits, and in those early years I formed friendships which continue 40+ years later. I was also privileged to meet and listen to actors, writers and other creative people whose TV and movie work (and books) I've admired and enjoyed.

Of course, I also found conventions to be a good way to meet fans who bought and read my books (especially in those days before the internet), and it was flattering when they wanted to know what I was working on next. So being at conventions was and remains a refreshingly low-tech way to keep the personal touch alive in an increasingly impersonal time when so many people keep their eyeballs glued to their digital screens at the expense of engaging with other humans face-to-face.

On Something People May Not Know About Him:

That I'm really shy. Oddly, I find it much easier to be on stage and talk to a roomful of hundreds of people than to make small-talk with someone I don't already know.

On Maryland Cons:

For years, I've encouraged people I know to come and experience such fan-run cons as Shore Leave, Farpoint and their related offshoots and predecessors. Though I've never attended the mega-cons like DragonCon or San Diego ComicCon, I went to a couple of WorldCons in Boston and Baltimore in the 1980s—and I didn't enjoy them. I found them too big, too sprawling, with too many people attending.

By contrast, the Maryland cons are labors of love for the fans who organize them year after year—just the right size to offer a wide range of programming choices and attract some big-name guests, but compact enough that you don't spend your day trekking great distances to get where you want to go.

I think most fans would find these conventions a real treat.

On a More Serious Note:

I would like to add one other thing—just a little cautionary reminder that being a passionate fan of something is supposed to be fun, not apocalyptic warfare! Whether it's sports, science fiction, TV shows or movies, I've occasionally seen people get so wrapped up in their own love of the subject that they take disagreements as personal insults. When this happens, I've seen friendships sundered, enemies made, and enjoyment curdled.

Unfortunately, the anonymity and indirect communication of the internet has made this worse. People say things online they'd probably never say face-to-face.

As dictionaries note, the word "fan" derives from "fanatic" —but every debate doesn't have to devolve into a cage match. Opinion isn't gospel. Disagree without being disagreeable. If a discussion threatens to boil over, just smile and walk away. If somebody else acts like a jerk, I'm not required to be a jerk in return.

In general, treat other people the way you'd like to be treated. You'll end up more respected – not to mention happier – than the belligerent brawler who has to win every battle.

The Convention Committees

Inge Heyer

On Her Job in Real Life:

I am a professor, teaching astronomy and physics at Loyola University Maryland in Baltimore.

On Her Personal History:

I was born and raised in Berlin, Germany, and completed my secondary education there before accepting a scholarship to attend Tenri University (Japan) where I studied Japanese. After earning an undergraduate degree in Astronomy and Physics from Smith College in Massachusetts, I earned a Master's degree in Astronomy from the University of Hawaii at Manoa, and a Ph.D. in Science Education from the University of Wyoming.

In addition to my professional work as senior data analyst at the Space Telescope Science Institute, I also served as the public information officer at the Joint Astronomy Centre in Hilo, HI, and served as Deputy Press Officer for the American Astronomical Society. I have earned Shodan in both Judo and Karate and am an irregular guest science blogger for startrek.com.

I currently teach astronomy and physics at Loyola University in Maryland. And if you have ever wondered how those beautiful Hubble images got into science fiction series like *Babylon 5* and *Star Trek*, you're looking at the trouble-maker who instigated this.

On Her Introduction to Fandom:

In 1971, *Star Trek* was first broadcast in Germany. Despite the rather poor translation, I was hooked immediately.

On Her Introduction to Conventions:

In 1982, when I attended college in Massachusetts, DeForest Kelley made an appearance at a local car dealership (don't ask me why). It wasn't exactly a convention, but it was the first time I realized that there were lots of other fans. It was there that I heard of Shirley Maiewski ("Grandma Trek") and joined the Boston *Star Trek* Association. The next convention was either the Boston Bash or one of the NYC cons, I don't remember.

On Her Years in Fandom:

Well, 2018 – 1982 = 36 years

On Her Current Connections to Conventions and Fandom:

I have been involved with Shore Leave ever since I moved to Baltimore in 1992 to work on the Hubble Space Telescope. I have been co-chair of Shore Leave since 2013.

On *Star Trek*:

Star Trek has been a major influence in my life, second only to family and education. While I enjoy reading and watching all kinds of things, *Star Trek* will always be special. It gave a young kid a vision of a future worth aspiring to, a future where, through the power of education and fellowship, you can overcome any challenge the universe throws at you.

On Her Con Jobs:

Science track coordinator, author track coordinator, document preparation (program book, flyers, etc.), helping out with various other things at times (dealers' room, art show, hotel, logistics), and now co-chair.

On Difficulties in Running a Con:

It's like herding cats: you have to have the right incentive to make the people want to go where you want them to go... with gentleness and subtlety... cats do not react well to show of force.

But seriously, planning ahead is the key ingredient here. Have team meetings every month, and make sure all the little details get done. Having a SOP manual is essential (otherwise you'll go nuts).

On Why She Continues Working at Shore Leave:

The happy faces and kind comments of the attending fans. While it may seem overwhelming at times, when everyone comes together and has a good time, that makes everything worthwhile.

On Her Favorite Activities at a Con:

Personally, it's getting books signed by my author friends. Listening to the various speakers would be a close second. Fandom has exposed me to so many different aspects of life and work that a regular professor would never get to know.

On Her Favorite Con Recollections:

Well, I don't know if this qualifies, but I always enjoy seeing our author guests huddle in a corner and plot new adventures. Many a book and anthology has been hatched at Shore Leave, and many books have been premiered at Shore Leave as well.

On Favorite Con Guests:

That would have to be Richard Dean Anderson. For me as a scientist, MacGyver is just the best (and I use his problem-solving skills in my physics classes all the time). Yes, I know he's not *Trek*, but he was apparently runner-up for the role of Ben Sisko in *DS9*.

On What Makes the Maryland Cons So Popular:

They are family-oriented, long-lived, and therefore have long traditions and a built-in fan base. I know fan families in the fourth generation. At every Shore Leave or Farpoint I know at least half the people there. It's like a huge family reunion every year. The con-chairs of the Baltimore-area cons talk to each other, and in many cases the committees even overlap. We keep going because it's family, not because we want to make money. And because it's family, we want to do a good job.

On Meeting People at Cons:

Almost all of my friends come from fandom. And the few I met outside fandom didn't stay outside for very long. Two of my doctoral advisers who knew nothing of fandom are now con coms themselves.

On Something People Don't Know About Her:

Probably very little. Some may not know that I am a black belt, and some may not know that I speak Japanese.

Melissa James

On Her Real Life Job:

I teach individuals with disabilities for the state of Maryland.

On Her Personal History:

I'm a lifelong Baltimorean, raised in the city. I now live in Baltimore County. I'm single; no kids of my own, but I'm a godmother, an aunt, a great-aunt, and a great-great-aunt. What else? I'm a teacher. I was a volunteer organist and choir director for almost twenty years. I'm active in the state chapter of the National Rehabilitation Association. And, of course, I'm a member of the *Star Trek* Association of Towson, the fan club that puts on the Shore Leave convention. I'm also a member of Watson's Tin Box, a Maryland-based Sherlock Holmes group.

On Her Introduction to Fandom:

I guess my introduction to fandom was reading *Star Trek Lives!* by Joanie Winston. I would read my brothers' high school English books, becoming familiar with classic science fiction short stories, and I would read their Marvel comics. One of my brothers gave me *The Making of Star Trek* by Stephen Whitfield. *Star Trek* had just finished its second season when the first edition of the book came out in paperback, so I wrote the third season episode titles in the back of the book. I read that book over and over until it fell apart.

As far as meeting fans in fandom, some of my friends in high school, Denise, Kathy, Cathy, and Regina, were *Trek* fans (a.k.a. The Denebian Slime Devils later), and we went to *Star Trek*-themed events at local libraries. We realized that the Baltimore area had an active fan base.

On Her Introduction to Conventions:

The first convention I attended was Balticon 9 at the Pikesville Hilton in 1976. Later that year Denise and I went to Bicentennial-10, a *Star Trek* convention in New York City, celebrating the tenth anniversary of *Star Trek*. We stayed with my brother and his family; we certainly couldn't afford to stay at a hotel! Kathy, Cathy, and I ran into Baltimore fans at a *Star Trek* convention in Atlanta; that eventually led to STAT and Shore Leave. The August Party conventions in the late '70s and early '80s were a huge influence in showing us what a fan-run convention could look like.

On Her Years in Fandom:

43! Time flies.

On Being a Con Chair:

It may sound cliché, but when it all comes together, it's a great feeling to be part of something that makes people happy and allows them to express creativity. You have to listen and understand people's points of view, whether it's those of your committee members or the fans. You have to trust that your committee knows what they're doing; they've been working on the convention all year. And if you're not organized, forget it.

On Difficulties in Running a Con:

Different things. In the early days, having to cut the autograph line. Trying to remember all the details and pieces of information. I was on a panel at Philcon several years ago; the topic was "So You Want to Run a Convention," and there were seven of us on the panel. One guy asked our advice about starting a convention and we all exclaimed, "Don't!" It's a lot harder now. There are many, many conventions out there, mostly pro, with deep pockets. Some actors now have contracts to only appear at certain pro cons, and it's harder for the fan-run media conventions to compete with that. And there's always another convention on "our weekend."

On the Funniest Thing at a Con:

Regina and I saw a performance of "The Empire Striketh Back: A Shakespearean *Star Wars*" at this year's Balticon by The Cohesion Theater Company. They played multiple roles with puppets and props. It was great. There have been many hilarious skits performed at cons over the years, as Masquerade entries or as plays. Some of the hall costumes are very funny, like the giant dinosaurs in Trek uniforms. It's fun to watch fans, especially the really young ones, interact with the unexpected.

On the Denebian Slime Devils:

Singing with the Denebian Slime Devils is a great opportunity to be silly and hang out with your closest friends. We'd still get together socially even if we weren't performing at cons, but where else can you do a parody of *Jurassic Park* to the tune of "MacArthur Park," complete with dinosaur puppets? Unless you're Weird Al. We keep saying we'll do a CD, but I think 2019 may be the year we actually do it.

We've been singing as the Slimes for 39 years now, not counting high school field days. Shore Leave 41 will be our 40th anniversary!

Picking a favorite song of ours is a challenge. I don't think I have an absolute favorite, but there's the "Whale Song" about *Star Trek IV*, the "Wrath of Khan Rag," "Back in the Capsule Again," and "I See Clones of Jango, Jango, Jango." For something more serious, I like "Pure Imagination," about Universal's *Harry Potter* theme park.

On Influential People and Media:

TV influences: *Bonanza, Star Trek, Twilight Zone, Outer Limits, Dark Shadows*. BBC's *Sherlock*. *The Big Bang Theory*, certainly. Movie influences? The Twilight movies- NOT the vampire ones—I'm talking about the cheesy horror movies that were on when we'd get home from elementary school. *Galaxy Quest*—one of my favorite memories is of my brothers and their families laughing their heads off in the theater. People? My mother, who wrote song parodies for fellow teachers' retirements; my brothers; fans who encouraged us, like Bev Volker, Nancy Kippax, Marion McChesney, and Roberta Rogow. Performers: Tom Lehrer, Weird Al Yankovic, Spike Jones, The Capitol Steps, Stan Freberg.

On Con Jobs:

I've run programming, guest relations, information, pre-registration, and served as comptroller. I liked scheduling the programming, which consisted of only two or three tracks at the time. Once I had a programming committee meeting, and I set up a chart like one in an old Alan King skit about network programming. That was fun. Pre-registration gives me the chance to meet and talk with a lot of people.

On the Reasons Why She Continues Working the Cons:

Because no one wants my job(s)! (Laughs) I still want to help put on a con that I would like to attend. I've almost burned out a couple times, but people have been there to help me keep my act together. And I enjoy seeing the club members and committee people and running into past club members and committee people!

On Her Favorite Con Activities:

I enjoy going to filk performances, singing with my friends, going to Masquerade, trying to see a panel about a show I like. Sometimes I'll catch a guest talk. I enjoy talking to people at the Shore Leave table at other conventions. Once in a while, I'll actually be on a panel. That's fun and nerve-wracking at the same time.

On Her Con Recollections:

That's going back quite a while! I remember, at Balticon in 1976, there was a presentation with storyboards about a movie coming out the following year about a boy *and his sister* (no surprise later about Leia) who were fighting against an evil empire with a force that was in all things or something like that. It sounded dumb—it's a good thing I'm not in the movie business.

Also, at a Balticon: The Flying Karamazov Brothers were performing—this is before they appeared on TV—and they didn't have enough money to get home. So, a collection was taken up in the ballroom to pay their way back. Fans can be exasperating, but they are some of the most generous people you'll meet.

On Con Guests:

Rene Auberjonois and his wife Judith are nice, down-to-earth people. Bill Campbell was a generous soul. He and his wife Tereza gave back to the Hollywood community to ensure that people in every level of show business were taken care of and not forgotten.

On People Who Have Made an Impression on Her:

Gary Lockwood once told us at Registration that Shore Leave was the best organized convention he'd ever been to, and that we could keep going for a long time "if we didn't screw it up." Then there's Lisa Stanton, from Erie, PA—she comes every year to help at Registration and hardly sees any of the convention. She's made costumes, props, and decorations out of all sorts of items. She is super-talented and creative.

On Something People Don't Know About Her:

I'm not really comfortable in large crowds!

Sharon Van Blarcom

On Her Real Life Job:

Acquisition Logistician for U.S. Navy contractor at Naval Air Station, Patuxent River, MD.

On Her Brief Personal History:

I have been interested in fantastic worlds and science fiction all my life. I remember watching *Batman* and *Lost in Space* on TV when I was too small to remember much else. I read a lot of science fiction and fantasy growing up. *A Wrinkle in Time* is one of my all-time favorite books. I found it when I was in 5th grade as our school librarian set out a contest for all 5th and 6th graders to read all the Newberry Award books that had been published to date by the end of the school year.

I graduated from Salisbury University in Maryland with a degree in Business and Finance and met and married my husband John a few years after that. As of this date, we have been married 31 years and have two children, Tim and Cyndi.

On Her Introduction to Fandom:

I discovered a Creation con was scheduled for the Hyatt hotel in Crystal City, VA in the mid-late 1980s, I think through an ad in *Starlog*. I went there and discovered fandom was an actual experience one could have. I had a blast meeting other fans and finding all the cool stuff you could find in a vendor's room.

On Her Introduction to Conventions:

I found out about OktoberTrek and Shore Leave at that Creation con. Once I went to a true fan-run convention, I never went back to a Creation con again. I was an attendee at the first OktoberTrek, a helper at the second and third OkoberTreks and was invited to be on the programming staff for the first Farpoint. I then became Farpoint's programming chair and held that position until becoming con chair in 2001.

On Her Years in Fandom:

30+

On Influential Media:

Of course, *Star Trek*, as it is what got me into fandom in the first place. My favorite book series is *The Time Quartet* by Madeleine L'Engle, the *Foundation* series by Isaac Asimov and the *Dune* series by Frank Herbert. All of these books require one to be more than a passive reader and give you different ideas and points of view to consider. I'm also a huge fan of the *Harry Potter* books and movies, as it is a fandom that I share with my children and several other family members. And there's the *Star Wars* Universe and, of course, my Disney/Pixar obsession.

On Being a Con Chair:

My husband will say it's "too much." The con chair is the ringmaster, keeping all of the pieces of the convention puzzle moving into place at the right time and keeping an eye on the big picture. It's about staging a successful weekend for the fans who choose to spend their hard-earned money at Farpoint, as opposed to the many other ways they could spend their leisure time. My work as Farpoint con chair is split into two big areas—the stuff I *have* to do to keep things moving, and the stuff I love to do because it's fun. Keeping things moving involves handling the finances (setting and managing the budget, filing taxes, paying bills, ordering supplies, etc.) and putting together the master calendar of activity for the year to ensure we've got everything planned and ready to go on the first day of the convention. The master calendar specifies when and where we'll have committee and/or programming team meetings, as well as identifying the other conventions we plan to attend for publicity. The love-to-do stuff includes working with the wonderful committee that puts all the various pieces of the Farpoint puzzle into place each year. I'm very lucky to have a team of strong, dedicated and talented people to work with. I also love to attend other conventions representing Farpoint. I'm very proud of our con, and I enjoy introducing what we do to attendees at other events. In this day and age of the giant comic-con, what Farpoint does as a fan-run convention is not as well-known amongst fans. Showing comic-con attendees our program book and schedule with its over 200 hours of events, and explaining that their convention membership ticket includes one to two complimentary celebrity signatures, can be amazing. That's because comic-con attendees have never experienced the differences between a fan-con programming model and a comic-con programming model. I love it when we blow their minds with the phrase "celebrity signature at no additional charge."

On the Challenges of Being a Con Chair:

Keeping our identity as a fan-run convention intact is a challenge. Right now, conventions are judged on how many celebrity names are on your guest list, and I spend a lot of time at publicity events talking about the benefits a fan-run convention offers over having a dozen different celebrities in a row to sign autographs. Don't get me wrong—there's a place for the convention with the large celebrity lineup. That type of event has financial resources we simply don't have, and is able to bring some very big celebrity names to meet their fans. But I strongly feel there is still a need and a place for regional, fan-run conventions. We just have to talk a lot more and as loudly as possible to get the word out.

Each Farpoint committee member is head of a particular organizational department—programming, registration, operations, vendors/dealers, etc. Any time you have a large and diverse group of people working together you will run into clashes of personality and/or expectations of who is doing which job. As con chair, I have to walk that fine line between captaining the "ship" and moderating the discussions. I try my damnedest to be as fair as possible with group consensus being the goal, but there are times when "no" has to be the correct and final answer.

On Strange Things She's Experienced at a Con:

It amazes me the "friends" that will pop up when Farpoint happens to bring in their favorite celebrity. I'll have met someone casually or not heard from an old friend for a long time, and then Farpoint books "Ms. X." Suddenly my casual acquaintance or long-lost friend is my *best* friend. It's also strange how people will assume that, just because they know me or another convention committee member, they are entitled to free tickets or perks. These instances luckily aren't constant but happen often enough to be disheartening.

On the Perks of Being a Con Chair:

The biggest perk for me is putting on an event that brings happiness to so many people—especially when someone says, "I go to a lot of conventions but Farpoint is my favorite because I feel so welcome." That is our mission, to be a place where fans can get together, enjoy each other's company and learn from each other. Of course, getting hugs from, and sit-down face time with, our celebrity guests isn't a bad perk either!

On the Longevity of Farpoint:

It's a result of the fandom love. Farpoint was founded by Steve and Renee Wilson with the mission of providing fans a place to share their passions and knowledge with each other—to make those connections that are sometimes missing in our everyday lives. Everywhere else, "nerds" can be considered "unusual" or "strange." Farpoint is truly centered on the fans and the fan experience, and I feel that resonates with our attendees.

On Her Other Con Jobs:

I started out as a helper and then a staff member for programming. That led to me being the programming chair and ultimately con chair. Picking a favorite isn't possible. I've enjoyed (mostly) every minute, and each job has its own pros and cons.

On Her Favorite Farpoint Activities:

I love the activities Farpoint offers that many cons today do not, such as featuring our Masquerade costume contest as the main stage offering on Saturday evening. Most comic-cons do a costume parade type of presentation versus the full show with celebrity judges that we and other fan run conventions do. I also enjoy our Friday evening opening ceremony, which is a chance for everyone to gather and start the weekend off with some fun and laughs.

On Her Favorite Con Story:

This is one of my very favorites because I am a huge *Next Generation* fan. One year, when I was still programming chair, I was put in charge of picking up Jonathan Frakes at the airport Saturday morning. He was appearing at Farpoint Saturday and Sunday that year. Part of Jonathan's arrangements included his not staying at the Hunt Valley Inn but in downtown D.C. Patrick Stewart was doing a play there, and Jonathan wanted to visit him. We were, as usual, using the McCormick Suite at the hotel for con operations. Since Jonathan didn't have a room at the HVI, he was supposed to use the McCormick Suite parlor as his green room. Steve Wilson, as con chair, threatened all committee and staff with "Don't try to get into McCormick to hang out and mess up the parlor with food and trash, because our guest will be in there, and if you do it I'll have to kill you." You know, typical con chair stuff. So, I go to the airport Saturday morning and successfully pick Jonathan up, although it did require a double take from me because Jonathan had shaved off his beard. When I mentioned not recognizing him right away, Jonathan told me he had shaved his beard off for a while because it scratched his baby daughter's skin when he was playing or cuddling with her. I joked with him that some of the fans may not recognize him without the beard.

We arrive at the hotel and reach the McCormick Suite main door on the 2nd floor. And... my key doesn't work to let us in. Now, this was when the electronic locks and key cards were ridiculously unreliable (it took the hotel years to get any kind of reliability out of them). So, there I was, in the hallway with Jonathan Frakes (and no security staff), trying to figure out how to get him into this room. Option one was for us to go up to the 3rd floor, where I had one of the sleeping rooms connected to the loft level of McCormick (it's a two-story suite). But my room was a mess, so that was going to be embarrassing. Then option two popped into my head. I knew that Renee Wilson's mom, Beverly Volker, was in the adjoining 2nd floor sleeping room to McCormick, and her door was one step to my right. Bev was in there watching Steve and Renee's son Ethan (around five at the time) and a couple of the other family little ones while their parents were working the con. So, being stranded in the hallway, I tap on the next door and Bev Volker opens it. Jonathan is standing behind me, a few paces back. The hallway lighting was a little dim during that time.

(SCENE)

Me: "Bev, my key isn't working. Please open the door to McCormick."

Bev: "I can't. Steve said not to."

Me (starting to panic): "You have to. We have to get in there."

Bev: "I can't. *He*'s in there."

Me: "Who's in there?"

Bev: "Jonathan. Steve will be really mad if I let you in. He told me not to let anyone into McCormick while Jonathan was in there."

At this point Jonathan is chuckling behind me, and I'm also trying not to laugh.

Me (pointing over my shoulder): "Bev, this is Jonathan. We need to get in."

Beverly peers over my shoulder into the dim hallway and after a moment realizes I really am standing in the hotel hallway with our main celebrity guest, trying to get into the locked room next door.

Bev: "Oh my goodness. It is you, isn't it?"

Jonathan is full-on laughing at this point. Bev sends little Ethan through their adjoining door to let us in, and while we're (finally) entering I say:

"I told you your lack of beard was going to cause an issue!"

(END SCENE)

I'm lucky Jonathan Frakes has a good sense of humor.

On Her Favorite Con Guests:

Well, based on the previous story, obviously Jonathan Frakes is up there. I also adored John Billingsley and his wife, Bonita Friedericy, as they are just a lot of fun and really care about the fans. The same goes for Lee Arenberg, who to this day always says "Farpoint is still my favorite con" when he sees me (which isn't that often). Felicia Day is another favorite as she is extremely open to joining in on the convention activities and giving back to the fan community. I also love our Farpoint regulars, the guests who come every year and help us put on our show.

On Why She Continues with the Hard Work:

For the people I've met and continue to meet. Every time I'm ready to throw in the towel over something, a convention-goer will come up to me and thank me and the committee for providing a time and place for all of us to gather as a community. The loyalty of our regular attendees is something that encourages me and reminds me how lucky I am to be a member of fandom.

On Who Has Made a Lasting Impression:

Oh. My goodness. Too many to count. Working on Farpoint has shaped me and provided experiences I would never have had and friends I probably never would have met. For that, I am very grateful and blessed.

On Something People May Not Know About Her:

I have finally had to admit I'm a reality competition show junkie. *The Amazing Race, Top Chef,* and *Project Runway* are all favorites. My sisters and I text each other every Monday night during *Dancing with The Stars*. I have curtailed my habit in recent years, though, after horrifying Steve and Renee Wilson with my musings about turning the Farpoint children's program track into a kiddie beauty pageant. That was when I was laid up with a back injury, and I was using a marathon of *Toddlers and Tiaras* to distract myself from the pain. Trainwreck TV like that show served the purpose well. I had just watched an episode that walked viewers through how much money the pageant runners can make from a single event (it can go into the high five figures, if it's a big enough event), when the Wilsons came to visit my house-bound carcass. I made the comment about the children's track being a kiddie pageant, and Renee replied "I think we'll all be quitting the committee at that point," with Steve adding "Oh, we *so* need to get you out of the house!" And, I guess overall that's what fandom does. It gets you out of the house.

Renee Wilson

On Her Real Life Job:

In the real world, I work in Project Management for Howard County Fire and Rescue. I was born in Baltimore, and now live in Elkridge, Maryland.

On Her Introduction to Fandom:

My introduction to fandom was through my mother, Beverly Volker, who had a passion for *Star Trek*, *Alien Nation* and *Starman*. I attended my first convention, a Philcon, when I was eight years old. My mother and her sister, Nancy Kippax, created a fanzine called *Contact*. It was a very popular zine in the 1970s and 1980s, collecting stories and poems about the friendship (*just* a friendship, Mom insisted!) between Kirk and Spock, backed by some amazing artwork. A lot of work went into putting together the fanzines. My father was the art director, and did all the early artwork. My sister, my brother and I were the collators. In those days, most zine publishers were too poor to pay for copies to be collated and bound, so Mom would bring home cases of loose pages, and we would circle the dining room table, putting them together in order. Then we would GBS bind them with spiral combs. It was quite the labor of love! I also wrote a poem or two, and produced some artwork. *Contact* produced eight regular issues, two Christmas specials, and a full-length novel. The first issue was released in 1975, and it lasted until 1987.

On Conventions:

The Volker family (and other assorted members of the "*Contact* Crowd") attended New York conventions twice yearly, one at Labor Day and the other in February—Febcon. The *Contact* zine premiered at these conventions, so we would all caravan to the Statler Hilton in New York City and man a dealer's table for the weekend. In the evenings, the group had *loud* room parties. Hotel security knocking on the door was not an unusual event. I, being young, often fell asleep amidst the noise. When security showed up, Mom would point to me sleeping and say, "How could we have made a lot of noise? There's a *child* sleeping here!" I remember waiting for hours in the registration line at the Taft hotel and then having to wait forever to check into our room. The drivers would then all take their cars out to New Jersey to park where it was cheaper. They'd ride the subway back into the city.

We carted probably a thousand copies of the latest issue of *Contact* to every con. No one in the dealers' room took credit cards then, and the zines sold for $10 to $20 each. We wound up carrying a *lot* of cash. Banks weren't like they are now, either, so you didn't just have a branch of your neighborhood bank in Manhattan. So mom, being always inventive, would carry around several thousand dollars in her bra all weekend.

Like most con kids, I was dressed up as Trek aliens for the costume call (its name until OktoberTrek switched to the grander "Masquerade" in 1990.) When I was about eight or nine, Mom made me a blue silk dress and sent me on stage as the Metron from "Arena." [Editor's Note: A popular episode from the original *Star Trek's* first season, based on a story by SF author Frederic Brown.] Flash forward 20 years, and I'm at dinner at the Hunt Valley Szechuan with Michael and Beverly Ansara, and Allan and Arlene Asherman. Allan, who has this encyclopedic knowledge of TV, movies and comics, kept looking at me across the table. Finally, he said, "Renee, why do I keep thinking of the Metrons when I look at you?" He had judged that costume call!

I remember meeting William Shatner at Starbase Atlanta in 1984. He was signing autographs. In those days, autographs were free, and you might stand in line for hours waiting for one. No one had ever heard of a "photo op." If the celebrity had time, you pointed your Instamatic camera and took a picture, maybe posed, maybe while he was signing your program book. Anyway, Shatner ran out of time and had to get to the airport, but he walked the line as long as he could and signed as he walked. That's how I met him.

At those old cons, we met people who became lifelong friends. You can still do that, of course; but in those days, you knew we were all there because of *Star Trek*, and that everyone had at least some interest in it. Today, there are so many sub-fandoms, you don't know if the person you're talking to has even seen the same programs you watch.

Fan-run cons also have always been pretty safe environments. As kids, my cousins and I had freedom to run around at the cons and explore the hotel. If we got into trouble, *everyone* would know, and *everyone* knew our mothers. My kids grew up in the same safe environment.

On Starting Clippercon, OktoberTrek and Farpoint:

The Shore Leave convention had been around for about five years when Marion McChesney, my mom, my Aunt Nancy, and Martha Sayre (then Bonds) and a few others decided to start their own convention called Clippercon. Marion was Chair, and my mom was Assistant Chair and Programming Chair. The sponsoring organization was listed on hotel paperwork as "Contact Associates," but Marion was the financial backer.

Most of the Clippercon committee had been involved at some level with organizing Shore Leave as well. In the early years, the Shore Leave Dead Dog Party, where the committee members gather to relax and celebrate another con finished, for good or ill, was held at my house on Sunday evening. Mom and Aunt Nancy had lifetime Shore Leave memberships, and everyone in the Volker family knew the committee members.

The Contact Crowd members were still attending the New York conventions, but those were winding down. FebCons were no more, so that weekend was free for Baltimore fans. The group decided they wanted more con experiences, and closer to home. Marion always said she started the con just so she could pick the guests, but, if you knew Marion, you knew there was a lot more to it than that. Marion just loved fandom. We were her other family, and she would do anything for us. Marion was a fandom whirlwind. She lived in a huge storefront house in Hampden (Hon) and drove an ice cream truck that had been left to her by her dad. He had been murdered while driving his route, and she took over. She had been publishing a beautiful zine, *Vault of Tomorrow*, for a few years before we started ClipperCon. It was a Trek genzine, meaning there was no theme and there were no focus characters. It was just full of stories based on *Star Trek*, and, like *Contact*, it featured work by the best writers and artists in fandom. Marion kept publishing zines and running cons (although she branched out into other fandoms, like *Man From U.N.C.L.E.* and *Blake's 7*) until her untimely death in the Fall of 2000.

I was 16 years old in 1984, when we held the first ClipperCon at Hunt Valley Inn. Nichelle Nichols was our big guest, along with Howard Weinstein and Allan Asherman. I think Jesco Van Putkamer, the NASA scientist who had worked on *Star Trek: The Motion Picture*, was there too.

I assisted with the timekeeping of the panel rooms while Mom was programming chairperson. The convention was smaller than those we hold today, with a main ballroom, a couple of panel rooms, and a film room. The entire *Contact* crew was involved with the convention, including Suzanne and Mike Elmore, Terri and Geri Sylvester and all of my family.

Marion McChesney decided to step down from running the con, calling our 1988 convention "Clippercon 6: The Final Voyage." Shortly after that, she moved to California. We all thought. "This is it! We're done!" But then... Mom had a cookout, as she often did, and invited half of fandom, as she often did, and, with the Summer sun shining on us and the food making us feel happy and fulfilled, someone said to someone else, "You know, it wouldn't be that hard to do this again." Steve said we should have it in October, and Sandy said she would front the money. We agreed to have guests from classic *Trek* and *Next Gen*, which was the only other game in town at the time. Mom called Marion out West and said, "Are you sitting down...?" OktoberTrek was born.

It was a huge success. We pulled fans to the con in record numbers, but, three years later, Sandy also had had enough. Running a con is stressful, and it's very easy to lose money. Plus, OktoberTrek '92 wound up on Fox 45 News one evening, accused of peddling smut to minors, because there were slash zines in the dealers' room. It was nothing new, and our dealers knew better than to sell to minors. But the mundanes at Fox 45 thought it was shocking, and accused us, with no evidence, of something we hadn't done. It didn't hurt our reputation in fandom, but it hurt to have those things said about us.

Steve (my husband) took over the remaining three-year contract with the Hunt Valley Inn and renamed the convention Farpoint, with Sandy's support and blessings. It was a controversial changeover, since Steve was so young and had fresh ideas about running the conventions. In fact, there was a split among the con committee members who were not ready to hand over the con reins to Steve. My mom stepped up to be his co-chair for the first few months. That helped smooth ruffled feathers. After the first con was over, people seemed to forget their objections, and Steve was the boss.

On Influential Media:

I admit that I'm not into science fiction. I'm certain that if my mom had not been into *Star Trek*, I probably would not have watched the television show. However, I do like watching the original *Star Trek* episodes and most of the movies that have come since. My favorite fantasy film is *The Wizard of Oz*, and I adore Christopher Reeve. Superman is my hero. (But, while I like Henry Cavill, I do not like his Superman movies.)

On Acting:

I've acted in a couple of the Cheap Treks shows. Cheap Treks is the best-remembered of the names that our group of friends performed under. My husband Steve, as well as Dave Keefer and Lance Woods, had done a few plays at Shore Leave. Back in the day, Shore Leave ended the con with the "Shore Leave Showcase," a play or group of skits put together by the committee or their friends. Wanting to try their hands at writing and directing, Dave and Lance founded "Cheap Treks," and Steve founded "The Not Ready for Paramount Players." They both began with *Star Trek IV* parodies, and cast each other in them. Steve's was "The Voyage the Hell Home," a musical, God help us. Around 1990, they merged the groups under a single name. I was Saavik in "Voyage the Hell Home," as well as an Andorian (painted blue all over!) in "Beach Planet Romeos." I also did "Have Browncoat, Will Travel," "P for Producer," and "Con Suite." I find it amazing that Cheap Treks (or whatever we called ourselves!) did over 50 shows together. I've moved on to participating in Steve's radio plays. It's a different kind of acting. The group was tired of doing the plays with months of rehearsals. Radio shows really only require a read-through and a tech rehearsal. That's nice, but not having rehearsals as an excuse to get together has cut down on the social interactions of the group. The creativity kept us together, as it did my mom's *Contact* group 40(!) years ago. It took a while for the con audiences to understand what we were doing, but the radio plays are now anticipated and enjoyed by the fans.

On Raising Her Sons in Fandom:

I love it! I'm so proud of how they have embraced it. I'm so glad they have that environment to grow up in. They don't actually know life without it. They are the next generation of fandom, and I really think the experience has made them diverse and well-rounded individuals. It was at the cons that Christian discovered his love of acting, and Ethan realized that there were other people in the world who shared his passion for action figures. Now Christian is getting his Bachelor of Fine Arts in acting at Towson, and Ethan has a top-rated action figure review blog and has been published by Sequart Press.

On Con Recollections:

I've had some memorable interactions, usually involving my sons. I remember when I was at dinner with Peter Jurasik of *Babylon 5*, and all Peter wanted to do was hold my baby, Christian. When I offered to take him so Peter could eat his meal, he replied, "I don't need food. I need *this*."

Jonathan Frakes was especially kind to five-year-old Ethan, since he had a son of the same age and was missing him.

Felicia Day was such a cool guest at Farpoint! Christian was nine years old the first time she joined us, and Prometheus Radio Theatre had asked her to appear in a show called "Waste of Space." Felicia was playing the victim of a mad scientist—Christian! At tech rehearsal, when she saw that Christian, a young boy, was to be her leading man, her expression clearly said, "You're kidding, right?" However, she dove in and they read through the scene they had together. Now, in this play, there is a point where Felicia and Christian's characters switch bodies and voices. I was astonished when at one point, Christian took hold of Felicia's chin and said, "No. Do it again!" and shaped her mouth with his hand so that her delivery matched his Orson Welles impersonation. My fourth-grader was coaching our celebrity guest on acting! Felicia was a very good sport, and seems to have good memories of Christian.

On Con Jobs:

I continue to work at Farpoint after all these years in fandom, because I am dedicated to making sure the con is successful and maintains the true spirit of my mom and the fans I grew up with. I want other kids to have the chance to grow up in the fandom I knew, and other parents to have that opportunity. I've done almost every con job there is, and now I guess I'm one of the faces of Farpoint. I guess there are worse things to lend your face to!

Steven H. Wilson

On His Real Life Job:

I am Chief Technology Officer for Howard County Fire and Rescue. I've been with the Fire Department for almost 22 years, and worked for Howard County for 31. I was born in Fairfax, Virginia, but consider myself a Howard County native since I moved here when I was less than a year old.

Currently I work alongside my wife, Renee. A lot of people say they could never work with their spouse, but I think we make a good team. Everything I've accomplished has happened in large part because Renee was there to support me.

On His Introduction to Science Fiction:

My brother was a *Star Trek* fan and watched the series in its first run. I would have seen it on television from the very beginning, but was too young to remember most of it. Indeed, I don't know if my first memory of seeing Leonard Nimoy on television is of him playing Spock, or of him playing Paris in *Mission: Impossible*. But *Star Trek* was just always there in my life. I played with a *Lost in Space* toy robot and looked at *Voyage to the Bottom of the Sea* View-Master reels. I caught *Lost in Space* in reruns beginning around age 6, and it quickly became a favorite.

My father was also a bit of an insomniac, or at least a night owl. He watched TV until the test pattern came on, and, since we shared a room for most of my childhood (16 rooms and we lived in four of them—long story!), I watched the late show most nights. In those days, that meant science fiction movies. My father was a physicist and an engineer, so he enjoyed critiquing their technical aspects.

On Influential Media:

Because of my brother and father, I cut my teeth on *Trek, Lost in Space* and films like *The Day the Earth Stood Still, Forbidden Planet* and, a guilty pleasure, *Voyage to the Prehistoric Planet*, which I later learned was a recut of a Soviet film which was an utter masterpiece. My sister, like pretty much everyone of her generation, was a *Dark Shadows* fan. I loved it too.

I got into the *Star Trek* books written by James Blish very early. They were the first chapter books I read. I recently had to confess that my first actual novel-reading experience came at age seven, with *Spock Must Die!* I didn't even know what a "novel" was! That was an interesting book, because it actually contained some hard science. It gave me a taste for literary SF, which I feel a lot of media fans my age lack to this day. *Star Trek* did not invent science fiction, and is really a pretty watered-down example of the genre. A lot of people don't realize that.

I would grab Ray Bradbury and Arthur C. Clarke novels even though I sometimes struggled with reading the prose. I remember reading the first page of Bradbury's "Chrysalis" over and over again, trying to get into the story. *2001* just blew my mind, because I wasn't sure what the hell was happening at the end. Between Jack Kirby's wild comics adaptations of it, and my English teacher, Gail Saunders, explaining to to me, I came close to figuring it out.

I discovered comic books courtesy of ABC-TV's Saturday-morning cartoon, *Super Friends*, and re-runs of Adam West's *Batman*. I was madly in love with Yvonne Craig's Batgirl (in a chaste, respectful way at age eight!) I think she predisposed me to love super-heroines. My brother had a stack of war comics, which were of little interest to me; but they contained house ads for superhero comics, and I was fascinated to learn that there was also a Supergirl, a Black Canary, and a whole selection of heroines in the Legion of Super-Heroes. Wonder Woman I had seen on *Super Friends*, and Mera I saw when I discovered the 1960s Aquaman cartoons.

Cartoons were important to me. The Animated *Star Trek* was "my" *Trek*, and is, to this day, my best-loved version. It came years later, when I was old enough to appreciate it. It was kid-friendly, and I was nine. And I had it all to myself. My brother and sister were too "grown up" to watch it. Ballantine Books started to publish novelizations of the half-hour scripts—ironically much longer than the novelizations of the original, 60-minute episodes!—and I discovered a guy named Alan Dean Foster, who is still one of my favorite authors.

My first comic books, when I started buying my own, were issues of *Wonder Woman* and *Supergirl*. Courtesy of the 1975 Marvel Comics calendar I learned of the Scarlet Witch (still probably my favorite) and started reading *The Avengers*. After that, my tastes turned to comics about heroic teams—the Legion, The Justice League, the X-Men, the Champions. Maybe I liked the idea of heroes in friendly groupings because I didn't have a lot of friends. I was a skinny, non-athletic kid who liked to read and watch TV more than I liked people. That probably had something to do with it, but my imaginary friends liked each other and didn't find fault with me.

TV became pretty mundane, after discovering books and comic books, but I still found things to enjoy. *The Six Million Dollar Man* and *The Bionic Woman* weren't comic book-level fun, but they were fun. (Guess which I preferred!) And *Space:1999* introduced me to darker, more philosophical stories with its first year, and then introduced a kickass (not to mention smart and adorable) super-heroine named Maya in its second.

In high school, a dear friend—Beatrice Kondo, still one of my closest friends, and now an evolutionary biologist—introduced me to the work of Robert A. Heinlein. I consider that the final, critical step in my fandom evolution. Heinlein's voice was unique, and his ability to put fully developed characters into science-driven scenarios with real-world political challenges left other authors in the dust. His impatience with stupidity, coupled with an obvious compassion for humanity, resonated with me. I had found a true mentor, even though, sadly, I never met the man in person.

There's a medium I'm willing to bet no one else will mention, and that's toys. I was devoted to my Lego sets (just generic building sets, in my day) and action figures. I loved my 8-inch, cloth-costumed Mego figures and their playsets. I loved my 24" *Eagle* spaceship [from Space: 1999]. When the toy companies didn't make enough for me, I made my own. I still have hundreds of character figures made with paper, magic marker and duct tape. Toys let me engage in imaginative adventures of my own, to supplement the stories that formed in my head as I read and watched my heroes. They stimulated my creative impulses and brought me great joy. I still have my collection of well-loved toys from childhood, and I still buy new ones. Building a new Lego set is amazingly therapeutic. I don't play with my figures anymore, but I love just having them around. They remind me that my "fictional" friends are out there, maybe just a couple of translations or rotations away, populating the dimensions of the multiverse, which are not infinite, but surely stretch out to the Number of the Beast.

On His Introduction to Fandom

In the wilds of Clarksville, MD, I had little chance to interact with other fans. Occasionally ordering something from Majel Barrett's Lincoln Enterprises, or Heroes World, I would sometimes get flyers for cons. I hoped someday to attend one, but, for year, my fandom was long-distance fandom. We had no cable TV, and there was no public access to the Internet. At a very young age, I bought the book *Star Trek Lives!*, by Jacqueline Lichtenberg, Sondra Marshak and Joan Winston. I wasn't sure what it was, but it had cool thumbnails from all the (then) existing *Star Trek* novelizations on the cover. I didn't read it cover-to-cover, I just flipped through it in amazement. It had interviews with the *Trek* actors, and told tales of them appearing at conventions. I didn't even know what conventions were until then! It also talked about fan fiction, and described people who built replicas of the *Enterprise* bridge in their garages. I felt that "Here's this exotic land I'd like to go to someday."

When I was 15, a Creation Con came to town, to Baltimore to be exact, and I went with my best friend. There were no guests related to *Star Trek* at this con, but I did find an 8"x10" photo of the bridge crew for a dollar. I enjoyed having intelligent conversations with Marvel artists and writers.

A year later, the *Wrath of Khan* came out. I didn't have high hopes for the second *Star Trek* movie. After all, everyone already knew, courtesy of *Starlog*, that they were killing Spock. The clips I saw on the *Merv Griffin Show* (God help me!) looked a bit cheesy, if I'm honest. But I bought the novelization of the movie a few days before it opened in theaters. There were no gag orders or non-disclosure clauses in those days, which kept the book from shipping until a week after the premiere. Nobody gave a damn about spoilers in 1982!

Low expectations or not, the novelization was by Vonda McIntyre, whose novels *The Entropy Effect* and *Dreamsnake* I had loved. I started reading on the way home from the store (I believe Mother was driving. If not, well, I'm still alive.) and couldn't stop until I was done. I fell in love the character of Saavik, and ultimately fell in love with the movie. The younger cast, Kirstie Alley, Merritt Butrick and Ike Eisenmann, were closer to my generation, and they were on the *Enterprise. Star Trek* was opening up for new people and was not a stagnant franchise. I loved the plot of Kirk's growing awareness of becoming middle-aged.

The following year, the cast began appearing all over the country at Creation Cons, and I began attending faithfully. I saw Jimmy Doohan, Walter Koenig, Merritt Butrick and George Takei, all in Washington, D.C. It was patronizing those cookie-cutter cons that led to my becoming a part of the real, grassroots fandom I had been reading about nearly all my life.

On Writing His Own Fanzine:

The weekend *Wrath of Khan* came out, I was in a car accident and sprained my leg. I had totaled my mom's car, and my friends and I had gone to the ER. In the days that followed, I was wracked with guilt, partially immobile, and bored out of my mind! My dad had recently purchased a used IBM Selectric typewriter, and I, fueled by my excitement over the new *Trek* film, had just powered through

David Gerrold's book, *The Trouble with Tribbles*. Read it if you want to know how to plot a story. Writing a *Star Trek* story becamse my therapy. I had always wanted to write, but had managed only one original short in 6th grade, one piece of *M*A*S*H* fanfic in the 10th, and, in 7th and 8th grade, a handful of *Justice Society, Legion of Super-Heroes* and *Space:1999* fan fics. I'd started and outlined a bunch of others, but those were my completed output. I decided to project what happened after *Wrath of Khan* ended. Interestingly, I did not bring back Spock. I wrote more of a mood piece about Kirk finding friendship and renewed interest in living via his young crew.

When I finished my story, I wrote to the *Star Trek* Welcommittee, of whom I'd read in *Star Trek Lives!*, and who still got mentioned in *Starlog* and the *Best of Trek* books. I ordered "Protocols," their guide to producing a zine, and then corresponded with one of its authors, Judy Segal, who kindly read my story. She was an agent and gave me constructive, honest feedback. I sent the story to a few zines, but no one nibbled.

Life got in the way of my writing career. I started dating a girl I was crazy about, went to college orientation, went through a breakup, and started college in a kind of a fugue state. My story was still kicking around, but nothing had come of it, and I was depressed and lonely, in no shape to negotiate the College Park party scene. I remember spending lots of late afternoons and evenings in the library, reading old magazine articles about *Dark Shadows*. It was airing again in our market. It was a ridiculous, melancholy show which fit my ridiculous, melancholy life. A young lady in my computer science class decided I needed befriending before I melted into a puddle of angst on the lecture hall floor. She saw me writing a new opening to my fannish opus in my spiral notebook, instead of copying down Dr. Basili's wisdom. She confessed quietly, "I used to buy zynes." (Note the long-I pronunciation. It meant she'd only read the word, never hearing it spoken. A lot of people pronounced it that way, then.) With a little arm-twisting, I let her read my story. She convinced me I should publish it myself—wasn't that the point of fanzines anyway? I decided she was right—I needed to do something creative. Having left high school, I didn't have the school paper to give me ulcers or the yearbook to keep me up late nights working or the musical to rehearse for. I was lost. "Get back your command," I heard Dr. McCoy saying in my head. "Get it back before you turn into part of this collection."

(Okay, Reader, get that smirk off your face. You're a geek, or you wouldn't be reading this book. If fictional characters don't speak in your head and turn your mundane, little life pretentiously into great drama for you, you're doing your fandom wrong.)

Two years after I began my fanfic writing career, my dad struck again to propel it forward.

My dad retired right as I was graduating high school. I joked that he just wanted to keep being the one to get the most mail, as my college letters were pouring in, and so were his consulting offers. Anyway, he started his own consulting firm, turning my old bedroom into his office, and he bought a shiny new Xerox copier. Upon playing with it, I realized it had the quality to turn out a very respectable fanzine. So I typed up my story and drew six pencil illustrations to accompany it. *Et Walla!* My first, 40-page fanzine sold for $1.50 a copy, 'cause, hell, I wasn't paying for printing! I just needed to recoup the cost of mailing, listings in adzines, PresType, layout tape and typewriter ribbons. I kept careful records and was scrupulous about the "no profit" status of my zine. I re-invested every dime I made.

I printed 40 copies and hauled them to a Creation Con in Crystal City. I walked around the dealer's room and stopped passersby, saying, "Would you like to buy a fanzine?" I sold ten or twelve copies, and some people came back later to tell me how good it was. They had read it while sitting/standing the autograph line! At the same con, I also got a letter from Carole Frisbee, who was a BNF [Big Name Fan], living in northern Virginia. She had bought one of my zines, and she wrote to tell me what a good writer I was and that I was carrying on the *ST* traditions. Needless to say, I was on a high from all of the positive feedback.

My friends and I did hit ClipperCon on a Sunday. We saw Nichelle [Nichols] and got her autograph. We heard Allan Asherman and Howie Weinstein speak. We bought cool stuff in the dealers' room.

I wasn't prepared to know all the ways a fan-run con was different from a Creation "show," but I knew this con had a different feel. When I saw that there was another con—Shore Leave—in the same hotel in July, I knew I needed to be there, selling zines. And I was. I think it was there that I met Roberta Rogow, who offered to agent my zines and did a fantastic job.

By then, *Star Trek III* had come out, invalidating my fanzine sequel. But readers at Shore Leave encouraged me to continue my story as an alternate universe series. I went home and started writing. My brother and I started a short, quarterly humor zine. I was in business.

But I wasn't *quite* on the "inside" with local fandom yet. I wrote to Marion McChesney, who published *Vault of Tomorrow*. I sent her art and writing samples. She complimented my artwork, but politely declined a little continuity piece I offered that explained how Kirk lost the *Enterprise* after *ST:TMP*. It wasn't until later, when I was "family," that I became a contributor to the bigger-name zines.

On Meeting Renee Volker:

At the second Clippercon, I was back in the dealer's room for the weekend. Still on the outside, I had no awareness of the pretty, blonde teenager who was keeping time for the panel rooms. I was too busy selling zines to eat. The only thing that got me out of the dealers' room was the morning jog with George Takei—and that happened before the room opened!

But at that ClipperCon, a 34-year-old fan named Jan Davies bought one of my zines. She read it, loved it, and wrote me an LoC (Letter of Comment). She gave me her phone number and said, since she was local to me, I should give her a call. We became good friends. She was working on her own fan fiction at the time, and I was willing to beta read (*not* a term then!) and contribute illustrations. I still have my pen-and-ink of a female Spock! She had befriended the local zine community and was trying to get published in *Contact*, which I knew only from Welcommittee and DataZine listings.

After a few months, she asked me if I would like to come and meet area fans. She took me to a collating party at Marion McChesney's, where *Vault of Tomorrow's* fifth or sixth issue was being assembled. There I met zine publishers Bev Volker and Nancy Kippax, of *Contact*, as well as Geri Sylvester, who did the Shore Leave Showcases, and was thrilled to meet another actor. She threw her arms around me and said, "My God! Welcome!" And, indeed, I felt welcome. Marion put listings for my zines on the final page of the latest "*Vault*," and they all said, "Congratulations! You're a Big-Name Fan!"

A BNF. Me. Wow.

Bev's snarky husband, Russ, added, "Yeah, that and a dime will buy you a cup of coffee." And I'm pretty sure Marion narrowed her eyes and said, "Coffee hasn't cost a dime for years, Russ."

Marion was always very literal.

A week or so later, Jan took me to a STAT meeting, to meet the folks who put on Shore Leave. After the meeting, she asked if I "minded" riding along with her to Bev Volker's house. "I know it's just a bunch of women sitting around talking about their health issues, but they are *Star Trek* fans." I said I didn't mind, so I wound up on Bev's couch, listening to everyone talking about *Star Trek* and gynecologists. At some point, two teenage girls crept in and sat in the corner. One of them was a blonde with gorgeous legs (she had these shorts on that should have been illegal) and blue eyes that seemed taking in every sight there was to see in the universe and commit them all to memory. Her picture was on the wall, and she looked like Bev, so I gathered this was one of the daughters. I could not stop looking at her, and I couldn't speak coherently when they packed me into the back of a station wagon next to her so we could all ride to the Hazelwood Inn for dinner. I think we each said, "Hi," to each other, and perhaps made idle comments about the food. I don't know who even told me that her name was Renee.

SPOILER: It was a setup!

I kept going back to the Volker's house every Saturday, because Renee was there. I went with them to see Leonard Nimoy in New York at a Creation Con at the Penta hotel. It was my first time in New York, and I brought my female best friend, Jamie. I didn't see Renee react, but Renee and Jamie later assured me there were glares. Then we went to Shore Leave, where I was in charge of films. Renee followed me everywhere, and I bought her dinner for the first time. There was a dealer, who would put your picture on a button for you, and we stopped and had a couple made with her sitting on my lap. Apparently, after we left a room party in her mom's room Saturday night, with lots of giggling and laughing in our wake, Bev said, "I'll be damned! They finally noticed each other!" One morning shortly after the con, I woke up one morning and found myself sleeping on something metalic. I fished it out from under my pillow and realized it was that photo button of Renee and me. It had been sitting on my desk. Apparently, I had gone and fetched it in my sleep, and held it close to my heart.

I had a problem.

Jan called to ask if I was thinking of asking Renee out. I said, yes, I was thinking about it. But I'd recently been through a shall-we-say challenging relationship, and I wasn't sure about diving back in to dating. Jan kept saying, "Well you should call her," and I kept saying, "I know, but what if...?" This was pretty typical of our conversations. Finally, she decided to cut through the crap and said, "Look, she's *waiting* for you to call her. This whole thing was a matchmaking attempt. The only reason I introduced you to Bev was because she wanted to meet you before I introduced you to Renee for *her* approval."

So I wrote Jan out of my will and resolved to order a voodoo doll in her image, and then I called Renee. I said something eloquent like, "I was wondering kinda if maybe if you're not too busy you'd like to see a movie if you're free but you don't have to it would just be as friends."

And she said, inevitably, "I *suppose*."

And the rest is hysteria.

On Acting at the Cons:

That weekend of breathless energy at Shore Leave earned me the title of Film Chairman, awarded by Chairman Gus Liberto. I was kicked off the Shore Leave committee, though, because I stopped attending their long meetings—I had more fun things to do on weekends, now that I had a girlfriend. I still managed to work guest relations at the next Shore Leave (VIII), escorting Majel Barrett and Robin Curtis for the weekend. But I guess the thing that stuck was the Showcases. As I mentioned, I had let the committee know I had acting experience, and had taken a few theater courses as I got my journalism degree. So I was fresh meat. I wound up playing a Klingon Moe Howard, Sarek, and the memorable role of "man" that first year.

And then Marion did this thing...

Marion, being a zine publisher, faithfully attended Media West Con, and, in 1986, she was so impressed by a play they did there that she got the rights to produce it in Baltimore at Shore Leave. The show was *Star Trek III: The Search for Cole Porter*. Obviously, it was a musical, and I was cast as David Marcus. Boogie Knight Dave Keefer was Scotty, and Lance Woods was cast as my Dad. I had never met the guy. (Lance, that is. My Dad and I had been introduced.) We had great fun in rehearsal, and I decided to have more fun with Lance during the performance. I was to die off stage, screaming into the back mic before Saavik uttered her deadpan, "Admiral, David is Tango Uniform," (or whatever she said.) Instead, I shrieked, "Flee, Father, I am killed!" And then proceded to give a strangled cry over Lance's next dozen lines. When the show ended, in lieu of curtain call, I staggered out, knocked some set pieces over, dropped, shook my legs in the air, and pulled my jacket over my face, finally dying. Marion blurted out, "What the *hell* was that?" But I had earned Lance and Dave's respect... If you call spending the next few decades being written into shows in drag "respect."

On Writing Plays:

Even before the Cole Porter debacle, I had thought a humorous Trek musical was a good idea. After it, I thought it was an idea I could do even better. (I was 21, I thought I could do everything better than everyone.) So, sight unseen, I decided to parody *Star Trek* IV at the next ClipperCon. The movie premiered in November, so I had about eleven weeks to mount a show. I wrote *Star Trek IV: The Voyage (The Hell) Home* in five days. At Marion's annual Christmas party, I invited Lance Woods and Dave Keefer to be in it—and they invited me to be in *their* "Trek IV" parody at Shore Leave. From then on, the conventions had dueling *Star Trek* parodies with Dave and Lance premiering their shows at Shore Leave cons and me performing my shows at ClipperCons, Fan Outs and Oktobertreks.

On Meeting Influential People:

I came to the cons wanting to be a professional writer, and I made a point of meeting Howard Weinstein, Bob Greenberger and Ann (A.C.) Crispin. Ann was first to have a look at my work. I gave her a copy of my first fanzine. She *gutted* it! "I won't let you call this a story," she said. "It's a collection of angst." She told me *Star Trek* was a dead end, even though it had opened doors for her. But don't let me paint Ann as utterly discouraging. She was a kind and loving person. At that same con, while I was on the run one Saturday morning, she stopped me and asked (always the mom!) if I had eaten. When I said no, I only had about five dollars and I was just going to have coffee, she insisted on buying me French toast. Howie Weinstein was there too. He had only met me the night before, but he insisted that, even if I was only going to have coffee, I should sit down at a table with them to have it. I was touched by their kindness, even if Ann did continue to hammer on my to forget about *Star Trek*.

Months later, at a con in North Carolina, Howie pulled me aside and said not to take Ann's advice too much to heart. Writing a *ST* novel was lucrative and guaranteed to land an author on the *New York Times* Bestseller list. He offered to sponsor me. I started and abandoned at least five novels over the next few years, but never sold one. In the course of all that mentoring, however, Howie became one of my dearest friends. He still encourages me in my writing. Recently, I followed his example and tried my hand at historical fiction, selling a story on my first try to Howie's publisher, Five Star Press. I think he was happier about it than I was. And, speaking of influence, Bob Greenberger, then editor of the DC Comics *Star Trek* comic, helped me realize a lifelong dream.

On Writing Comics:

At an early ClipperCon banquet, I sat with Bob and asked him how one got into writing comics. Bob crisply replied, "You need to write a story with a beginning, middle and end." I think I said, "*And...?*" Then he handed me a business card and told me to send him three one-page pitches for comic stories. After the con, I took up the challenge and sent him pitches for *Star Trek, Hawkman* and *Legion of Super-Heroes*. Bob wrote back and said, "You were serious! And you *can* write a beginning, a middle and an end." At the time, I didn't realize such abilities were rare.

Bob liked my story outline, "Planet of the Dead," wherein Kirk is put on trial by the ghosts of a bunch of redshirts, and Uhura is confronted by the ghost of the child she never had time to have. But Bob didn't need a Trek story, he needed a new author to script a 16-page *Warlord* story for DC's new talent "Bonus Book" program. I had never read Mike Grell's John-Carter-like epic, even though I was a huge fan of his work. So I bought a bunch of issues and Bob and I hammered out a plot. It was pencilled by Rob Liefeld, who, a year later, was a comics superstar. I didn't do as well, but Bob always let me know when there were story openings. Ultimately, his encouragement allowed me to sell four issues of *Star Trek*, which I'm happy to say are remembered by fans with fondness.

On Firebringer Press and Prometheus Radio Theatre:

Firebringer Press and Prometheus Radio Theatre are pretty much Jack Williamson's fault. NASA scientist and SF author Yoji Kondo and I became friends after I went to high school with (and occasionally dated) his daughter, Beatrice. Yoji traveled the country doing cons, and had a list of friends that read like the SF section in the library. Whenever he had a local event, he would invite me along. In 1995, he invited me to a Writers of the Future dinner in DC. He introduced me to the great Jack Williamson as a writer for DC comics. Jack knew lots of people at DC Comics and asked me what I was writing now that DC had lost the license to *Star Trek*. I told him "nothing," because I didn't know of a paying market. The venerable Grandmaster shook a finger into my face and said, "Shame on you! You always write, and it doesn't matter if you get paid." I went home that night and started writing. Haven't stopped since.

I created a fictional universe populated by young, misfit space cadets who crewed a ship called the *Arbiter*. I was going to do a novel, but it was slow going. Then, at Farpoint 2000, we had an empty hour in the ballroom on a Saturday. A couple years before that, my friends had done a live radio show, and I had enjoyed acting in it. And I had several plots for my "Arbiter" characters waiting for me to write them. So I said to Sharon Van Blarcom, my program chair, "What if I wrote a radio show?" I drafted the Cheap Treks crew, asked audio wizard John Vengrouskie for pointers, and borrowed a sound effects library from my friend Lew Aide. The audience listened, did not throw vegetable matter, and applaused when our announcer, Paul Balze, asked them at the end, "Should we keep doing this?" We did. We produced some CDs, got played on local FM station WAMU, and even won the prestigious Mark Time Award. In 2005, I was approached by a podcasting network and asked to do content for them. By then, we had done probably ten episodes of what was now called *The Arbiter Chronicles*™. I had finally found the format for that Arbiters novel, and I knew I wanted to put it in the hands of readers, not editors. Don Sakers led me into the dark forest of micro-press publishing, and Firebringer Press was born. And with podcasting, I had a built-in market for the audiobook! My first novel was positively reviewed by *Library Journal,* and the podcast version was ranked as one of the original "classic" podcast novels. The podcast has gone out of production, but Firebringer is still publishing, and I'm actively blogging about the trials and tribulations of inheriting my Father's never-completed house.

Renee and Steve Wilson (Joint Interview)

On OktoberTrek:

Steve: Fandom was the backdrop to our life, from our first meeting, to our engagement and marriage, to the arrival of our children. Once I was drafted as a member of the Volker family, I was also drafted onto the ClipperCon committee. I guess I did everything—film co-chair, assistant in the dealers' room, program book, and, of course, the plays. We had a few dustups over the fact that producing the show was not considered "a committee position." When ClipperCon transition to OktoberTrek, Sandy Zier ended that conflict by making me entertainment coordinator. I also planned the Friday night live show and the Ten-Forward dance. (The Ten-Forward, by the way, was born at the ClipperCon V wrap meeting, as we all complained about how bad the service was in the bar. Martha Bonds (Sayre) suggested that the con should have its own, dedicated bar on Saturday nights. George Laurance said we should also play music, and I, being one of the few *Next Gen* fans on the committee, said, "We can call it the Ten-Forward." I doubt anyone knows that, and I fully expect a Harvard study to be produced, proving it never happened. But we invented the Ten-Forward Dance!)

Renee was pregnant with our first son, Ethan, when Sandy confessed to me that she wasn't sure there would be an OktoberTrek in 1993. I started working on a business plan, intended to save OktoberTrek. Instead, when Sandy said, "Nay, enough!", we used it to begin Farpoint.

On Farpoint:

Steve: Farpoint wasn't as well-attended as Oktobertrek had been, probably because I downsized the guest list. Those big names cost money, and we had been running in the red. I was 27 years old and doing unfulfilling work as a librarian. It was a heady experience to be in charge of huge sums of money (to me) and booking actors for the cons. It was also very high-energy and damned exhausting! I was the face of the convention, and everyone wanted something. It was exciting, but draining. I always thought that each con it would be the last con for me. Finally, in 2000, it was. My dear friend, Marion McChesney, who had been con chair while I was promoter, had died. That loss left me stunned, with little patience and minimal interest in the convention. In retrospect, I don't think that was the right decision for me. I should have powered forward. Had I been meant to leave, well, I wouldn't still be here, 19 years later.

Renee: We asked Sharon Van Blarcom if she would be interested in taking over Farpoint. Sharon and Sandy Zier-Teitler became co-Con Chairs, with Sharon as the financial officer, and Steve settled in as Programming Chairman.

Steve: Actually, my taking over programming was the cost of Sharon agreeing to hold the money bag. We held a meeting and discussed dissolving Farpoint, Inc. and creating Farpoint Enterprises, going from a single-owner company to one owned by stockholders. Sharon will tell you that, at that meeting, I asked, "So who's going to run the company?" and looked pointedly at her. It was a bit more complex than that, but, well, we weren't overflowing with candidates!

As Program Chair, I viewed my job as the most important position at the con. (No, not because I was in it! I'd felt the same way about it when it was Bev's job, Renee's and then Sharon's.) They (programming chairs) make it happen. Doing programming at a con is hard— it takes over your life for most of the year. Now, keep in mind, I only said I'd help out for a transitional year. I kept trying to find a new programming chairman, but it turned out to be difficult to find someone who would last. I guess I didn't really have the con out of my system, nor did Renee. So, six years after "retiring" from the con, we were back as operations managers, overseeing programming and logistics. We became known as the "Table Nazis," because we are committed to keeping walkways passable.

Renee: I couldn't walk away. I grew up with this welcoming community. I wanted to continue that. I was raising my children in a warm atmosphere, a place where you can be yourself. There is such creativity. I've never known a "normal" life. How boring would that be?

Steve: You grew up with Fandom's Algonquin Roundtable—all that creativity in your house, every Saturday night. It gets into your blood.

Renee: But it was also kind of a secret. You didn't tell your friends at school that you were a *Star Trek* fan. One of the few times I did was when someone was reading one of Ann Crispin's books in class, and I said, "Oh, she's a friend of my family." No one believed me, so I had to bring in a copy of [A.C. Crispin's *Star Trek* novel] *Yesterday's Son*, which mentions my mom in the acknowledgments. I guess I kind of outed myself then.

Steve: Yeah, I was not at all mainstream. I was the kid who sat and drew "space ladies" in my notebook while the teacher was reading the phone book, or whatever it was teachers did in the front of the class. I never actually knew.

Renee: It's different for fans today. There's more acceptance. I think cons have had a lot to do with that.

Steve: Still, it's a tough job, putting them together. Both of us actually quit—again—about four years ago. But then they begged us to do the art show, so we were still around... It was hard not to say when we thought things were going off track, or to step in when there was a problem. In particular, we saw a common but destructive tendency to invest all the power in the "old hands," on the committee, which doesn't give the younger generation a chance to grow. Fan cons are like small churches—always in danger of losing their lynchpins to old age, disease and death, because they don't know how to bring in youth. So we started fighting for our kids and others' to be part of things. And I think everyone got frustrated by these two people who kept "quitting," and then staying to boss everyone around!

Renee: We finally sat down with the core con group and said, "You are never getting rid of us. We are committee members for life. We don't want jobs. We don't want anyone to have expectations. We just want you to listen to us."

Steve: Because, I know it sounds like we're full of ourselves, but, dammit, we've earned the right to be heard. And if you think we haven't, well, maybe it's time to part ways.

Renee: Sharon quite diplomatically asked, "Do you want to be deputy con chairs?"

Steve: And that seemed to make sense. "We don't want jobs," went out the window, but we are being heard. And, well, I think there's just too much of *us* in Farpoint for us to talk about walking away.

On the Future of the Con:

Renee: You have to have young people involved and treat them as adults, not half-committee members. They are not kids.

Steve: Even the actual kids, the younger teens, can be treated like adults to a great degree, and given responsibilities. Especially when it comes to dealing with younger fans, I always ask myself "What would Marty do?" The late Marty Gear was a legend in the Baltimore fan community. He was known for his amazing costumes, but more for his generosity and compassion. Marty never treated someone differently because of their age. He did not resent young people. He welcomed both new fans and the new fandoms they embraced. Marty valued people. That's the spirit of fandom.

On Favorite Con Guests:

Steve: I think the guest whose visits touched me most is Harve Bennett. Harve hadn't done a convention for decades when he contacted Sandy Zier and asked, "Is *Star Trek* fandom still out there?" He came to Farpoint, and, when we were introduced, Sharon told him, "Steve is the reason this con exists." At his Sunday talk he raved about how wonderful the con had been and how this was what he always wanted fandom to be. I was backstage, and I started tearing up. The man who saved *Star Trek,* and whose work had inspired me to write, loved our little con! When Harve came off the stage, I told him, "They say Farpoint wouldn't be here if not for me. Well, I wouldn't be here if it weren't for you." Harve gave me a big hug. We stayed in touch over the years before his death. I'll always feel privileged to have met him.

On Last Words:

Renee: I saw the first *Star Trek* movie 35 times in the theater with my mom and her friends. My mother had been an active part of the campaign to bring *Star Trek* back in some form. She said that was the central goal of organized fandom. *ST:TMP* was their payoff. They had done it! A lot of people trash-talk that movie, but it meant something very special to fans of the time. I hope the fans that have come on board later can have that sort of moment, whatever form it takes.

Cindy Woods

On Her Real Life Job:

I have been a legal secretary for far too long.

On Her Introduction to Fandom and Conventions:

I blame *Star Wars* and my friend, Betsy Childs (formerly Anthony). I was born on the Eastern Shore of Maryland in the small town of Easton. In my junior year of high school, in a gym class, I met a transfer student named Betsy. Normally, I would have just smiled and nodded—I was painfully shy back then, however, Betsy had, pinned to her purse, a large blue button which read "May The Force Be With You." The rest is history!

Betsy invited me to my first convention in 1979, a one-day con called Trekaday, held at the University of Maryland, College Park. The con was nothing more than a video room and a small dealer's room, but it was fun, and I was hooked. Next, we went to the very first Shore Leave convention. I won an award in the costume contest for my *Battlestar Galactica* Viper Pilot outfit. I was even interviewed for the local evening news!

In 1983, we went back to Shore Leave, and I dressed as Princess Leia in her speeder bike outfit. I remember having a fake "crown" of hair pinned to the back of my head for the costume, and I had to keep it on until the costume contest. We hadn't made room reservations at the hotel, so on the first night of the convention we ended up crashing on some guy's floor for 20 dollars apiece; I had to sleep face down to avoid detaching my hair piece. At the costume contest, Betsy and I were one of several *Star Wars* costume entries. (She dressed as Luke, me as Leia, both in our Endor ponchos, etc.) The entry ahead of ours was another Luke Skywalker and a Darth Vader. The Vader costume consisted of the helmet and a black graduation gown, so, they played up that fact. In their presentation, Darth Vader was finally earning his diploma, with proud son, Luke, cheering him on. I got caught up in the moment and started cheering from backstage. Vader saw me and threw out his arms. Without thinking, I spontaneously ran onstage to give Darth Vader a hug and the crowd went crazy! We lost out on an award that night but gained a couple of friends in Will Burnham (Vader) and Thomas Atkinson (Luke). In turn, they introduced us to artist Sophia Kelly. Sophia offered Betsy and me crash space in her room at no charge, and the five of us stayed up until the wee hours talking about *Star Wars* and other stuff. At one point, Betsy happened to ask, "You don't collect the toys, do you?" I was (and still am) an avid toy collector. We found out that both Will and Thomas were collecting the toys as well, so we had much more to talk about!

On Filk Singing:

Besides costuming, I became interested in the Friday night filksing. (Everyone probably knows the story, but someone at a long-ago convention had meant to use the words "folksing" in a program. Instead, they typed "filksing" by mistake, and it stuck!) [Editor's Note: The typo in fact appeared in the title of an essay submitted to, and rejected by, the *Spectator Amateur Press Society*. The essay was (erroneously) titled "The Influence of Science Fiction on Modern American Filk Music." It was written by Lee Jacobs.] I had heard groups like The Denebian Slime Devils and the Boogie Knights and thought, "I could do that." I entered a contest and wrote a *Trek* parody song. I was told I probably would have won, had someone not at the last minute submitted a parody of 'Bette Davis Eyes' called 'Gary Mitchell's Eyes.' The Denebian Slime Devils chose to perform my song on stage; I was honored. Other filksongs I wrote that got to be popular were a version of "Little Red Corvette" called "Little Dead Smurfette" and a parody of the Dan Fogelberg song "Run for the Roses" called "Children of the Stars," written to honor the *Challenger* astronauts.

On Star Wars:

I am a major *Star Wars* fan. The town of Easton, Maryland only had one theater when I was growing up. The Avalon Theater was an old thirties-style movie palace with an orchestra pit, a player piano and velvet curtains. By the time I saw movies there, the place was falling apart. Easton would never get first-run movies; instead, we'd see them about a month after they had been released. My dad knew the guy who ran the place. Once *Star Wars* arrived there, I had only to walk up to the ticket booth and wave at my dad's friend. He'd nod his head, and I would walk right in. For *Star Wars'* entire month-plus run at the Avalon, I saw both showings of the film each night.

During Betsy's brief stint in college, she invited me to see a viewing of *Star Wars* being shown by a college film club. Little did I know that the print we were getting to see included cut scenes not in the wide release of the film. The cut with Luke and Biggs scenes!

On Con Jobs:

Back in the day, Suzanne Elmore ran Masquerade, and I helped out as her first lieutenant. We set up the Green Room and tried to make the masquerade organized and centered around the costumers. The idea was to make it more than just an entertainment event for the audience. I also belonged to Suzanne's theatrical troupe called Con Artists; they performed serious dramas at several Shore Leave conventions. Many years later, I started assisting Royal White with the Farpoint art show. After a few years, Royal stepped down and recommended to the committee that I and my friend, Heather Mikkelsen (another helper of Royal's) take over the show. Heather and I ran it for quite a few years.

On Being Programming Chair:

A few years ago, the Farpoint programming chair position opened up. I was starting to tire of the art show, and I got it in my head that I could do programming, because I'm organized. After a brief discussion with Heather (we are a team, after all), we jumped into programming. Heather handled the database aspect of the job;

I handled the scheduling. This year, I am handling the majority of the programming duties (with assists from Heather), and Heather is taking back control of the art show (with on-site help from me). It is definitely a challenging job!

On Cheap Treks:

I had the honor to work with Cheap Treks and its various iterations over the years they performed. I performed as stage crew, "Stage Mommy," actor and director in various shows. Some of my most cherished memories are working on those shows and with those incredible people.

On Her Toy Collection:

I learned that the Travel Channel was airing a show called *Toy Hunter*. Toy collector and dealer Jordan Hembrough would travel across the country, scouring people's attics, basements and storage for hard-to-find/unusual toys for his collection. At the end of the first episode, the show ended with "If you have a collection you think Jordan should look at, please e-mail us at..." So, I did. They asked for pictures. I sent pictures of the shelves in my 'toy room.' Within ten minutes, I was on the phone with someone from the Travel Channel; on a Sunday a few weeks later, a crew arrived to film a segment at my house! Jordan was a great guy and fun to work with. It was an interesting experience; the producers wanted me to act as if I didn't know what treasures I really had. I chose not to, and Jordan and I had a lot of fun! After a full day of filming, which involved moving many of my toys to my sunroom (my toy room was tiny and cluttered and had no space for lighting and cameras, etc.), Jordan and I literally had 15 minutes to discuss what items he wanted to buy from me. I ended up selling him a small pile of toys and made about $250. I came to understand that the persona that Jordan showed on TV was not who he really was.

As a footnote to this story, a couple of weeks later, I was in the McDonald's drive-thru picking up dinner, when the McDonald's employee handing me my food stopped, looked at me for a second, then asked, "Were you on *Toy Hunter*?"

On Fandom and Attending Conventions:

Quoting Gonzo from *The Muppet Movie*, "There's not a word yet for old friends who've just met." That's what cons are to me.

Sandy Zier-Teitler

On Her Real Life Job:

Legal Document Processing Specialist.

On a Brief Personal History:

I was born at Sibley Hospital in Washington, DC. I currently live in West Virginia, but lived most of my life in Maryland—first in Prince George's County and then in Ellicott City. In 1994 I met my soulmate, Bruce Teitler and we were married in May of 1996. In June of 1999, I traveled to Los Angeles at the invitation of Carolyn Kelley to attend the Paramount memorial tribute to DeForest Kelley. I returned home the evening of June 24 to find that my husband... my true soulmate... had died in his sleep.

With regard to pets, I have never been without a pet ... rabbits, guinea pigs, cats, dogs, goats, many varieties... though if you really had to pin me down, I'm a "dog" person at heart, and it's thanks to one of my dogs that I made a friend in someone whom I admired (More on this later).

On Her Introduction to Fandom:

In a strange sort of way, my dad was responsible for introducing me to fandom. My dad was a big western fan. We were watching this new show called *Star Trek*, and, when my dad saw [popular Western film actor] DeForest Kelley as one of the stars, we became *Star Trek* fans for life.

On Her Introduction to Conventions:

I attended a *Star Trek* convention with a coworker in the mid-1970s. I do remember it was in Washington, DC, but I really don't remember any more than that. This same coworker took me to a convention in New York in the early 1980s. While these details are vague, I realize, it was indeed my introduction to fandom as well as to conventions.

On Fanzines:

In 1982, the videotape for *Star Trek, the Wrath of Khan*, was being released, so I went to my local video rental store to preorder my copy. The girl at the desk and I struck up a conversation about *Star Trek*, and we immediately became friends. She asked me if I knew anything about fanzines and I, having never heard the term, said that I did not. Well, my new friend, Michelle Holmes, offered to lend me some of her fanzines to read. I was hooked immediately. In May of 1983, she was going to MediaWest and offered to purchase some zines for me. Well, of course I took her up on her offer and a new obsession was awoken.

One of the fanzines she purchased was an issue of *Contact*. *Contact* was a well-known example of the "Hurt/Comfort" genre. These stories usually focused on Kirk and Spock, with one of them being "hurt." McCoy also made frequent appearances. So I wrote to one of the editors, someone by the name of Beverly Volker, and expressed my interest in future issues of her fanzine. Well, a few days later, I received a call from Beverly and after a somewhat long discussion, she invited me to come to a Saturday afternoon/evening meeting. It goes without saying that not only did I accept the invitation, I *had* to invite my new friend, Michelle Holmes; after all, she was the person who had set this whole series of events in motion. If I had not met her at the time I did, my life might have taken an entirely different path.

So, Michelle and I made our way to Beverly's house one Saturday afternoon. We found ourselves sitting in the presence of not one, but three very well-respected zine editors—Beverly Volker and Nancy Kippax (Bev's sister) of *Contact*; and Martha Bonds of *Gateway* (among others). After a very enjoyable visit, we were invited to join them at their Saturday night get-togethers affectionately called the "Contact Crowd." Michelle and I quickly immersed ourselves in this great group of people, which also included Marion McChesney (*Vault of Tomorrow* editor), Mary Mills, Cheryl Bobbitt, Suzanne Elmore, Carol Frisbee, Merle Decker and several others. I apologize for forgetting names.

On Conventions:

In meeting with the fanzine people, I learned that Marion McChesney was chairman of an upcoming convention, ClipperCon. *And* it was assumed that we (Michelle and I) would be willing to work this convention, to be held in February (Yes, we were indeed willing). This was my first experience at working a convention, and I immediately fell in love with it.

When Marion decided to end ClipperCon, we had a barbeque at Beverly's house and it was the general consensus that no one really wanted ClipperCon to end. So, a few people twisted my arm (yes, it was a conspiracy) to take on a "replacement" convention, bribing me with the ability to have DeForest Kelley as a guest. Okay, so I gave in. I chaired OktoberTrek for three years. Our guests were, for the first year, DeForest Kelley and Gates McFadden (first time the two "doctors" had appeared together); for the second, we had Jonathan Frakes, Nichelle Nichols and LeVar Burton (who actually called me to request to be a guest!); and, for the third, we had DeForest Kelley back, along with Brent Spiner. It was a great three years, but I really didn't want to go to a fourth. So, after the third OktoberTrek, I called it quits. That's when Beverly Volker, Steve Wilson and a couple others decided to run with the ball, so to speak. Farpoint was born, and still lives. Right now, I am co-chairman of Farpoint, but, through the years of the various conventions, I have worked registration, programming, preregistration. As current co-chairman, I am responsible for being a liaison with the hotel.

On Giving Advice About Running a Con:

First, be sure you know what you are getting into. Obviously, finances are a big part of it, and don't plan on making money. A fan-run convention is a labor of love, and you really have to enjoy it to put together a great fan-run convention. Luckily, with OktoberTrek and now, with Farpoint, we have a great group of people. Some of the committee members were but mere toddlers when I first met them. Also have a focus. Is it going to be strictly a "one-show" convention, or a general media convention with multiple shows represented? The

On the Difficulties of Running a Con:

Finances, finances, finances. If you are a new convention, it will be difficult to establish yourself to bring money in before the convention to cover expenses. I (we) were lucky in that we were involved with Marion and the "*Contact* Crowd," who were well-respected in the world of fandom. The first thing that must be done is to get a contract with a hotel. Many things have to go into consideration including the type of programming, how many attendees you want to have, etc. Again, we were lucky here in that we followed Marion, who had a great reputation with the hotel, and OktoberTrek continued that reputation to allow Farpoint basically to take over our time slot and contract.

On Her Years in Fandom:

Technically, I'd say since 1983, once Michelle Holmes and I became involved with the "*Contact* Crowd." The only reason I am not including the two conventions I went to with my coworker in the 1970s is that I really didn't think I'd become as involved as I eventually did.

On a Zine of Her Own:

Well, my first introduction to fandom was through Michelle and fanzines, so I was part of the zine community from the beginning. I started helping Beverly and Nancy with *Contact,* typing and proofing the typed copy (this was at a time when a fanzine was not created on a computer but typed on an actual typewriter).

Not long after I really got interested in fanzines, Michelle Holmes and I figured we knew the characters enough that we could do one. My brother was a printer, so I talked to him first. He was willing to print and bind for expenses, so *Mind Meld* was born. Michelle and I would be the editors. Of course, our first issue had a lot of familiar names in it—Beverly Volker, Nancy Kippax, Martha Bonds, Merle

Decker, Gina LaCroix (a great hurt/comfort author with whom I'm still a friend). As with conventions, finances are a big part of getting a zine off the ground, and while authors and artists did work for copies of the zine, there are still other expenses (flyers to solicit preorders, printing costs in general). We were able to get the first issue off the ground, and we took off running. Again, this was because of our involvement with the "*Contact* Crowd" and their reputation. Because of my love of McCoy, he, of course had to be one of our focuses. It was a general zine that focused on the friendship between Kirk, Spock and McCoy. In fact, not long after we got *Mind Meld* off the ground, I saw an interview with Gene Roddenberry who said that he felt that Kirk, Spock and McCoy made up the "perfect person." That seemed logical. The first issue of *Mind Meld* was published in 1984. Again, luck was on our side because of our involvement in Baltimore Fandom. (It may be interesting to note here that the major "pro con" never really broke into Baltimore fandom because of the strong fan base.) Michelle stayed on board for two issues of *Mind Meld*, but after the second issue; she was in school and training and it became a little too much, so I figured I'd take on *Mind Meld* by myself. I ended up doing five issues of *Mind Meld* by myself but will always be grateful to Michelle for initiating my involvement in fandom in general and fanzines in particular.

On Her Current Connection to Fandom:

I am co-chairman of Farpoint. That is the limit to my involvement at this time. I take care of hotel relations.

On Influential Media and People:

Movies/TV shows: *Star Trek* (obviously), many of the *Star Trek* novels. People: So many to name, so afraid I'll forget someone, but to avoid this list from becoming a novel, I'll list the people who I felt had the most influence: Michelle Holmes, Beverly Volker, Nancy Kippax, Martha Bonds, Mary Mills, Marion McChesney, Sue Keenan (president of DeForest Kelley's "official" fan club), my dad, Gina LaCroix, DeForest Kelley, Steve and Renee Wilson.

On Her Favorite Con Activities:

Basically, seeing friends who I only see once a year, which is at Farpoint. Because I don't live in the area anymore, I don't get to see anyone other than at the convention itself. I also love looking at the art work in the art show.

On Her Favorite Con Recollections:

This has to be the development of my friendship with DeForest Kelley and his wife. I first met him at Shore Leave convention in 1986. My mother had crocheted an afghan, celebrating the 20th anniversary of *Star Trek*, to raffle off to benefit the North Shore Animal League (DeForest Kelley's charity of choice). I was able to meet De and Carolyn only briefly, but, during that very short meeting, we learned he and I were both dog lovers. He sent my mother a copy of his poem "A Big Bird's Dream," autographed to her.

Fast forward to the beginnings of OktoberTrek. Without going into too much detail, we had decided we wanted to try to get DeForest Kelley and Gates McFadden as guests. I was friends with Gates' assistant at the time, and with Sue Keenan's connections to De, the initial contact with them went much more smoothly than one would think.

De and Carolyn and I had become pen pals, writing back and forth about anything but the convention and *Star Trek*. They learned my dog, Radar, would be at the convention. Of course, they insisted that they had to meet him. When they arrived in Baltimore, I took Radar to their hotel, where they met. Radar got many head pats, and De and Carolyn were rewarded with a lot of tail wags. The next morning, Carolyn saved a doggie bag for Radar with his name in calligraphy on the front of the bag. That was the true beginning of our friendship. Knowing I was a major football fan (specifically the Washington Redskins), De would often call me after Sunday's game to congratulate or commiserate with me.

Through the years, I received many letters from De and Carolyn. Well, let me clarify, RADAR received many letters from De and Carolyn. See, back during the first OktoberTrek, De was presented with a lot of chocolate gifts (he was a well-known chocaholic). I packed them up so I could ship them to him, to avoid him having to take them on the plane. Well, Radar, being a chocaholic himself (and yes, luckily, he was a dog that could eat chocolate), got into the box and ate some of De's chocolate. And, being a dog of refined tastes, he didn't pick the general chocolates—he chose the Swiss and German chocolates. I told Radar he'd have to write a letter of apology to De, which he did—with my help, of course. In the letter, Radar told De that he was including a pound of Hershey Kisses to try to make up for his weakness. By the time Radar was finished with the apology, what De got was empty Hershey Kiss wrappers. De and Carolyn both really got a kick out of this, and Radar got a letter back, saying he was forgiven. They also included their own empty chocolate wrappers.

Through the years, the "chocolate gag" was referred to in letters between them many times. Radar also received more than his share of autographed pictures of De, including one from *Star Trek V* (with a full growth of beard) which said, "To Radar—from your fuzzy actor friend, Love, DeForest."

In 1991, De received his star on the Hollywood Walk of Fame. I was privileged to receive an invitation to the reception following the ceremony at Paramount. Sue Keenan, as well as two other friends, were also invited. We had seats up-close-and-personal to the ceremony, and, when De made his entrance (picture this, there's the Galaxy Theater which has a two-story escalator), his entrance was down that escalator to the *Star Trek* theme. We were seated at a table together, and, as De brought a friend around, we were introduced as "good friends."

There are many stories I could tell, but there are two others I must share. When Radar was reaching the end of his life, he had a stroke one weekend. Bruce (my husband) and I decided it was time to call the vet and send Radar off to Rainbow Bridge. My vet had always said he'd come to the house to do this, which he did that Monday morning. I called De and Carolyn over the weekend, and we had good cry together. About a month later, I received a letter from De, handwritten (which is significant because by this time Carolyn was doing 99% of the correspondence), and in the letter was enclosed a eulogy for Radar. Talk about bringing tears to my eyes! He referred to the running "chocolate gag" and said that "Radar was swinging on a star, chewing on my chocolate bar."

Finally, while I hate to finish this story on a sad note, I fear I must. In 1999, De died. About two weeks before De's cancer was publicized in the media, he called me and said that he wanted "[his] friends to know about the diagnosis before the media got it out." While I knew we were friends, the fact that he and Carolyn thought to call me was just a heartwarming feeling, in a sad sort of way. When he died, Bruce and I were on vacation. I was invited to Paramount's private memorial service for De on June 23. Bruce could not afford to accompany me, but he said I had to go—to be there not only for myself, but also for Sue. So, to Paramount I went. I returned home the evening of June 24 to find that Bruce had died in his sleep. This time period is still, to this day, very surreal to me.

On Her Favorite Con Guest:

The obvious answer to this is DeForest Kelley. Meeting him and becoming friends with him and his wife was definitely a highlight of my life. If I had to name a non-*Star Trek* guest, while it would be difficult, it would be a toss-up between Melissa McBride and Laurie Holden.

On Why She Continues Working at Farpoint:

It's the source of many of my current friendships as well as friendships with those who are no longer with us. We are a family. This couldn't be illustrated more than at Farpoint 2018, where, the Thursday before the convention started, my sister died suddenly. My immediate family knew that, with no plans being made for the weekend, I would be immersing myself in the convention.

On a Con Person Who Has Enriched Her Life:

Again, I can't pick just one. Beverly Volker has to be one of them. After my mother died, she became my second "mom" and even made my wedding dress for me. Sue Keenan is another. I would have never been able to contact DeForest Kelley, and eventually become friends, if it hadn't been for her.

On Something People May Not Know About Her:

When I was in high school, I raced on roller skates (not derby, just racing) and did freestyle and dance, for which I had several trophies and medals.

Miriam Winder Kelly

On Her Job in Real Life:

Currently, I work in real estate, on the mortgage end, part-time. I retired from the Baltimore City Department of Public Works as a Civil Engineer 3.

On Her Personal History:

My parents were Holocaust Survivors, with my mother at Auschwitz and my father at Matthausen, so we had no close U.S. relatives. I started reading SF and fantasy in third grade at the Enoch Pratt branch library at Park Heights and Belvedere Avenue. I watched *Twilight Zone* and *Rocky Jones* on TV. I took a tiny black-and-white TV to the University of Maryland to watch *Star Trek*. I received a Bachelor of Science in Civil Engineering with a minor in Environmental Engineering.

In July, 1975, I went to LaunchCon 3. Patrick J. Kelly, Jr., was the con chair. A group of cars caravanned from his apartment in Arlington, Virginia, to Cape Canaveral, Florida. It was awesome to watch the launch of the Apollo, which then docked with the Soyuz. Afterwards, we went to Disney World (and rode on Space Mountain).

Back home, Patrick, one of the founders of the Baltimore Science Fiction Society, started to escort me to BSFS meetings. I joined the L5 Society and was a pro-space activist. SP Somtow, Jack Chalker, L Sprague de Camp, and his wife Catherine Crook de Camp were among those who came to our engagement party. Our engagement cake was Smaug the Dragon! Patrick and I married in September, 1981 and honeymooned at Worldcon in Denver. After the con, we traveled to New Mexico and had a meal with Pat's friend, Roger Zelazny, and his lovely family, before visiting the Bandelier National Monument.

I applied to be a Mission Specialist astronaut and got a rejection letter in the first batch! The L5, now National Space Society, meetings were held in our living room (until Pat died in 2004). Yearly, we went to Andrews Air Force base on Armed Forces Day and set up a booth to promote Space education and SF.

On Her Introduction to Fandom and Conventions:

I attended Unicon at the University of Maryland as either a freshman in 1970 or a sophomore in 1971. I purchased a Kelly Freas rough at the art auction. The University of Maryland had SF movies, including showing the *Trek* blooper reels!

On Influential Media:

Twilight Zone! The ethics of the show helped influence my commitment to the Reconstructionist philosophy of Judaism. I went to my first Worldcon in September 1976. Robert Heinlein was the Guest of Honor, and three young guys brought their movie to the con: *Star Wars*—I still have my one-page mimeo! I have a fondness for *Wandering Stars*, an anthology of Jewish SF stories.

I also have been subscribing to the *Forward, Science News* and *Fantasy & Science Fiction* magazines for many years. What you read matters!

On Becoming Involved with Balticon:

My first Balticon was in 1975, held at the Pikesville Hilton. I was staff in 1976, but don't remember what I did.

On Her Jobs Held at Balticon:

After becoming a parent, I took over Children's programming. Currently, I'm the Science Track scheduler. Prior to the con, inviting scientists to be volunteer presenters. (True story: I cold-called a top researcher in physics. He laughed hysterically and said *"No!"* After work, he went home and told his family that some crazy person called and asked him to present in the Balticon Science Track. His daughter told him "I attend Balticon every year and you need to accept!" He was an excellent presenter!) I purchase pretzels, chips, and cookies at Utz and Stauffer in Hanover and York, PA prior to the con. I also purchase 18 dozen donuts for the volunteers and bread for the con suite in Patrick's memory. At the Con, I make sure there are no holes in the Science Track due to last minute cancellations. I prepare the Friday "Meet the Scientist" social, also in Patrick's memory. During the year, I'm the unofficial publicity *yenta* and scheduler for the volunteers to staff the BSFS/Balticon fan tables at other cons. Also, I'm the Young Writers' Contest (http://bsfs.org/bsfsywc.htm) organizer.

On Why Balticon Succeeds:

1. There has been a science track at Balticon for more than 40 years!
2. It's very harmonious. Folks support each other. Balticon truly supports the big tent: *Star Trek, Star Wars, Dr. Who, Marvel, Red Dwarf,* Anime, Larping, Gaming, art, music, movies and more.
3. Balticon has the best con suite!
4. There's diversity of Programming

On Her Fan Art Collection:

I have 170-plus original pieces including pieces by Kelly Freas, Mark Rogers, Joe Bergeron, A. Beck, L.W. Perkins, Steven Fox, Jannie Wertz, Michael Whalen, Robin Wood, Steve Stiles, John Picacio, Rick Sternbach, Vicky Wyman, and others.

On Her Favorite Con Activity:

I like going to someone else's con as a fan, so I don't have responsibilities.

On Her Favorite Con Story:

The story that gets the most attention is when I watched *Star Wars* at the Kansas City Worldcon seven months before it came out. Then it was seeing *Star Wars* at the Senator Theater on York Road with my father (who fell asleep during the movie).

I enjoy recounting stories from Isaac Asimov or Kelly Freas or Hal Clement—greats who are no longer here. I loved the science panel "Extending Human Life" with Ben Bova, Dr. Richard Nakamura, Dr. Thomas Talbot and Dr. John Cmar. The panelists were electric. I always enjoy Dr. Thomas Holtz's Dinosaur Science updates at Balticon

On Her Favorite Con Guest:

Hal Clement—what a gentleman! Although, Vinton Cerf of Google is a close second.

On the Person Who Has Made a Lasting Impression:

It is my late husband, Patrick J. Kelly Jr., father of our daughter, Alexandra, now 27. I went into labor with Alexandra on Saturday of Balticon, but she missed the "dead dog party" since she was born at 1 a.m.

On What Cons Give to Her:

1. Fun. I chose a profession to clean up the environment, but that is not happening at this time. I need fun to counteract my frustrations.

2. When you discuss religious ethics with someone, they become defensive. Being able to discuss ethics with someone in an SF/Fantasy setting removes the personal threat to them.

On What People Don't Know About Her:

Not telling! Most people already know that I am a chocoholic, caffeine addict and "abby-normal."

The Stage Crew

Bob Ahrens

On His Real-Life Job:

I have been in automotive repair since 1980. I currently work as a Parts Specialist at a Honda dealer in Cockeysville, Maryland.

On His Personal History:

I was born in a small New Hampshire town called Hudson. As a middle son of a Navy man, we moved frequently and often without notice. At one point, our family tore up roots and moved four times in one year. It was hard keeping friends. After about 1982, my parents decided to move once more, but I elected to stay and try to finish college. All bets were off, however, when I met a certain little redhead, married her, and raised a daughter near Perry Hall, Md. I have a redheaded wife, a redheaded daughter and a red Dachshund. I am so outnumbered...

On His Introduction to Fandom:

My earliest exposure to *Trek* was covertly staying up to watch an episode, about 1968, peering through the upstairs banister as my mother watched in the living room.

On His Introduction to Conventions:

I scraped enough paper route money together to attend a con in D.C. in about 1976, and was lucky enough to tag along with Lance Woods to the first Shore Leave in 1978.

On His Time in Fandom:

That makes it roughly 42 years.

On Being a Member of the Boogie Knights:

Not long after my senior year of high school began, I met Lance Woods, John Scheeler and David Keefer (my best man and two ushers). The four of us achieved great things at Glen Burnie High, cruising the mall, going to Wildwood, appearing in plays together and forging life-long bonds. Mostly to pass down-time backstage, we'd regale each other with lines discovered from Monty Python and the musical genius of "Weird" Al Yankovic… in other words, we got silly. A couple years later, David had a costume entered in a Masquerade at Hunt Valley—a Vulcan Elder robe, I believe. Anyway, he was not happy with the presentation he'd come up with, so he ditched the ears, and came up with a new one at the last minute, and thus Theodoric of York, Medieval Disc Jockey was born. The four of us were bowled over with the audience response, and the rest of the day was spent trying to come up with goofy 10th century song titles Theo would "play" on the air. Yes. Once again, we got silly.

Then … Dave got quiet and contemplative …"Why not? Let's do it!" We all thought he was kidding, or drunk, or crazy. Lance was beginning to stash away sharp objects. Then we began to come up with characters for ourselves, with thought-out back stories and biographies for us all. The Boogies were born.

On His Current Connections to Conventions:

It's hard to imagine what life was like before these cons. I certainly haven't had many fond memories that weren't somehow related to fandom and these wonderful friends I've kept over 40 years.

I can look back on meeting most of the casts of each iteration of *Trek*, with few notable exceptions, and they've all been wonderful, personable and friendly. But now, it's less about the guests and more about family. As our lives drive us on the tide to distant shores, the con has grown to be more a celebration of my personal relationships with my closest friends. While life attempts to split us up, it's fandom that brings us back together.

On Influential Media:

Obviously, *Star Trek* was, of course, the catalyst, then, ten years later, George Lucas came along with permission to be *nerds*. When *Star Wars* did so well, it was as if the whole world was saying, "We're right with you, pal. SciFi is cool!" We were no longer the weirdos... ok, maybe we were. But it seemed okay to be so. We didn't have to hide anymore. We were free to come out of the basement and into the light.

Nowadays, if it has the name Spielberg on it, I'm in. Here's my $14.00.

On Working at the Cons:

My first stint of volunteering was working Con Security, checking badges, and helping out in Masquerade. If entertaining the folks in the ballroom as Syd the Vicious counts as a job, then that was my favorite. That and the plays. C'mon, acting silly with your best friends in front of five hundred people? Wouldn't it be great to get paid for that every day?

On Raising a Daughter in Fandom:

I wasn't sure I was totally on board with that at first. It's one thing to do it to yourself, but ... I mean... I'm a *dad* now. What I do, good or bad, affects a different person. That's a whole new level of responsibility. But you get that anyway, fandom or no. So, just like God, I'd let her see Dad doing it, and if she could embrace that, she'd let us know. Rachel actually isn't much into *Star Trek*, or even *Star Wars*, but The Doctor moves her like no other. Now that they've made The Doctor a woman, I think the bloom is off the rose, though.

On His Favorite Roles in Cheap Treks:

I've been lucky enough to act with these people, help write some shows and direct once or twice. Just being in the same room with them was such an honor. Yes, I consider them close friends, but they're also all so talented, I felt like an interloper at times. Why do these brilliant people keep me around?

One year, I got to play Hal O'Dally in "Bolt Upright", my biggest role, and one of the few original scripts penned by Lance. I think it was his best work, and to be a part of that, bringing his genius to life with my own humble skills as an actor… well I just hoped I was doing it justice.

On His Favorite Activities at a Con:

These days, working with George Laurence and Conventional Magic takes up a lot of free con-time, so I mainly try to catch Masquerade and see the headline guest, but the rest of the time is spent catching up with everyone I haven't seen since last year. It's a big family reunion.

On His Favorite Con Story:

Back in the days before *The Next Generation*, it was hard to go to a con and stay for all three days. Hotel suites were (and still are) pricey and were often sold to capacity before you even thought of going that year. On Shore Leave weekend, a friend decided to defray costs by taking ten bucks a head for a bit of floor space. A ten-spot and a sleeping bag.

Twenty-six of us spent the night in that room—with T. Alan Chafin in the bathtub!

On His Favorite Con Guest:

Are you kidding me? Do you have to ask? George Takei—"St. George of the Helm." There can be only one.

On Attending Maryland Conventions:

Well, they're *here*, and everyone I know makes a concerted effort to come here at least once every year. If I'd had time and funds, I might try San Diego Comic-Con, but never all the time. It's your hometown for a reason. You're dug in, you've put down roots. The home con is something you've invested in. Like a marriage, you make a commitment. You keep having the con here, I'll keep showing up.

On What People Don't Know About Him:

Ostensibly, I show the world a smart, confident, outgoing, well-adjusted family man. Nothing further from the truth. What they don't know is how much I fear I'm not even in the same league… everyone I call a friend is so mind-dazzlingly talented and so good at what they do, I couldn't even come close. It's why I love them all so much. I am in awe of them, and I hope they never lose what they have so much of.

Lewis G. Aide

On His Personal History:

I hail from a military family, with parents Fou and Sue. At the age of 13, I watched the first episode of *Star Trek*, "The Man Trap," in my family's Augusta, Georgia living room when it aired in August 1967. I fell in love with the show, as did my father, Fouad, and we watched every week through its three seasons' run. I was heart-broken when the show  went off the air. I truly thought I would never see anything as good as that again on television.

On His Personal History:

I followed in my dad's footsteps and went to West Point, graduating in 1976. I was stationed in such far-flung places as Frankfurt, Germany, Fort Gordon, Georgia, Seoul, Korea, and Fort Meade, Maryland, with jobs in the Signal Corps related to electronic communications. It was at West Point, during my freshman year, that I developed my fascination with computers and came to understand how they worked.

On His Introduction to Conventions:

While at West Point in 1974, I saw a TV commercial for the International *Star Trek* Con in NY, run by Bjo Trimble. [Editor's Note: Lew is most likely referring to the 1974 "Star Trek Lives!" convention, chaired by Al Shuster. According to Fanlore, it was advertised as "The International Star Trek Convention," but the West Coast-based Bjo Trimble was not part of its staff. Rather, Bjo was organizing a Trek con in California at the same time.] As a sophomore with weekend leave, I took a bus to the city and entered the hotel where I thought the convention was to be held. I wasn't sure I was in the correct place until an Andorian walked by me in the lobby. After checking in, I took an elevator to the dealer's room. The elevator stopped, and Walter Koenig walked on. It was my first meeting with a *Star Trek* actor. At that con, all of the principal cast members of *Star Trek* were present. [Editor's Note: DeForest Kelley, Walter Koenig, Nichelle Nichols and George Takei and D.C. Fontana are recorded as the Trek guests.] I became a full-fledged fan when I purchased a Captain's shirt with the appropriate insignia and then went out on to the streets of New York to buy the requisite black pants and boots of Captain Kirk's uniform. I even sewed the correct braids on to the sleeves. I bought a phaser pistol and tricorder, which were made by independent artists, as there were no official products at that time.

On Entering Maryland Fandom:

In 1985, I heard about Shore Leave in Maryland. I went, volunteered my services and never left the video room all weekend. I ran the video room all by myself, and I'm sure the con committee was grateful for my help. With this auspicious beginning, I have been an active member of fandom for 38 years. I've worked at the various Maryland cons, including ClipperCon, OktoberTrek, Shore Leave and Farpoint. In 1993, I joined Conventional Magic, a group of technical artists run by George Laurence and John Vengrouskie. My role was to assist the video director, John Reynolds, who was recording the weekend's events in the ballroom with only a single camera. That same year, I offered my services to Farpoint for desktop publishing of its program book. This was the first time that a desktop publishing was used instead of the cut-and-paste method by the Maryland conventions.

On His Role at Conventions:

I became Video Director for Farpoint and Shore Leave in 1994. I stopped using a single camera and introduced a video switcher that allowed me to do a multi-camera video recording with live switching between cameras. My other technological innovations at the Maryland conventions included hotel maps in perspective, showing the various convention areas. I also worked with the area fan acting groups to video tape credits synchronized with music, produce 3-D generated video including some blue screen work, and implement the first con-based live blue screen effect for one of the productions. I was a camera man for many Cheap Treks productions, as well as the video editor, audio editor, and sound effects editor. I also provided all the equipment used to record at the cons. I made copies of the Masquerade video to sell to fans, and a master tape was then provided to the con committees of all the ballroom activities.

After 20 years of running the video, I've stepped down and become Video Director Emeritus. I provide advice and guidance to new video staff and work as a roving trouble shooter for tech in the various con rooms.

On His Favorite Con Experiences:

One of my favorite con experiences was when I assisted in announcing the death of a popular character from a past convention masquerade, called K'Elvis, and portrayed by T. Alan Chafin. T. Alan and I made fake newspapers with headlines announcing the death (by Jolt Cola overdose) and printed them to be distributed around the convention.

Another time I was at a helpers' breakfast in a con suite, when a striking woman with red hair came over to me and said hello. I didn't realize that it was Suzie Plakson, K'Ehleyr in *Star Trek: the Next Generation*, until after the verbal exchange. I was thrilled because I had always admired Suzie.

On Something You May Not Know About Him:

I regard myself as a big fan, and I have always enjoyed helping at the cons, or with any endeavor, without expectation of reward. Something you may not know about me is that I am actually the "Roadside Aide." I regularly assist people whose cars have broken down on the highways, or who are having medical emergencies. I was inspired by a TV show called *That's Incredible* in the early 80's. The show profiled a man who cruised highways in a pickup truck loaded with supplies and wore the Lone Ranger's costume, minus the mask. He was known as the Road Ranger. The impetus of my own work as a Good Samaritan was a three-car collision that I happened upon in the 80s. I had to drive far and fast to get to a phone to call 911 and procure assistance for the injured. The very next week I bought myself a cell phone and started taking Red Cross courses. I've taken CPR and AED training, and I am a state-certified Emergency Medical Responder. I've acquired medical equipment and vehicle supplies for my car. I've changed about 80 flat tires over the years. I've even dealt with medical emergencies at the cons. I never accept payment for helping people, and I tell people to pay it forward or give to charity.

George Laurence

On His Real Life Job:

I am a museum exhibit designer and fabricator. I've been working with the museum community since 1980 and have been involved in some pretty cool stuff. I have worked on the Apollo 11 command module, the Enola Gay, and to my fandom delight, the 12' original series *Enterprise* in which I designed and built the mounting cradle to hang it from the ceiling of the Air and Space Museum, back in 1991. They have since done an entirely new refit of the exhibit in 2015. My company, Museum Acrylics, has done hundreds of exhibit projects since 1996 for art and history museums, as well as science centers throughout the country.

On A Brief Personal History:

I grew up in northern New Jersey and graduated high school in 1976. I was, and still am, an academic/non-sports nerd, and was heavily into history, model railroading, and of course, *Trek*. I went to the University of Maryland and majored in Industrial Technology and plastics, graduating in 1981. It was Maryland that changed everything. My first marriage was in 1985. My second was in 1996 to Stacie, who is a fan and whom I met at OktoberTrek in 1994. In 1997, my daughter Maeggie was born, and that was the best thing ever to happen to me. Stacie is a stained glass artist, and Maegs is pursuing a career in museum education. She will graduate in 2019 from Walsh University. For many years, I have embraced local Ohio history. I run arts and history festivals here, and do colonial era living history woodwork at a local historic site. I am also involved with the historic canal research. I have always been into historic preservation and restoration of old things, such as our houses, antiques and railroad passenger car interiors. We have a wonderful railroad museum in this area. I collect Revolutionary War New Jersey-related stuff, vintage American Flags, and New York Subway objects.

On His Introduction to Fandom and Conventions:

I was in algebra class freshman year in high school (1973), when my friend Bob, who had a copy of the *TV Guide*, showed me an ad for a *Star Trek* con in New York. I only lived 45 minutes from downtown so four of us went to the second-ever *Trek* con. For $5 a day, you could see almost the entire main cast. It was unbelievable to see the "Bloopers" for the first time and, my God, the dealer's room! I was hooked. Each year we would go and slowly got involved. It was a blast to be a helper for the first time, in which I was part of the human wall that kept the crowd away from Shatner. Once I started college, I had somewhat forgotten about cons, until I was in the Colonial Ballroom Lounge in the Student Union at Maryland and ran across a bunch of people rehearsing for a play. They were doing short *Trek* skits for the August Party Con. [Editor's Note: The Colonial Ballroom Lounge was still hosting rehearsals for The Not Ready for Paramount Players' shows a decade later. Sadly, changes to the space since have left it unsuited for future bands of thespians to use.] I asked what was going on, and well… the rest changed my social life. I joined the committee and had an idea to do a one-day con. Trekaday was born in 1977. I ran several more one-day cons and then worked on August Party for four more years. We would go to other cons, and my first Shore Leave was in 1980. I got involved with Clippercon, Starbase Baltimore, Fan-Out and other fannish craziness. As well as con administration things, I really loved coordinating operations and tech.

On His Years in Fandom:

Going to cons for 45 years (that's scary). Involved with some aspect of running them for 41 years.

On Influential Media:

Other than *Trek*, *Babylon 5* did it for me. I love time travel, so any film, show or book works for me.

On Conventional Magic:

In 1983, a truly visionary and driven man by the name of Dick Preston, from Vienna, Virginia, asked me if I was interested in helping him run Starcall. It was a half fandom/half science con in Rosslyn, Virginia. He pulled in a truly wacky and talented sound man by the name of John Vengrouskie, whom he knew from local Jewish Community Center gigs. A video guy, Pat Darby from Bethesda, rounded out our three-man group, and Conventional Magic was born. I came up with the name. Pat's wife, Cam, joined us as another camera person (yes, that's weird). In the beginning we actually thought about making it a real company. Way too much bureaucratic BS! Once the IRS invented the LLC, it was easier, but by then we were all too busy with life to do that. Besides, I hate paperwork. In 1986, the Shore Leave committee asked us to get involved. Shore Leave's Marion McChesney (truly a sweetie) also ran Clippercon, and I joined that committee. We also helped with tech and operations on *Galactica* and even *Blake's 7* cons. As time has gone on, we've brought in others like Lew Aide, who has been the most reliable and great-to-work-with ConMag person we've ever had. He took over for John Reynolds, who ran our video for a few cons. We have had several other sound, lighting and video people throughout the years.

On What He Does at Cons:

My work begins three months before the con. I am responsible for all operations coordination. That includes the physical layout, what goes where and when, and all tech equipment and staff. I generate floorplan drawings, schedules and lists, which, in concert with the committee, will enable the con to run smoothly (hopefully). I delegate many duties to key personnel, which in turn make this all happen without problems. Coordination of tech crews and contractors includes audio, video, lighting and hardware. In the past few years, we have started using professionals in these positions. The tech demands have become too advanced for "home" equipment and capabilities to keep up with the state-of-the-art. I miss the old days of 16mm film, hand-held video VHS and four-channel mixers.

What is something that went haywire while you were working the convention?

Scheduling can easily get off target. Some guests (certain starship captains for instance), can cause timing to be totally screwed up. With an experienced con committee like we have at Farpoint and Shore Leave, we work together to fix things. It is so important the con-goer never sees or hears problems on the front end.

On Introducing His Daughter to Fandom:

Her first con, she was four months old. Her next time was at eight years old, and she had fun. It wasn't until she was 16 that it caught on. She's always been a "fan girl," but she discovered it's OK to like Anime and other fandoms as a teen. She went to a small jock-centric/anti-nerd high school in which she did not fit well. Although, she threw discus junior and senior years and broke records. They liked her then (go figure). At Shore Leave she developed friends as kindred spirits and is always in contact with them.

On His Favorite Con Recollection:

Jadzia Dax! I was on the light board during masquerade and like usual, there was a stage blackout. This was a full blackout which included the judges table as well. Terry Farrell was a judge, and she maybe had had some liquid courage. She stood up and said loudly, "I'm Dax, so turn the f****** lights back on!" You could have heard a pin drop. From that point on, the committee stopped allowing the guests to drink before or during masquerade. And yes, I turned the lights on.

On His Favorite Con Guest:

I was watching B5 one night, and I noticed that Kosh was later played by Jeffery Willerth. I went to high school with a Jeffery Willerth. (Nah!) He became Associate Producer in the last season. Marilyn Mann told me early on, that Pat Tallman (Jeff's wife at the time) was a guest. I didn't think about it at the time. About two weeks before Shore Leave, Marilyn tells me her husband is coming, too. I said, "wouldn't it be funny if..." It's Saturday, midday in the ballroom and he is about to come on. As I was doing my stage manager duties, he walks backstage and I say "Hi Jeff, do you remember me?" He says "Oh my God, George!" What's funny is that we never really hung together. We BS'd over drinks later.

On the Con Person Who Made a Lasting Impression:

My wife Stacie.

On Why He Continues Working at the Cons:

I like what I do.

The Entertainers

David Keefer

On His Real Life Job:

I retired from federal government service in 2015, after working for thirty-three years as an analyst for the US Government Accountability Office (GAO). Before that I was a Banquet Manager for a local catering company for six years.

On His Personal History:

I was born in September, 1961 in Baltimore, Maryland, to an electrician and a housewife. Mom's pregnancy was a bit of a surprise, since my parents had been married (and childless) for 22 years; when my mother told my father the news, he said, "I'll believe it when I see it." The hospital where I was born no longer exists, perhaps as some sort of warning.

My mother was always reading and read to me before I could even hold a book, passing on her love of the written word. It was she who always stressed the importance of education, and I was the first member of our family to earn a college degree. Dad, on the other hand, taught me more of the "outdoors stuff," like fishing, crabbing, baseball, how to plant a decent vegetable garden, and how to make basic repairs around the house. I miss them both dearly, though I do hear their voices in my head on a daily basis. Oh, and the house where I was raised no longer exists, either. Another warning, perhaps?

I was one of those weird kids who loved school. (Well, maybe not junior high; some of those kids were a-holes just for the sake of being a-holes.) High school was especially fun for me (except for Calculus... Yech!), because I finally started to meet and hang out with people who had similar interests to my own: movies and science fiction. It was here that I met the people who would become my convention co-conspirators for many years to come: Lance, Bob, and John. It was also here that I started writing parodies. Lance and I co-wrote and directed "Star Bores" for our high school's variety show in 1978, and then our senior class play, "Seniorman," in 1979 ("You'll believe a Gopher can fly!"). Yeah, our school mascot was a gopher; welcome to the suburbs.

In 1986 I met the love of my life and future wife, Mary, at Balticon. She has been an inspiration to a lot of my writing and has always been supportive of my convention-related endeavors. We have since raised two beautiful daughters together, who have also attended numerous conventions and even participated in masquerade a few times. We currently live in southern Maryland with four dogs, three cats, one guinea pig, and several fish tanks.

On His Introduction to Science Fiction:

Science was always my favorite subject in school, and I was obsessed with the Apollo Program; every launch, mission, and splashdown had me glued to the television. However, I credit Jerome Beatty, Jr.'s *Matthew Looney* series of children's books as my first real introduction to science fiction. Then, of course, came the *Star Trek* re-runs...

On His Involvement with Conventions:

I got involved with attending conventions in high school. Friends of mine attended a convention called Shore Leave and had a great time; so some of us went to the next available convention, which was Balticon 14. I guess I was hooked from that point on.

On His Years in Fandom:

I guess it's been since 1980. Wow... *that long?* Now I feel even older. Thanks a lot, Diane!

On His Current Fame or Connection to Conventions:

Fame? You think I have fame? *Bwah-ha-ha-ha-ha!* Oh, you're talking about that stuff I do at conventions...

I am one of the two remaining (still active), founding members of the filk/parody group The Boogie Knights (founded 1982), one of the founding members of the comedy troupe Cheap Treks (1987-1997), and I currently serve as masquerade emcee at both Farpoint and Shore Leave.

On Influential People or Media in his His Life:

People: My mother for teaching me to read at an early age and my wife for being so supportive. Also, Lance, Steve, Bob, and John, my "partners in crime" from Cheap Treks and Boogie Knights.

Books: Early works of Robert Heinlein, Larry Niven, Ben Bova, Alan Dean Foster, Isaac Asimov, Spider Robinson, Robert Asprin

Movies: *Planet of the Apes* (the original), *Rollerball* (also the original), *Star Wars* (before it was called Episode IV), *Superman: The Movie, Blade Runner, Star Trek II: The Wrath of Khan*

Television: *Star Trek* (original series), *Star Trek: The Next Generation, The Twilight Zone, Lost in Space, Quark*

On Costuming:

I think some, if not all, of these won some sort of award. I really don't remember.

- Condorman (Best Recreation, Balticon 16)
- Theodoric of York, Medieval Disk Jockey
- The K-Team
- The Honeymooners on Krypton

On Creating the Boogie Knights:

At that point in my life, I was playing Dungeons & Dragons almost every weekend. I noticed that nearly all of the filkers I heard at conventions were doing songs about *Star Trek* and space travel, but no one was covering fantasy, mythology, and medieval history. So, I figured it was about time someone did. Fortunately, my friend (and frequent dungeon master) John Scheeler was musically inclined...

On What the Boogie Knights Means to Him:

It's just something that keeps me off the street corners.

Seriously, though, it's become a major part of who I am. Being able to create and perform song parodies that people enjoy is kind of a rush. Seeing the face and hearing the laughter of someone enjoying one of our concerts for the time is the ultimate reward.

On His Favorite Boogie Knight Song:

My favorite BK song is probably "Top of the Wall." It also was the favorite song of the late great Robert Asprin, who was one of our biggest fans. If I had to pick a favorite BK song that I didn't write (but wish I had) I'd have to say "Castle Transylvania."

On Cheap Treks:

Wow... I honestly can't remember all of the shows that I wrote, co-wrote, directed or co-directed during Cheap Treks' ten-year history. So I'll just list a few that were my personal favorites, in no particular order:

- Jupiter 2, Enterprise 0
- A Hard Day's Light Year
- Fandom at the Opera
- Deep West Nine: A Fistful of Latinum
- Federation's Most Wanted
- The Ex-Files: This Way to the Egress
- KT2
- Conquerors of the Ionosphere

After Cheap Treks was dissolved, I wrote and directed a few more under the banner of Misfit Toy Productions:

- Scully the Vampire Slayer
- Ring, One Each: Force Nine from Rivendell
- Ring, One Each: Alternities

On Writing and Directing More Parodies:

I would definitely consider writing one if a good idea came along; in fact, I have three or four partially-written scripts on a flash drive somewhere. Thing is, I have a hard time handing off a script to someone else to direct. Maybe it's ego, maybe it's just being overly-protective of my scripts. So, the answer is a definite maybe.

Not sure if I'm up for directing again yet. The problem with directing and producing plays for conventions is time: having to essentially give up one out of every seven days to rehearse (yes, we rehearsed). Plus, there were the inevitable problems that one must deal with when producing such an undertaking with a large cast and crew. There are times when I really miss it; then I wake up.

On Being a Masquerade Emcee:

I like to go back into the green room before masquerade and go over each entry's paperwork. I want to be sure that I can pronounce every entrant's name, their character's name, any script they want me to read, etc. If it's not obvious to me when I look at the sheet, I seek out the entrant and go over it with them. I don't know if other masquerade emcees do this now, but I remember too many instances in the past where things were mispronounced, misread, or generally mishandled by an emcee. I used to compete, and I know that costumers are under enough stress to not have to worry about someone getting their name right or screwing up their script.

Crazy masquerade stories? Not that I can recall; every masquerade I've done has gone smooth as glass... [insert nervous laughter while vigorously knocking on every piece of wood in reach]

On His Favorite Con Recollections:

Once when I was auctioneer for a charity auction, I described a Captain Kirk action figure as "The William Shatner doll... Wind it up and it over-acts." Jimmy Doohan, who was sitting at the table right in front of me, laughed so hard he almost fell out of his chair.

I remember getting a book autographed by the late Isaac Asimov. The rather busty young lady I was dating at the time was also in line. When she reached the front, Asimov asked her age. When she told him she was twenty-two, he replied, "You grew those in twenty-two years?"

On Favorite Con Guests:

I don't think I really have a favorite, but I always enjoyed listening to George Takei and Jimmy Doohan speak.

On Maryland Cons:

Maryland conventions have been a place to meet people with similar interests to my own and hang out with friends I only see a few times a year. They've also provided a platform for my creative endeavors that I probably would have never found elsewhere. And I met my wife at one, for which I will be eternally grateful.

On Something People Don't Know About Him:

Let's see... I collect yo-yos and decks of playing cards, I'm a major league procrastinator, I don't know how to use a sewing machine, and I would someday like to write children's books.

Cheralyn (Cher) Lambeth

On Her Real Life Job:

I actually have multiple jobs, but I mainly freelance/contract as a costume, prop, and puppet builder for the entertainment industries (film, TV, theater, exhibits, etc). Some of my past work includes films (*The Muppet Christmas Carol; The Net; The Patriot; The New World; Evan Almighty; Leatherheads; The Hunger Games*), TV shows (*Dinosaurs!; Homeland; Outcast*), theater (*Sesame Street Live!; Avenue Q*), and live/interactive properties (*Star Trek: The Experience* at the Las Vegas Hilton, and sports mascots such as Sir Purr for the Carolina Panthers).

On Her Life and Hobbies:

Currently, I live and work in Charlotte, NC, although I do a great deal of travelling for my various jobs. I also travel quite a bit to various conventions as well as to pirate festivals where I perform with my stage combat group The ShadowPlayers.

Another of my hobbies is paranormal research/investigation (AKA ghost hunting), and I have a book out on haunted theaters. It fits quite nicely with my Ghostbusters cosplay (I'm team captain/founder of the Southern Belle Ghostbusters), as I've actually gotten some of my best ghost stories from people who've seen me in my Ghostbusters gear and who've said "I've got to tell you this ghost story I have, I know *you'll* believe me!"

On Her Introduction to Fandom and Conventions:

Even before I was first introduced to fandom, I always enjoyed playing dress-up and making costumes and props (cosplaying before it was a thing!). I learned how to sew at a pretty early age, when my mother finally got tired of trying to come up with all the elaborate Halloween costume ideas I had, and taught me sewing, so that I could make them myself. It wasn't until I saw *Star Wars* for the first time, however, that I realized there was a whole other world out there of costumes, props, alien creatures, and special effects, and I was hooked. After that, I looked for any other sci-fi shows I could find—I got caught up in *Star Trek* reruns, stumbled on *Dr. Who* completely by accident, and fell in love with the original *Battlestar Galactica* (a costume from that show was one of my first complete costume recreations).

It was some time after that that my mother discovered our local university hosted a small student run sci-fi convention called StellarCon and suggested I might enjoy attending. I was still in middle school at the time, so I went along with another friend for the day and fell in love with the convention scene, especially meeting and talking with other costumers. StellarCon has long since gone by the wayside, but I've continued to go to cons ever since.

On the Star Wars Stormtroopers:

I'm proud to say that I'm one of the earliest still-active members of the 501st Legion. I joined the 501st in 1998, shortly after seeing and meeting other troopers at DragonCon that year and have been trooping ever since! My participation in the 501st has given me some amazing opportunities: I've had the chance to travel all over the world, working various *Star Wars* Celebrations and other events (such as going to South Africa to work with Adidas on promoting their line of *Star Wars* shoes and clothing). I was one of the lucky troopers who marched in the 2007 Tournament of Roses Parade. I also have been on stage as a trooper with "Weird Al" Yankovic at many of his concerts, serving as background with other stormtroopers to his *Star Wars* parody songs "The Saga Begins" and "Yoda." I've always been a huge fan of "Weird Al," so it was an exciting experience to have the opportunity to be part of his concerts! The first concert I participated in was especially exciting. At that particular location, they had been unable to get local cheerleader performers as they usually did for the song "Smells Like Nirvana," and one of Al's crew came up with the idea of using stormtroopers instead. I had less than an hour to work with one of my fellow troopers to choreograph a routine with giant red pompoms (in armor!) for the song, but the look on Al's face as we were led out on stage before the start of the song was priceless. I'm glad to say we carried off the routine without a hitch!

I've also been very glad for the chance to do some good with my hobby and participate with my fellow troopers in numerous charity events such as children's hospital visits and fundraisers for the Make-A-Wish Foundation. Most especially, I'm proud to be a part of the "Pit Crew" for R2-KT, the pink R2 unit built in honor and memory of Katie Johnson, daughter of 501st Legion Founder Albin Johnson. Katie was diagnosed with a brain tumor at the age of six, and sadly passed away from it not long after. R2-KT was built especially for her by the R2 Builders, and KT now travels the world, serving as a goodwill ambassador in the fight against pediatric cancer and other childhood illnesses. The Builders had been concerned that they might not finish KT in time before Katie passed away, and one of the group (Andrew Schwarz) painted his own R2-D2 pink to serve as a stand-in while the "real" KT was being finished. I actually transported the stand-in KT from Farpoint convention (where I had picked it up from Andy) to Columbia, SC, in the front seat of my Toyota Echo! We later presented the real KT to Albin at the following Shore Leave.

Lastly, one of my favorite anecdotes from my time in the 501st comes from an appearance our group made with the North Carolina Symphony for a science-fiction themed concert. The narrator for this event was none other than George Takei, and we were looking forward to meeting him. I was dressed as Princess Leia, to help round out the contingent of stormtroopers and other *Star Wars* characters, and we were waiting in the green room for the elevator to take us up to the orchestra level. The elevator arrived, the doors opened, and there with a group of Symphony officials was George Takei. I exclaimed, to let the others know, "It's George Takei!" And, without skipping a beat, he responded, "It's Carrie Fisher!"

On Her Stage Combat Group:

As mentioned above, I perform with a stage combat group called The ShadowPlayers and have traveled to numerous festivals, conventions and other events performing sword-fighting shows with them. Currently we perform mainly at pirate-themed events, but in years past we've done lightsaber "battles" at conventions, *Star Wars* movie premieres, and other events.

On Influential People and Media:

There are so many people and things that have been a positive influence on me that it's hard to list them all, but I think it's safe to say that George Lucas and the *Star Wars* films have most definitely influenced my life in fandom (the 501st wouldn't exist without them!). I've also been greatly influenced by the Harry Potter films, and by the works (movies, TV shows, and books) of/about Jim Henson.

On Costuming:

I have several favorite costumes, including many of my Harry Potter costumes, my Marty McFly from *Back to the Future*, and most especially my recreation of Sarah's ball gown from the film *Labyrinth*. If I had to pick a single favorite, however, it would probably be my Ringwraith-on-a-horse costume from *Lord of the Rings*. This is a costume/puppet hybrid that combines the Ringwraith costume with an almost-life-size horse puppet, so that I'm giving the illusion of a rider on a horse. Many people have assumed there are two people operating the costume, and one time someone came up to me and said from a distance they thought there was actually a horse standing there! This costume has won numerous awards, including Best in Show at Farpoint 2003.

One interesting story related to that costume is that I wore it to Dragon Con the year after *MythBuster* Adam Savage had gone to San Diego Comic-Con disguised as a Ringwraith. While I was standing in the hotel lobby at the con, one con attendee came up to me and said, "OK, I just have to ask—Adam, is that you in there?"

Other awards I've won include Best in Show at Dragon Con for Marvin the Martian; several Champion's Cups, Most Humorous Presentation, and Workmanship awards at Shore Leave and Farpoint. These days, I more often participate as a costume judge at competitions, but I still compete whenever I can.

On Her Costuming Book:

My costuming book is titled *Creating the Character Costume: Tools, Tips, and Talks with Top Costumers and Cosplayers* (published by Routledge Publishing). It was a fun book to write and is divided into two sections. The first has information and resources on the different aspects of creating a costume (patterning, stitching, crafts, wigs, armor). The second section includes interviews with costumers and cosplayers in multiple aspects of the craft—fellow professional film/TV costumers, convention cosplayers, historical re-enactors, museum curators, academic instructors—discussing the different sides of costuming in their particular field.

On Her Other Books:

In addition to my costuming book, I also have my ghost book (*Haunted Theaters of the Carolinas*) and a puppetry book (*The Well-Dressed Puppet*), and I recently edited a cook book for an historic site I work with in Charlotte (Historic Rosedale Plantation). I'm currently in the middle of writing another puppet book *(Introduction to Puppetry Arts)*, and have several other book projects planned and/or in various stages of production.

On Luna-C:

I've had some great roles with Luna-C—Princess Leia, stormtrooper, Commander Susan Ivanova from *Babylon 5*, Sarah from *Labyrinth*. My very favorite, though, would have to be Harry Potter in our production of "Potter Live in 45." I feel that's one of the best scripts our group has produced, and I greatly enjoyed acting it at Farpoint in 2009.

On Being Stranded Inside a Dalek:

I was just recently talking with my fellow Luna-C members about the time at one convention I had performed with the group onstage in my Dalek costume. It was a costume I needed help getting into and out of; after the performance, the other cast members wandered off to see the rest of the con, completely forgetting that I was still in the Dalek! I had to wander around in costume by myself until I could find one of the other Luna-C folks to help me out.

On Her Favorite Con Activities:

I especially enjoy meeting and talking with other costumers and fellow fans. I've made some lifelong friends at the various conventions I've attended, some of whom I actually only see in person at the cons.

On Her Favorite Con Recollection:

One con story that definitely rates as a favorite is the time I was at a small convention (GalaCon) in Virginia with several fellow *Battlestar Galactica* fans to see Richard Hatch. One of the other con guests there was Walter Koenig, and my friends and I felt we'd be glad for the chance to meet him as well. We joined the line for his table (a small group of *Galactica* costumers seemingly out of place in a long line of other attendees all dressed in *Star Trek* uniforms), and were waiting patiently when Walter Koenig himself strolled casually down the line towards his table. Surprisingly, no one else seemed to take much notice of him; we caught his eye and timidly waved at him, and, to our surprise, he walked straight over to us, leaned in, and whispered, "What are you all waiting in line for?" We replied, "You! We're waiting in line for you!" at which he laughed, took our con booklets and signed them, and then continued walking to his table. I don't think the *Trek* fans there were very happy with us at that moment, but it's definitely made for a great story!

On Convention Guests:

I can't really pinpoint any one favorite con guest. Over the years, as I've attended conventions first as a fan and then as a guest myself, I've had the opportunity to meet and get to know quite a few other con guests, many of whom have since become good friends. Some of those include *Star Wars* authors Timothy Zahn and Michael Stackpole;

puppeteer Mike Quinn (who performed Salacious Crumb and Nien Nunb in *Return of the Jedi*, and who has worked on numerous productions for the *Muppets*); John Morton (who played Dak in *The Empire Strikes Back*); and numerous others. I'm always very glad for the chance to see and catch up with them at the cons we attend!

On Attending Maryland Cons:

I first started attending Maryland conventions (namely Shore Leave and Farpoint) with my fellow Luna-C performers, first just as fans and then as guest performers. I've also been a guest myself at Farpoint in years past and definitely enjoy catching up with friends at both cons. They hold a special meaning and memories for me; it was Farpoint where I picked up the stand-in R2-KT to take to South Carolina, and the following Shore Leave where we presented Albin with the "real" KT. Farpoint and Shore Leave both served as a central meeting ground for many of my good friends in the 501st for many years. (In fact, I believe it was one Farpoint that I "officially" wore my biker scout armor for the very first time to a con, although I can't pinpoint exactly which Farpoint it was.) I also have friends trying to persuade me to attend KatsuCon with them. That has sadly often conflicted with Farpoint, but I still hope to get to that one at some point.

On Something People Don't Know About Her:

Before I began pursuing a career in film/TV, I actually started school on an Air Force scholarship in the AF Reserve. I didn't continue my career in the Reserve, but it was definitely a good experience to have, and I'm glad now I had that opportunity. In addition, I found a good use for my flight suit as part of my *Ghostbusters* gear, and years later turned my (now-vintage) Class A uniform into a *Stargate* costume.

Dean Rogers

On His Real Life Job:

In real life, I am the Executive Assistant to the Executive Head of a private school in Northern Virginia. My job consists of maintaining the front office and working with students—from babies to 4th graders—and generally assisting the Executive Head.

On Some of the Exciting People He Has Interviewed for the Rogers Revue:

Let's start with my first red carpet for *Night at the Museum: Battle of the Smithsonian* in March 2009. I was at the after party for the movie, and I was in the company of the late comedian Robin Williams. He was very funny and one of the sincerest gentlemen that I ever met. We got a picture together during that night and it hangs on my wall to remind me how I got started. Since that red carpet, the list has grown exponentially. I have sat down with comedian Kevin Hart, talked to Robin Wright before she became first lady in *House of Cards*, and had fellow game show host John Davidson perform a mini concert before an interview. In regards to A-listers, I have talked to, in the same week, Natalie Portman for *Jackie*, and Denzel Washington for *Fences*. I've interviewed directors like Ken Burns, Christopher Nolan, Amy Heckling, The Russo Brothers, Paul Schrader and Ava DuVernay. I even got to talk to one of our Apollo Astronauts.

Don't worry, sci-fi actors are a-plenty. I talked to Tim Russ, Rene Auberjonois, John DeLancie, the casts of *The Guild* and *The Tick*—and Caitlin Blackwood! (If you want to see who we interview, follow us at therogersrevue.com, and on social media follow @TheRogersRevue on Facebook, Instagram and Twitter.)

On A Brief Personal History:

I am a true native of the DMV—Born in the District, raised in Maryland and living in Virginia for the past five years. I am a graduate of Bowie State University, with a B.S. in Communications: Broadcast Journalism. My hobbies include amateur photography, reading, writing short stories, listening to my iPod and traveling.

(Personal Note: I am recently divorced)

On His Introduction to Fandom:

I got involved with the world of fandom when *Star Trek: The Next Generation* premiered on WDCA TV-20 in Washington, DC. When my mother found out that I liked this show, she told me about her time watching the original series. We bonded over our love of *Trek* by watching *Star Trek* and *TNG* together. She even waited in line to get tickets to the *Star Trek* 25th Anniversary exhibit at the Air & Space Museum. It was there that I first got to talk to fellow *Trek* fans like me and know that I am not alone in my love for this amazing sci-fi series.

On His Introduction to Conventions:

My introduction to conventions was on Sunday, January 9, 1994. I was a few weeks' shy of thirteen when I first heard of the Imzadi Tour by Creation. The guest stars were Marina Sirtis and Jonathan Frakes. Since my mom was a fan of *Trek* as much as I, she took me downtown to the Renaissance Hotel. Dressed in my *TNG* Command Uniform, I got my first taste of the conventions and never looked back. I even got to talk to Ms. Sirtis herself. She was very friendly to me. As soon as the convention was over, I found out that I had gained a cousin that day as my aunt gave birth to a baby girl named Chanel. It was a road to a new world that would continue today.

On His Years in Fandom:

I have been a fan of *Trek* since the premiere of *Star Trek: The Next Generation*. Seeing the Galaxy Class Starship blazing across the stars, I was instantly hooked. Special thanks to my mother, Sharon, who not only embraced my fandom but helped me develop it over the years.

On His Current Connections to Conventions:

I am known for the sci-fi gameshows I have been hosting since 2008. I was one of the youngest members of the Farpoint and Shore Leave security team up until my mid-twenties when I decided to finally hang up my hat and try new adventures within the fandom community. In 2004, I was interviewed for a little documentary called *Trekkies 2*. In fact, you can catch me in the Baltimore segment.

On Game Shows:

Ever since I was a young boy, I've been fascinated by the wonderful world of game shows. I love everything about them: the flashing sets, the theme music, the contestants—but most importantly, the charming men and women who host them and entertain us for thirty minutes. Where else can you get a daily dose of trivia that might come in handy one day? Among my favorite gameshows were *Wheel of Fortune, Jeopardy!, Scrabble, $ale of the Century, The Joker's Wild, Hollywood Squares* and *The $25,000/$100,000 Pyramid*.

Well, it's not every day that you meet someone who has been a contestant on two gameshows. My first was *Who Wants to Be a Millionaire?* I went to the NYC auditions in the summer of 2003. There, I took a multiple-choice test and was interviewed by the contestant coordinators. At the end of the day, I was given a card letting me know that I was in the contestant pool and that I could be called at any time to be on the show. I was called three weeks later.

I went back to NYC in late September to tape my episode. I got a tour of the studio, met fellow contestants, and went through a series of trainings to on how to be a great contestant. Then I waited in the green room, not actually knowing if I was going to called to be in one of the five episodes taped that day. I was the last contestant on the first episode. I got to meet the lovely Meredith Vieira on stage, with the studio audience, cameras, and lights surrounding me. By the end of my fourth question, the horn blared and that was the end of the episode but not the end of my run. We said goodbyes for episode one and then I had to change clothes and get ready for day number two which taped fifteen minutes later.

I ran the board and won $64,000 for my efforts by walking away from a question on *The Little Prince*. Not a bad showing for the years' worth of trivia floating around in my head. Many years later, in January of 2015 , I was attending the NBC4 Health and Fitness Expo and Meredith was one of the guests. When we reunited, I told that it was great to meet her again and that she had given me $64,000 on *Millionaire*. She was floored, and she gave me the biggest hug I have ever received.

Now, this was my first game show experience, if you want to know about me being a winner on *Wheel of Fortune* in 2013, you'll have to ask me in person. I'll be happy to tell you all about it!

On His Convention Game Shows:

The sci-fi gameshows are just like the gameshows we love on television but with a sci-fi/fantasy/horror twist. With every gameshow, we do a regular version with the audience first. I want to make sure it can be adapted for conventions before I create numerous sci-fi based questions. So far, the fan reaction has been great because of the atmosphere and the fun we have for that hour. As of this writing, I have created adaptations for *Jeopardy!*, *Family Feud*, *Press Your Luck*, *Blockbusters* and *Hollywood Squares*. While most of the gameshows are well-known to everyone, I will explain Blockbusters.

Blockbusters has three contestants play in each round, with a solo contestant playing against a team of two related contestants, referred to as the "family pair." The solo contestant plays behind a red desk, while the family pair play behind a white one.

The game board consists of four interlocking rows of five hexagons each. Within each hexagon is a different letter of the alphabet, representing the first letter of the correct answer to a question. For example, if the letter P was chosen, a sample question might be: "What 'P' is an herbivorous North American mammal whose body is covered with thousands of bristles called quills?" The correct answer would be "Porcupine." Contestants attempt to complete a connecting set of hexagons to win each round: in red from top to bottom for the solo player, and in white from left to right for the family pair. The solo player has the advantage of being able to win with as few as four hexagons, while the family pair must connect at least five. In addition, the two members of the family pair are not allowed to discuss the questions. All questions have one-word answers.

With the popular Sci-fi Jeopardy!, we developed our own Tournament of Champions at Shore Leave 34 in which we brought back nine winners from previous shows for the weekend to compete for the top prize!

On Anecdotes from His Game Shows:

There are too many to name! Sci-fi Squares is always a standout show for me, because of the panel of the nine or sometimes ten stars who bring the funny to Shore Leave. I have a feeling that the panel's job is to crack me up, and the panelists succeed every time. It's people like Rachel Wyman, Chris Carothers with his impressions, Paul R. Seiber, fellow sci-fi gameshow host Chris Bunye, the voice of the games, Bill Hensel, the daring contestants and the rest of the gang that makes it all more fun and exciting! I am hoping one day some of the Hollywood guests can join in on the fun!

On Influential People and Media:

Influential people include LeVar Burton, Isaac Asimov, Marina Sirtis, Jonathan Frakes and, of course, my mother, Sharon Rogers, who kept me into *Trek*. Favorite sci-fi movies include Fritz Lang's *Metropolis*, *Star Trek II: The Wrath of Khan*, *E.T.*, *2001: A Space Odyssey*, *Space Camp*, *Back to the Future*, *Fahrenheit 451* and *Rollerball*.

On His Roles in Fan Films:

From 2007 – 2016, I had the pleasure of playing helmsman-turned-navigator Roy Adam Morris in the web series *Starship Farragut*. I started working with Farragut in March, 2007, with the episode "For Want of a Nail." They filmed the outdoor scenes at Smallwood State Park on a cold March day. I was brought on as a still photographer and took some behind the scenes shots for the episodes. The crew was impressed by the photos. I thought my job was done, but I got a call a few weeks later, asking me if I would like to be part of the bridge crew for that same episode. I didn't hesitate to respond that I would gladly be part of it.

In May, I traveled up to Ticonderoga, NY to film "FWOAN" on the sets of *Star Trek Phase 2*. To be fitted for a uniform was one thing, but when I got into the turbolift and they opened the doors for the first time, I was crying on the inside. I never thought that I would play *Trek* for real. I got to my first station, helm, and I got to practice with the buttons and look at the bridge in all her glory. It was my first taste of being on a film set, and I soaked it all in. The crew asked me what I would like to name my character. I was blown away by the request, but I already had a name in mind, Roy Morris. Morris was the name of my Naval Junior ROTC instructor at Friendly High. He was a Radar Intelligence Officer who had once engaged a MiG-17 in May, 1972. Before I left Friendly High, I promised my captain that I would do something as a dedication to him, and this was perfect.

So, in my first episode, I was a helm officer. When we filmed our next episode "The Price of Anything," Morris was switched to navigation. I didn't mind—he's still a pilot, after all. One of the best parts of "TPOA" was that I got to perform my first stunt on-camera. It took a lot of practice to get it done right, but it looks amazing in the final product.

Overall, I had a great time becoming Roy Morris! I was in six episodes, two vignettes, shot stills for every episode I was on, and I became director of photography for one of the spin-off episodes. I would sum up the experience as being in Space Camp for a week, except I was helping to create movie magic and new adventures in the Final Frontier.

On His Favorite Con Activities:

Among my numerous favorites are listening to guest stars during their hour, Vic's Place, since I love to karaoke, and the 10-Forward dance, because a Starfleet officer and Klingons can really cut a rug.

On His Favorite Con Recollection:

The one that sticks out in my mind was Shore Leave 27 in July of 2005. This was the weekend when I was getting ready to commission my Starfleet Chapter, the Sovereign class USS Top Gun, NCC-75029. Unbeknownst to me at the time, the Region 7 staff decided to pull a prank on me. They decided to transfer to another ship some of the members needed to launch the chapter. I was in a bit of a panic, and the remaining crew and I were feeling a bit down because we didn't have enough members to launch that weekend. During the Region 7 meeting, the Region 7 staff, the shuttle operations command officer and the chief of operations finally explained that they wanted to launch us in a memorable way. Some of my crew were even in on the prank. After the dust settled, my new Starfleet chapter launched that Saturday!

During this convention, I decided to do something special for the crew. At the time of Starship Top Gun's commissioning, we were given a certificate of chapter charter. I decided to make the certificate very special by not only having the top brass of Region 7, but also the guests of Shore Leave 27 sign it. So, on this certificate, we have signatures from two Starfleet Commodores from *Star Trek* (Matt Decker played by William Windom & Jose Mendez played by Malachi Throne), *Babylon 5*'s Patricia Tallman, *Stargate*'s Alex Cruz, *Blade Runner*'s Joanna Cassidy, and authors Peter David & Robert Greenberger. What a way to launch a great Maryland SFI Chapter.

On His Favorite Con Guest:

My favorite is Robert Picardo. He's funny and very down to earth. At a convention in Arlington, VA back in 2001, he was walking past me in the hallways and approached me. I was shocked as he asked me "Excuse me, but I like your suit. How much could I give you for it?" I had to tell him that the suit was not for sale, but I told him where he could find one like it. We had a good laugh and went on our ways. Then, the next day as I was getting his autograph, he saw me and asked me if I had changed my mind about the suit. I said, "No, this suit is staying with me."

The most recent story comes from Awesome Con 2017, where I was meeting Wil Wheaton. When I approached him in the autograph line, he noticed that I was wearing the *Wheel of Fortune* shirt that they gave me for the show. He asked "Were you on *Wheel of Fortune*?" I answered "Yes, I was." He went crazy and was like all "fanboy" with me. He told me that he and his wife were fans of the show and asked how I had done and what had I won. Once I told Wil I had won, he was floored and asked for the date of the program. Talk about a role reversal, especially since, just moments before, I had had a difficult choice of deciding what Wil photo I wanted him to sign. I had finally decided on the *Stand by Me* photo with the late River Phoenix. One of the best guest encounters of my life.

On Who He Has Met Who Enriched His Life:

I would have to say Frank and Gina Hernandez because they were at my first convention back in 1994, and we've been great friends ever since. The best part of the friendship is that all three of us got to work together on Starship Farragut for five years. I started on Farragut, and Frank and Gina joined in when we filmed "The Price of Anything." It's amazing when the friends you've known for years get to work together with you.

The other person who enriched my life is John Broughton. When I first met the crew of Farragut back in 2007, I never knew how much of a family I was going to be part of. John created a web series that was local to me, and, when I found out about it, I wanted to be part of it. It's truly amazing that we worked on a *Trek* fan film for many years, and then, when it came time to direct the short film "Trek: Isolation," he asked me to be the director of photography. I have never been a DoP before, but I was ready to take on the challenge; and what we did on film was amazing. Since then, we have worked on numerous projects, and he became one of the best men at my wedding. John is one of the best people I've worked with, and I am looking forward to the next film project we work on. I felt John helped me develop my skills in filmmaking, for which I am forever grateful.

On Why He Attends Maryland Conventions:

The Maryland conventions are unique, because they are fan-run and more friendly than the bigger cons that I have attended over the years. From my first con to the current one, going to the cons takes on a whole new meaning when it's a Maryland con. I started going to cons as a place to belong and to share a love of fandom. Nowadays, it feels more like a family reunion since many people I have met throughout the years have seen me grow from a young teen to the man I am today. With Maryland cons, you're welcome from the first step to the last goodbye. You have the experience of feeling that you can cut loose and be yourself, your true self. It was the at the Maryland cons that I found Starship Farragut, hosted my first sci-fi gameshow, and conducted my first sci-fi celebrity interviews.

On Something People May Not Know About Him:

My convention friends know so much about me that it's hard to know what they *don't* know about me. I would say one of my greatest interviews was Captain Eugene Cernan—the last man to walk on the moon in Apollo 17.

John Scheeler

On His Real-Life Job:

Insurance Underwriter

On a Brief Personal History:

I was born at Cherry Point Naval Hospital in Havelock, North Carolina. My father was in the Marine Corp and for the first few years of my life, we moved around a lot. My family finally settled in Glen Burnie, MD when I was 6 years old. I had a happy childhood and did okay in school. In college, I studied music with a concentration in voice. I've been doing musical theater since I was nine years old and currently sing with several groups.

On His Introduction to Conventions:

In 1978, David Keefer and I attended a very small convention in Towson called Cosmi-Con.

On His Years in Fandom:

40 years

On Influential Media:

Star Trek; Star Wars; Buffy, The Vampire Slayer (TV Series); Lord of the Rings; Hitchhiker's Guide to the Galaxy; Thieves' World; The Myth-Adventures of Skeeve and Aahz; and the game Dungeons and Dragons.

On the Origin of the Boogie Knights:

In 1980, David Keefer entered a Shore Leave Masquerade dressed as a Vulcan Ambassador. There were other Vulcan Ambassadors in the same Masquerade, so Dave decided to be original. He pulled off the ears, threw on a pair of cheap sunglasses and became "Theodoric of York, Medieval DJ." The following year, he re-created that persona for another Masquerade, but this time he invited several of his friends to participate with costumes of their own and become "Theodoric of York and his Boogie Knights." We wrote some song parodies which we strung together into a medley and performed a-cappella while the audience clapped along in a rhythm, much like a hit song from that era called "Stars on 45." We called ours "Stars on Two Score and Five." At Shore Leave in 1982, we were asked if we could develop a one-hour concert. We put our heads together and wrote a bunch of comedic songs. We performed the concert thinking, *this is ridiculous, who would possibly like this?* 36 years and seven CDs later, we're still going strong.

On His Favorite Parody and Song:

Favorite Parody: "Earth Magic Girls" (a parody of "Fat Bottom Girls" by Queen) because we have tight harmonies on that song.

Most Popular Song: "Arthurian Pie" (a parody of "American Pie" by Don McLean)

On the Success of the Boogie Knights:

Everyone enjoys good music, and everyone likes to laugh. We combine the two rather successfully and have earned a loyal following.

On Acting in Convention Plays:

As previously mentioned, I've been doing musical theater since I was nine. I guess that made me a logical choice to participate in some of the plays that were produced during the '80s and '90s. I was lucky enough to be friends with the people who were writing and directing the shows, so I was frequently cast in them. I even co-wrote one or two plays. I also directed one and was music director for another. It was always so much fun to get together with those people and brainstorm ideas for bits and ways to make each scene funnier. Those were good times!

On Working with the Guest Stars:

As the Director of Guest Relations for Farpoint, it is my responsibility to arrange transportation for our celebrity guests from the airport to the hotel and back and to assign someone to assist them with keeping to their schedules, collecting money during their autograph sessions, and tracking their sales. Often, I'm the one who drives the celebrities from the airport to the hotel and back, which allows me time to chat with them and get to know them a little. They can come to me with anything they need and I will arrange it, if possible and within reason. Although stressful at time, it is an interesting and rewarding job. I also have to be a buffer between our guests and their fans. This can sometimes become awkward, but for the most part, our attendees are polite and fun people who just want to meet the actors from their favorite movies and TV shows.

Some of our celebrity guests have never traveled to places like Maryland and our February weather both frightens and fascinates them. For example, Felicia Day grew up in warm climates and before coming to Farpoint, she had never seen, let alone thrown, a snowball! Her Guest Relations Assistant presented her with a snowball to throw before she left for the airport. It was hilarious to watch as she hurled it at one of her fans!

On His Favorite Con Activities:

I enjoy perusing the dealers' room, sitting in on guest talks, and, of course, performing as a Boogie Knight.

On His Favorite Con Story:

I don't want to seem as if I'm picking on her, but the first time Felicia Day came to Farpoint, we had just had a large snow storm and there was a lot of snow on the ground and piled in the parking lot at the hotel. As I was assisting in checking her in, Felicia asked me why there was a basket of cheese graters on the counter. I looked and spotted what she was referring to, which was actually a basket of complementary ice scrapers the hotel was supplying for its guests!

She had lived in warm areas her whole life and had never seen an ice scrapper! The fans being who they are, Felicia went home that year with several ice scrappers and cheese graters. She thought it was so funny!

On His Favorite Con Guest:

Lee Arenberg has been a guest at Farpoint twice, and both times he was an absolute delight to work with. All of our guests are fantastic, of course, but Lee seems to go to greater lengths to make you feel like a friend and not just the "guy who picked him up at the airport."

On a Con Person Who Has Made a Lasting Impression:

I would have to say author Bob Greenberger. I met him way back when the Boogie Knights first got started. He has taken the time to be a good friend over the years. I've stayed at his home and had dinner with him and his wife. His daughter is a current member of the Knights. There was one occasion in particular when Bob had a profound impact on my life. When I was about 45, I complained to him at a convention about the need to wear reading glasses, which I didn't have to do until much later compared to some of my friends. He said, "John, this will improve your quality of life," and he was absolutely right. Since then, I've never complained about doing things to compensate for getting older, since these things have, in fact, improved my quality of life.

On Something People May Not Know About Him:

I once attended a modeling workshop to see if I had what it takes to be a catalogue or fashion model. Those photos will never see the light of day, I can promise you that! As a model, I make a fine insurance underwriter.

Kathleen "Kathy" Scrimger

On Her Real-Life Job:

In real life, I am an elementary school teacher currently working with second grade students. I am also a full-time wife and mother of two grown children, which has been my most important job for the past 30+ years.

On a Brief Personal History:

I am a native of Baltimore, Maryland and was fortunate to be raised by parents who were pro-education. My dad made sure that my sister and I grew up to be independent women. I have a Master's in Education and over 180 hours in substance abuse education from the State of Maryland.

My husband of 30+ years is also active in fandom. My hobbies include working with Shore Leave and the Star Trek Association of Towson, sewing, reading, and traveling when possible. While I also love to cook, I do not like housework and have little free time.

On Her Introduction to Fandom:

My introduction to fandom occurred when I joined the Science Fiction Club as a student at Towson State College. That is where I learned about conventions beyond what I had read in magazines and newspaper articles.

On Her Introduction to Conventions:

My first convention was the World Con in Washington D.C. It was probably the best and worst way to get started in fandom. At that time, the science fiction community was not very welcoming of *Star Trek* and other media fans. It was a good thing my friend and I had a good grounding in science fiction literature. The dealer rooms were much more inclusive.

I attended my first *Star Trek* convention in Atlanta, Georgia in 1977, where I first met some of the people who would later help found the Star Trek Association of Towson.

On Her Years in Fandom:

Let's just go with over 40 years. I was a fan of shows like *Twilight Zone*, the *Outer Limits,* and *One Step Beyond* when I was sitting on my dad's lap.

On Her Current Connection to Cons:

At present, I am the Vice President of the Star Trek Association of Towson and have been working Shore Leave since its inception. This past year, I was the Emporium and Information at the Door chair. I am also a member of the Choir of the Robes of Many Colors in the Temple of Trek and a member of the Denebian Slime Devils. I attend at least three cons per year now that my children are grown. All of this keeps me pretty busy when you factor in what my job requires of me from mid-August until the end of June each year.

On Influential Media and People:

When it comes to TV shows, it is obvious that *Star Trek* in its many forms has played a major role in my life. I have been a science fiction fan since childhood. I think that this genre was really the first to expand women's roles in society. As a close runner-up, I would have to list the *Twilight Zone* for its ground-breaking work in early television, and *Babylon 5* because I enjoyed the character interaction and development. It would be hard to list all my favorite authors because there are just too many and each for a different reason. I am a hard-core film buff, so my favorite movies encompass all eras and genres. My favorite films would be a book by themselves.

On Her Con Jobs:

When Shore Leave began, jobs were done by whoever was available at that moment. I have worked on programming, children's programming, hospitality, and in recent years, I have been running the

Emporium. I am not sure I have a favorite. If you are a member of the team, you do what needs to be done. I do like being on panels and performing filk at other conventions.

On the Denebian Slime Devils:

According to Memory Alpha, an on-line fan site, they are creatures from Deneb VI. They have sharp teeth and long claws. They are tough and known to attack larger creatures to protect their eggs. One of the Klingons called Kirk a Denebian Slime Devil in the classic *Star Trek* episode, "The Trouble with Tribbles." My group adopted the name because we liked the sound of it and wanted to seem tough.

We're a Baltimore-based filk group that's been writing and performing sci-fi, media, and pop-culture song parodies since the mid to late 1970's. We do both serious and funny and have borrowed tunes from traditional melodies to current rock. We started singing together in high school and have been doing it ever since. The group consists of Melissa James, Regina DeSimone, Cathy Dougherty, Denise Masters, and myself. Grace Serio was a member for several years but has not been active in the past decade. Although all of us have written song parodies, Melissa is the principal contributor in this area.

On Her Favorite Slime Song:

I guess the all-time favorite would be the "Whale Song" to the tune of "The Hee-Haw Song." My current favorite would be "Jamie" to Pure Prairie League's "Amie." The latter gives us a chance to use multiple-part harmony.

On Her Favorite Con Activities:

My favorite activity is just hanging out and talking to people. Most of the time, I am working at Shore Leave, so I do not see programing that I am not a part of. At other cons, I enjoy going to panel discussions on various topics.

On Her Favorite Con Recollection:

One of my favorite memories goes back to Shore Leave V when George Takei sat in the audience during the production of "The Best

Little Pon Farr Palace on Vulcan." He laughed so hard that we could hear him back stage. George let us know that our hours of work on this silly musical were worth the effort.

On Her Favorite Con Guest:

There have been many great guests, but two of my favorites were Rene Auberjonois and Richard Biggs who came to Shore Leave in 1996 where I was managing children's programing. Both guests came in and spoke to the children and patiently answered their questions. Rene signed autographs for each child by drawing a small bucket, labeling it "ODO," and then signing his name.

On Why She Attends Maryland Cons:

I think the Baltimore area has some of the best conventions on the east coast and maybe anywhere. When our children were small, it was difficult to travel to more distant conventions. As someone who has known many other convention organizers over the years, I like to support my friends. We have grown into a thriving area for a variety of media-related conventions. Sometimes, I think there are too many conventions coming to the area.

On Someone who Made a Lasting Impression:

I met my husband, Weston, at Shore Leave III. He changed my life, and I will be forever grateful for his presence.

On Something People May Not Know About Her:

I doubt there is anything that my friends do not know by now. They have been with me through good times and bad for over 40 years. Though occasionally, I do find that they have not made the connection that I am Mrs. Trekwell.

Weston Scrimger

On His Real-Life Job:

I am retired from the Motor Vehicles Administration of Maryland.

On a Brief Personal History:

I was raised and attended schools in Baltimore City. I have a B.S. in Geography from Towson University. I am married to one of the founding mothers of Shore Leave and the father of two wonderful children who were raised around fandom. I currently live in Baltimore County and enjoy reading, watching movies and television, and occasional traveling. I am an active member of the Star Trek Association of Towson and enjoy attending local conventions.

On His Introduction to Fandom and Conventions:

My introduction to fandom was Shore Leave III. I heard about it from a radio or TV ad and attended on Sunday, which was my day off. I had a great time and decided to join the folks who ran the con. I have been active in fandom ever since.

On His Years in Fandom:

36+

On His Current Connection to Cons:

I recently stepped down as co-con chair of Shore Leave, but remain an active member of the Star Trek Association of Towson where I am involved with planning activities and until the end of Shore Leave 40, I was the leader of the Temple of Trek as "Dr. Trekwell." Since the Temple of Trek will have its rebirth in 2020, I will probably be involved in some capacity since my wife is a member of the choir. I plan to be in the dealers' room again next year at Shore Leave running my table as usual.

On Influential People and Media:

The list of books, movies, and TV shows is too long to expound here. I am an avid reader and so my favorites among the early authors include Robert Heinlein, Isaac Asimov, and Arthur C. Clarke to mention a few. If it is science fiction media, I have probably seen it. Of course, *Star Trek* and the shows that followed have played a significant role in bringing me into fandom and keeping me there. When it comes to people, I would have to say the members of the Star Trek Association of Towson (STAT) have been the most influential since they have been my friends and family for the past 30+ years. My wife, Kathy, who is active in fandom, has been most supportive of my fannish activities.

On His Con Jobs:

I have worked on every committee except art show. I also chaired several.

On the Highs and Lows of Being a Committee Member:

My low point as a committee chair occurred when Deforest Kelly walked out of the autograph line because his hands hurt. As head of security, I was left to deal with a mob of upset fans. My high point was having dinner with George Takei at Shore Leave V and talking about his career and his future plans. At that time, the club was so small that we were generally a committee of the whole except for con chair.

On the Temple of Trek:

The Temple of Trek developed out of a committee member's suggestion that we have a skit al la *Guys and Dolls*, and they wanted to do "Sit Down You're Rocking the Boat." With the Denebian Slime Devils as our first choir, I appeared in a three-piece suit using an accent similar to the televangelists who were making headlines at the time. The fans liked it and asked us to continue the Temple. The format is a basic order of service from almost any Christian church. Although we always planned each Temple, the fans added and changed what happened at each service. People asked for copies of the songs, and I started printing hymnals as well as copies of the sermons, which I sold, too. We began talking about Praise Trek University after Oral Roberts University was in the news about their pray ladder, so we introduced a pray step ladder. When the Bakers talked about starting a Christian amusement park, we started talking about Trekkerland with fannish themed rides until they opened a real one at Six Flags America. The services are very interactive, and you can count on the choir singing an opening and closing prayer. Since about 1990, we have taken up a collection for one charity or another. Although I announced at Shore Leave 40 that it would be the last Temple, another fan came forth and will have the Temple up and running again in 2020. I look forward to being in the congregation (audience) when that happens.

On Being Reverend Trekwell:

I suppose being Reverend Trekwell is like being myself. I enjoy sharing my love of science fiction, science fact, and all things fannish with others. I have made good friends doing the Temple. I think the Temple has lasted so long because it struck a chord with other fans who have been reviled, ignored, and ridiculed by main stream media for years as an uneducated bunch of crazy people who dress in weird costumes. The truth is we are, for the most part, people who are well-read, well-educated, and inclusive in our community. We are professionals in the outside world and have managed to change the way we are perceived by maintaining our beliefs about the future. We are now mainstream.

On the Fez and the Kilt:

The Trekkie Shriner grew out of an experience at Shore Leave VIII when the convention moved to the Omni Hotel in Baltimore. That weekend, a Shriners group shared the hotel with our convention and someone pointed out that it was probably the worst of both worlds to have the groups together. Borrowing generously from a song by Ray Stevens, the Trekkie Shriner appeared first at ClipperCon—at Marion McChesney's request—to tell bad jokes and pull pranks on guests. Most often, the Shriner wanted the guest star to recite tongue twisters. It was fun to do.

On His Favorite Con Activities:

My favorite activity is meeting and talking to other fans. That is the reason I started my dealer's table—so fans could come and talk about whatever interested them. My table is actually a one-man fannish flea market. It always leads to great conversations.

On His Favorite Con Recollection:

After attending Temple at ClipperCon, George Takei asked why the fans threw chocolate candies to me during the service. I taught George the magic phrase to obtain chocolate from the faithful fans of the Temple. The phrase is, of course, "Praise Trek!"

On His Favorite Con Guest:

That is a hard choice, but I really enjoyed the times we shared with George Takei at Shore Leave. He was a treasure, always willing to be out among the fans.

On Why He Attends Maryland Cons:

I do not like to travel far for a convention for a number of reasons. I am not fond of hotel beds, and I prefer to go home after a busy day and decompress before starting out again. I became accustomed to saving money by going home each day when the children were little and do not want to change now.

On the Con Guest Who Impacted His Life:

I would say William "Bill" Campbell, who I met at conventions in the early '90s. He was a fascinating person to know, and he helped the Temple raise money for charity. He'd had a long career in Hollywood and was involved with the Actors Home and Fund when I met him. He was a great guy and I am sorry for his passing.

On Something People May Not Know About Him:

I get scared before any stage performance, especially as Dr. Trekwell. Most people think I enjoy being in the spotlight.

Richard Siebigteroth & Cynthia Hardesty

On Their Jobs in Real Life:

Rick:

Middle School Science Teacher

Cyn:

High School Physics Teacher

On Their Personal Histories:

We have been married for 28 years. We live in Yorktown, VA with a 12-year-old daughter and two cats. Our hobbies have varied over the years. The first summer we were dating (31 years ago), we worked together on a Sixth Doctor (Colin Baker) costume, spending hours in fabric and craft stores searching for all the items necessary to create the costume. We also collect Hallmark ornaments together. Cynthia has collected Ewok memorabilia for years, and Rick collects Major Matt Mason toys (astronaut toys from the late 1960s). Together, we run Luna-C, a sci-fi comedy troupe, and build and show Daleks as the founders of Old Dominion Daleks.

On Being Introduced to Fandom:

Rick: I remember my dad waking me up at 2 a.m. to watch old movies with him like *Valley of the Gwangi* and *The Land that Time Forgot*. My grandfather worked at NASA Marshall Space Flight Center in Huntsville on the Saturn V, so I grew up with space adventures and science fiction.

Cyn: One of my earliest memories is being woken by my dad to watch *Star Trek* reruns with my brother at 6 a.m. on Saturday mornings. My dad was an engineer at NASA Langley, so I grew up exposed to science and science fiction.

On Their Introduction to Conventions:

Rick: My first convention was Coast Con, March 1983, in Biloxi, Mississippi. I went with some Air Force friends from our D&D group. We all piled into a Ford EXP and drove from Seymour Johnson AFB in Goldboro, NC. I wanted to meet author Andy Offutt. While waiting for his panel to start, we got to joking with another guy outside the panel room about some of the ridiculous peace bonding of "weapons" that had occurred at the convention. The man was wearing a scimitar necklace, and we joked that it should be peace bonded and proceeded to wrap it in a napkin and ribbon. When the panel room cleared, we were surprised to watch him go up onto the stage and introduce himself as the author, Andy Offutt. He still had the peace-bonded necklace on when we shared drinks in the bar later that evening.

Cyn: My first convention was Sci-Con in November 1983 in Virginia Beach, VA. I had just turned 16 years old two weeks prior. My best friend had passed away from cancer six weeks before and two very good friends, both a year younger than I, convinced their parents that taking a day trip would be a good birthday present, as I had not done anything to celebrate. That was my first exposure to the world of cosplay, filking, and fan-run panels.

On Their Years in Fandom:

35 years for both of us.

On Luna-C:

Rick: Shortly after I was stationed in Virginia, I had the opportunity to join Doctors in the House, a sci-fi sketch comedy group run by Kris Curling, as a performer and writer. My wife was pulled in as crew, doing backstage and tech work. When Kris decided to step down and dissolve the group, several members wanted to continue on, so my wife and I formed Luna-C. I am chief writer, director, and producer while Cynthia takes care of the organization. She ensures the scripts are assembled and sent to members, costumes and props are found, and generally keeps things running as smoothly as possible.

Cyn: Luna-C was a name I came up with in college. Cynthia is one of the names of the mythological Greek moon goddess Artemis, referring to her birth on Mount Cynthus. Luna is Latin for the moon. So, I had started signing creative works with Luna-Cyn in college. When we needed a name for our crazy comedy group, we chose lunacy, written as Luna-C.

On Their Favorite Luna-C Sketches:

Rick: Some of my favorites are the slapstick style sketches that get good audience response even if they're unfamiliar with the fandom it's based upon. I love performing "The Brutal Gourmet." It's a parody of a cooking show, featuring a Klingon attempting to demonstrate how to prepare several delicacies. After some communication issues, he decides to cook Tribble Surprise (it always surprises the tribble). Another fun sketch is the Whack-a-Goul'd *Stargate* sketch, "All That Glitters is not Goul'd," where Dr. Frasier has to use alternative methods to get a blood sample from a Goul'd symbiote.

Cyn: I like "Klingon Home Security." It's another slapstick sketch in which a large Klingon 'hides' under a lampshade and then proceeds to creatively deal with a thief that comes to rob his place. Unfortunately, it relies on having a smaller, younger cast member to play the thief, so we haven't done it in recent years.

On Luna-C Bloopers and Antics:

Rick: Honestly, it's hard to remember a lot of what occurs onstage or backstage during a show as the adrenaline is pumping. Ironically, many of our onstage bloopers, if they go over well, become written into the sketch. Of course, with the slapstick sketches, props sometimes don't work as planned. The Goul'd symbiote in the Whack-a-Gould sketch is supposed to emerge from the Jaffa's stomach pouch, but if it's a little too low and the stage angle is wrong it can appear to be emerging from an inappropriate area. Also, the actor playing the Jaffa has occasionally been hit a little too hard in a sensitive area. Backstage, we often dress props in costume pieces to relieve stress, such as putting a wig and Colin's coat on the Matt Smith standee or Hammond's hat on Casper's head.

Cyn: As the one usually running sound, I'm often the source of bloopers. We use whatever sound system the convention provides, so I'm usually working on unfamiliar equipment that continues to play unless manually stopped. The actors on stage have had to adlib to cover a late or wrong cue, such as "and I am waiting for the phone to ring" or answering only to have it ring again, in which case the "button's stuck." Sometimes the mistake is on the part of the actors. One time, they skipped an entire section of the sketch and the convention sound person asked if we should skip the sound cues as well, and I had to explain that we needed to wait as they would probably get back around to it and they did. My favorite backstage story is from the early days of Luna-C. We were at WarriorCon, a small convention aimed at *Xena: Warrior Princess* fandom. Kevin Smith who played Ares and Karl Urban who played Cupid were guests. We had a sketch called "Ares: Extra Dry" that was a bunch of deodorant puns, like "Having trouble keeping your 'Mennen' line." Kevin Smith agreed to read it for our show. Karl Urban was disappointed we hadn't asked him to participate. When we did a sketch with Aphrodite, Cupid's mom in *Xena*, Karl Urban grabbed a rubber band off the sound table, shot it at our Gabby who was turning down Joxer's advances and jumped up on stage declaring "She had it comin' ma!" Our actors had to adlib and work it into the sketch and did so.

On Influential Media:

Rick & Cynthia: *Star Trek* was the first exposure to science fiction for both of us, followed by the original *Battlestar Galactica*. *Dr. Who* introduced us to science fiction beyond the United States. For Luna-C, comedians like Mel Brooks and Monty Python, and shows like *Black Adder* and *The Muppet Show* have been influential to our comedic style.

Rick: My aunt got me into reading science fiction and fantasy, exposing me to many of her favorite books and authors, including Anne McCaffrey's *Dragonriders of Pern* and Roger Zelazny's *Chronicles of Amber*.

Cyn: I read my way through the limited children's section of our public library and discovered the rocket and atom stickers they used to place on library books to indicate science fiction. As I started into the adult section, I knew to look for books in those areas. Isaac Asimov's *Robots* and McCaffrey's *Dragonriders of Pern* still rate as my favorites.

On Fandoms:

Rick: *Doctor Who* and *Ghostbusters* are still among my favorites. *Doctor Who* has been interesting in recent years. I've been a fan since the time of the fourth doctor and have watched it explode in popularity. I sponsored a *Doctor Who* club at my school and have tried to expose fans of the new series to classic episodes.

Cyn: Beyond trying to keep up with the mainstream media, I still enjoy reading *Primeval* fanfic from a long-cancelled show about portals called anomalies that open to allow prehistoric creatures into the modern world.

On Costuming:

Rick: I've won multiple awards over the years for Workmanship and Presentation, Humor, and Best-In-Show. I usually inject humor into my presentations, so am happy to win awards for Most Humorous. I loved doing Londo Mollari from *Babylon 5* and have his red, blue and Emperor costumes. I think my first Best-In-Show was for "Sex and the Single Commander," a *Babylon 5* presentation with my wife as Timov and Cheralyn Lambeth as Commander Ivanova. My Sixth Doctor (Colin Baker) costume, while over 30 years old, is still one of my favorites. My Hagrid costume had Alan Ruck asking to get a picture with me for his kid.

Cyn: My favorite costume is my Ewok. Most of my costume work is on accessories and presentation, my favorite of which is my daughter's "Do you want to be a Dalek?" I found the karaoke version of "Do you want to Build a Snowman?" then rewrote the lyrics and sang the new version while Rick built the Dalek. Bella assisted by painting Dalek bumps. During the Masquerade, she rolled out to the correct location on stage and managed the tic-toc of gun stalk and sucker arm with the music, nailing the presentation. She won Best-in-Show for that and it inspired us to build Daleks and form Old Dominion Daleks.

On Raising a Daughter in Fandom:

Rick & Cyn: Bella has been attending conventions since she was six weeks old, but we did not put her onstage until she asked. Her first costume contest appearance was at age three as Sarah Jane in the Andy Panda outfit. Our efforts now go into her presentations. We involved her with children's programming when possible so she could interact with other children. It was a welcome outlet for her, inspiring an interest in fantasy. Although she is sometimes ostracized as the "weird kid" at school, attending conventions reminds her that she is not the only one with these interests, that she is not alone. When we saw John Barrowman, he took the time to offer Bella advice about dealing with bullies.

On Their Favorite Con Activities:

Rick & Cyn: Although we're busy with Luna-C performances and costume presentations, we enjoy catching up with friends in fandom and wandering the dealers' room. We rarely make it to panels anymore, but if there are big name guests that we have not seen before, we'll attend their talks. Bella enjoys wandering in the inflatable costumes. It's interesting to watch people's positive reactions to Baymax and Pikachu, Hammond with T-Rexes, or the *Ghostbusters* with Slimer and the Stay Puft Marshmallow Man. The Daleks also get interesting reactions when we roll at conventions.

On Con Fun:

Rick: We were performing at Big E Con, and it fell on Cindy's birthday. I managed to get the hotel to have a birthday cake in the room for her and gather our friends together to sing Happy Birthday.

Cyn: Once, when Nana Visitor was a guest, everyone was asking *Deep Space Nine* questions. I couldn't resist and asked her what it was like working as a guest on *MacGyver* with Richard Dean Andersen. She smiled at the change and launched into the subject, having several good stories of working on that show.

On Favorite Guest Stars:

Rick: It's hard to pick just one guest after attending an average of three cons a year for 35 years. Colin Ferguson stands out for agreeing to perform one of our sketches with us, reprising his role as Sheriff Carter from *Eureka*. In the sketch, his consciousness had been trapped in the appliances of the smart house. He was very complimentary about the sketch. I ran into Rob Poulsen in the hotel elevator while wearing a *Pinky & the Brain* print vest, and he commented, "You know I was in that show."

Cyn: I am a big fan of *Stargate SG-1* and was excited to see Amanda Tapping. Bella was only six weeks old and many questioned us for attending a convention so soon after her birth, but Luna-C was performing, so we were there. Amanda Tapping has a child just a year older and asked if she could hold Bella, but was afraid to wake her. Since I needed to wake her for feeding, I told her yes and she held Bella. We shared a moment as mothers.

On Attending Maryland Conventions:

Rick & Cyn: We enjoy the familial atmosphere of fan-run conventions. Those local to us are more literary than media, and we enjoy media cons. Many of our friends and Luna-C members live in the Washington-Baltimore area, drawing us north instead of south for conventions.

On Their Secret Identities:

Rick & Cyn: We do Mr. & Mrs. Claus at Christmas time, with Bella helping out as an elf.

Lance Woods

On His Personal History:

I was born in Baltimore in 1961 and have lived in that general area for most of my life, except for a few years when I was given time off for good behavior.

On His Real-Life Job

I work as the Senior Editor of Marketing at Diamond Comic Distributors, the world's largest distributor of English language comic books and pop culture items. Specifically, I write and edit articles for publications designed to help comic retailers run their businesses more efficiently.

On His First Convention:

My very first convention was the first Shore Leave, held in 1978 at Towson State University near Baltimore. I'd started watching *Star Trek* reruns in middle school and couldn't miss the opportunity to check out an actual con. From there, I started attending other conventions in the area, including Balticon, ClipperCon (which evolved into Oktobertrek and then Farpoint), the occasional August Trek/August Party, and others. These days, I get to far fewer cons. Farpoint, Awesome Con, and the Baltimore Comic Con are pretty much my annual itinerary.

On Influential Media:

As I said, I watched reruns of *Star Trek* in middle and high school (mid to late 1970s), which led me to cons, but I wasn't deeply into SF. Many science fiction books I encountered were just too technical, and I wasn't very good at science in school, so we weren't a good match. As time went on, my friends introduced me to concepts by Robert Heinlein, Larry Niven, and others and I appreciated how they dealt with characters as opposed to technology. Eventually, I read the occasional SF short story, and Frank Herbert's *Dune*, which I loved.

My biggest influences have always come from TV and movies. When I was 4 years old, I discovered the Adam West/Burt Ward *Batman* series. When Batman and Robin slid down the poles into the Batcave, it changed my life. (I had no idea I would end up working in the comic book industry.) As I grew older, I came to appreciate the finer points of the writing and acting in the show, and it influenced the way I approached writing comedy in my plays for conventions. When I pursued more "serious" writing, my influences broadened to include William Goldman (*The Princess Bride, Marathon Man*), Neil Simon, and—never straying far from the fantasy genre—Rod Serling.

On the Boogie Knights:

One night in 1981, after watching a filksing that, honestly, had very few decent acts, one of my best friends, Dave Keefer, turned to me and said, "We could do this." So, we did. The following year, Dave created Theodoric of York's Boogie Knights, and we—myself, Bob Ahrens, John Scheeler, and Barbara Thompson Helfer—debuted with him at Shore Leave IV. It felt great to contribute something unique to the con and to give everyone a good laugh. It amazes me that they're still performing, and it flatters me that their concerts not only include songs that I wrote or co-wrote more than 30 years ago, but that those songs still get laughs.

On Con Performances:

After watching numerous "plays" at convention showcases that involved hastily drafted fans standing on stage reading (badly) from scripts, I looked again to Dave Keefer (with whom I'd written stage parodies in high school), and echoed his words when he'd created the Boogie Knights: "We could do this." This was about four years after we co-founded the Boogie Knights, so we figured we could do for con showcases what we'd done for filksinging—especially after Dave and I performed in a hideous Cole Porter musical of *Star Trek III: The Search for Spock*. (The best thing about that experience for me was meeting Steve Wilson, for reasons that will become clearer later.)

The result of our labors was the acting troupe, Cheap Treks. For for ten years, we brought a lot to the stage: memorization, costumes, sets, and—most importantly—jokes. All those years of reading *MAD Magazine* and watching *The Carol Burnett Show* and *Saturday Night Live* paid off. No one was more surprised by our success than we.

Nowadays, my acting is pretty much confined to Steve Wilson's (told ya he'd be back) wonderful Prometheus Radio Theatre, where I don't have to memorize lines. Instead, I act with fans standing on stage reading from scripts. Circle of life.

On Radio Shows:

I love doing radio shows now. Most of the time, I listen to classic radio shows for pleasure. I like to hear how they presented certain things, then take those ideas and play around with them when I write a radio show. Steve has given us a new/old universe to play in before audiences that appreciate our work. Cindy (the Mrs.) and I are especially proud that our son, Greg, now joins us on the stage to do sound effects with her. We never set out to raise a fanboy, but it's nice that these shows have become something of a family outing.

Here's a radio-related aside while we're here: Shortly after graduating from college and realizing that I could tell a story, I hooked up with an aspiring agent friend who actually got one of my scripts through the door of NBC's *Remington Steele*, one of my all-time favorite series. My agent got a very nice rejection from the story editor of the series, who said that "he [I] writes well and plots carefully and should not be discouraged from future submissions." The letter was signed by a man named Elliott Lewis, who I learned many years later was a radio superstar—actor, writer, producer, director. I hear him and his work all the time on Sirius/XM's Radio Classics channel. And he couldn't use my stuff, but he liked it. If I'd known who he was, I probably would have worked harder at becoming a scriptwriter. But it's one of my most prized rejections, and I find it amusing that I ended up doing radio theatre decades after receiving it.

On His Connection to Cons:

I'm looking forward to Shore Leave 44 in 2022. It will be the 40th anniversary of Shore Leave IV, which saw the debut of the Boogie Knights. It was also where I met so many lifelong friends, including writing heroes Bob Greenberger and Howard Weinstein, and buddies Will Burnham, Thomas Atkinson, and Danny Coggins. I haven't been to a Shore Leave for many years, but I might break that fast for number 44.

The strongest connection I have to the convention scene is easily my wife, Cindy. We met at a Shore Leave in the 1980s (introduced in 1983 by the aforementioned Will Burnham) and crossed paths casually many times before we ended up together in 1994. I met the woman I'm spending the rest of my life with at a convention and our son is now graduating from high school. Who says cons are a waste of time?

On Costuming:

As should be obvious, I like performing to a laugh, and that includes con masquerades. I never worried about accuracy, workmanship, or blowing the house away with a fancy costume. I just wanted the Most Humorous trophies, and I was fortunate to win my share of them, usually when I collaborated with my friends on stage.

On Writing:

I'm the author of the novel *Heroic Park*, published by Firebringer Press in 2012. *Heroic Park* is based on *SuperHuman Times*, a podcast I created for Prometheus Radio Theatre in 2006. I also contribute short stories to Firebringer Press's *Middle of Eternity* anthologies, edited by Phil Giunta. I wrote the story "Dead Air" for *Somewhere in the Middle of Eternity* and "The Gravest Show Unearthed" for *Elsewhere in the Middle of Eternity*. My next story, "Bodies of Evidence," is scheduled to run in the third volume, *Meanwhile in the Middle of Eternity*, which we hope to release in 2019.

On Something Others May Not Know About Him:

I'm scared of everybody as a result of childhood bullying—even nice people. Conventions have helped me cope with that, too.

THE KLINGONS

Marc Okrand

On His Real Life Job:

Retired, but I used to be involved in closed captioning. I also devised Klingon and bits of other alien languages for *Star Trek* and a couple of other things.

On His Personal History:

I grew up in Los Angeles, went to college at the University of California, Santa Cruz, and to graduate school at the University of California, Berkeley. I moved to Washington, D.C. in 1978 and have lived there ever since.

On His Introduction to Fandom:

My involvement with fandom began with conventions, particularly my first ClipperCon in 1985.

On His Introduction to Conventions:

The first con I attended was a Creation event in Arlington, Virginia in 1984. I'd heard about it while working on *Star Trek III*. Walter Koenig mentioned to me that he was going to be a guest there. My first fan-run con was the aforementioned ClipperCon in 1985. I was invited to be a guest there after Mark Lenard (whom I'd met while we were both standing around on the Genesis Planet with not much to do—sounds odd, but it's true) said he thought I should give a talk at a con and that he'd suggest me to people in the Baltimore area.

On His Years in Fandom:

If we calculate from that ClipperCon, it would be about 33 years.

On the Origin of the Klingon Language:

I was hired by Paramount to devise the Klingon dialogue for *Star Trek III*. Producer Harve Bennett approached me (I didn't make a proposal to them) because I had worked on a little bit of Vulcan dialogue for *Star Trek II*.

What I created for *Star Trek III* took several months, but the language has grown a lot since then. It's never finished, so I'd say creating the language has taken about 34 years so far. Originally, it was difficult choosing words that sounded strange ("alien") but that the actors could pronounce comfortably, and also devising the grammar (and keeping track of why I made various decisions).

On His Involvement with the *Star Trek* movies:

I've been involved with all of the original-character movies (meaning the original cast and the J.J. Abrams films), except for *Star Trek: The Motion Picture* and *Star Trek V*. I could tell you stories about each of them, but what I liked best was working with the actors and being on the set when the Klingons were speaking (and being on the set even when there were no Klingons around). I was also impressed by how seriously the language was treated by everyone involved in the films.

On People Speaking the Klingon Language:

The number of truly fluent speakers is small, but recently there's been a surge of interest in the language, and the number of speakers seems to be growing.

On His Current Connection to Fandom:

These days I go to several cons a year including Farpoint, the conventions of the Klingon Language Institute, and others.

On Influential Media and People:

I'm fortunate to have a number of good friends among the people who organize the Baltimore conventions I've attended over the years.

Regarding movies, I'd single out *Galaxy Quest*, not that it influenced my life in fandom, but because my life in fandom made it possible to truly appreciate the film.

On His Favorite Con Activities:

I enjoy talking to attendees—not only about Klingon or *Star Trek*, but all sorts of topics—and, of course, listening to the stories the main guests have to tell. It's also fun to simply roam around the hotel surrounded by visitors from so many alien worlds.

On His Favorite Con Story:

The first ClipperCon I attended occurred shortly after my Klingon Dictionary was published. Since I suspected I might be asked to autograph the book, I thought of a Klingon phrase to use as an inscription. After my talk, an autograph line formed, so I was happy I'd thought about this ahead of time. When the first person in line presented his book, I wrote the Klingon phrase and signed it. He thanked me and went on his way. As soon as he was gone, I realized I'd made an error (I can't remember now what the error was), but there was nothing I could do about it. A while later, he came back and said that he'd looked all through the dictionary but couldn't figure out the meaning of the Klingon phrase I had written. I admitted that my inscription contained an error and offered to take the book back and give him another copy with a correct inscription. He immediately replied, "No way." I learned a bit about both fandom and collectibles that day.

On His Favorite Con Guests:

I'll leave out people I knew or worked with prior to their con appearances (and I assume this includes any con, not just Maryland cons). Among those whom I saw/met for the first time at a con, I'd say Jonathan Harris (the original Dr. Smith). Both on stage and off (I was lucky enough to be among some fans having dinner with him), he was interesting, delightful, and appropriately cantankerous.

On Why He Attends Maryland Cons:

To spend time with friends, most of whom I see only at the cons, and to catch up on what everyone's thinking and talking about. The feeling is one of family.

On Con People Who Have Made a Lasting Impression:

Not to weasel out of naming an individual, but I'd say several groups of people who organize and put on the cons (not just in Maryland, but particularly there). Among these are some of the most industrious, dedicated, generous, and caring people I've ever met.

On Something People May Not Know About Him:

Before I pursued linguistics, I worked professionally in radio (both commercial and noncommercial) in Los Angeles for five years or so.

Cheryl Jewett-Koblinsky

On Her Real Life:

In my real life, I work at Rockland Industries, Inc. as a Customer Service Agent. My company makes the blackout material for the curtains used in hotels. We also supply material to Walmart, JoAnn Fabrics, and Hobby Lobby to name a few.

I'm a native of Baltimore County and currently live in Parkville, Maryland with Bill, my husband of twenty-three years, our son Duncan, three cats, and a cockatiel. I have one brother and two sisters, none of whom are involved in fandom like I am. Occasionally, my younger sister and I will dress in our Steampunk outfits and go to an event or to High Tea.

On Her Introduction to Fandom:

My introduction to fandom happened back in the late 70s early 80s when I worked at the Hunt Valley Inn as a banquet waitress. This was in the early days of Shore Leave. On my day off, I thought it would be cool to take my sister and niece to Shore Leave to look around. I don't recall who the guests were, but I remember seeing and meeting this guy who was dressed as General Urko from *Planet of the Apes*. He did a great job because it wasn't just a mask that he had on. I think I worked a couple more of those conventions as a banquet waitress until I changed jobs. I didn't go to another fandom convention until I met my husband in 1991.

On Her Current Connection to Fandom:

I have been in fandom in one form or another steadily for 27 years or so. My current connections to cons and fandom are the friends I have come to know over the years. These days, I attend Shore Leave and Farpoint for the day just to catch up with familiar faces and chat for a while. I also like to peruse the dealers' room to see if they're offering anything new.

On Influential Media and People:

My father was a big influence, but not directly to fandom per se. My dad was a clown when I was a little girl in the 60s, but it wasn't his full- time job. He performed comedy magic dressed as a clown with my mom as his assistant to bring in some extra money. He was one of the original members of the Clown Club of Maryland and helped facilitate the beginnings of the Clown Club of America. Dad loved any opportunity to don a costume, especially at Halloween. My love of costuming comes from him, and to me, costumes and fandom go hand in hand.

As a kid I loved watching *Star Trek, Land of the Giants, Dark Shadows, Twilight Zone, Outer Limits, Lancelot Link,* and even some early *Dr. Who* with Tom Baker. In my teens, I loved to read mostly fantasy, science fiction, and horror. I frequently drew costumes based on what I read or saw.

On Her Roles at Conventions:

I have held several different jobs at conventions over the years. I worked in Public Relations for a couple of years with Shore Leave and ran Masquerade once. I have been both assistant and Workmanship Judge and a regular Masquerade Judge. Out of all the jobs I have held, my favorite was being part of Public Relations for Shore Leave. We would visit the Pediatric Unit at Sinai— some of us dressed in *Star Trek* outfits and a couple of us dressed in full Klingon complete with headpieces. We also visited several of the Enoch Pratt Free Libraries in Baltimore City, sometimes with a guest star. These visits were intended to encourage children to read. We would have some kids come up with us and give them a line or two to read. Sometimes, it was sad to hear a child struggling to read when you know they should be much more proficient. Some of the guests who joined us include Tony Todd and Michael Ansara. Tony was totally involved with the kids. On both the hospital visits and the library visits, we handed out book markers, books that we would pick up at the dollar store that were age appropriate, and also give out *Star Trek* trading cards. I was even on TV a couple of times dressed as a Klingon to promote a convention.

On Costuming:

I love costuming, and since my son is now older, I have been easing back into it. My favorite group Masquerade was "Pirates of the Caribbean." We were all dirty as if we hadn't bathed for a long time, but we also learned a valuable lesson. We wanted to recreate the underwater scene from the first film complete with transformation to skeletons. Rather than the usual skeletal glow-in-the-dark green but wanted the effect to be blue. I'd learned that laundry detergent glows blue under black light. Unfortunately, this resulted in chemical burns on our faces. Never again! Lesson learned. Another favorite was a Cardassian known as "Da Bitch." Up to that point, we had never seen a Cardassian at a convention. My father came to the Hunt Valley Inn to help me apply the makeup since I knew it would be awkward with the wheelchair if my husband helped. I had to explain to my dad how the appliances went on because he had never done anything like that before. Applying the makeup was a piece of cake to him since he understood contour and highlight. I won a Workmanship Award for Best Makeup that year.

As a member of a Klingon group, I've won a lot of Masquerade awards. Early on at a Vulkon, my husband and I performed as "Sonny & Cher" Klingons and sang "I Got You Babe," which netted us a First Place in the *Star Trek* category. My most prized award was the only overall Workmanship Award that I had to split with someone who did Captain Jack Sparrow. It was for the work I did on an outfit for my son Duncan. The character was Yun-seong from the video game *Soul Calibur II*.

On Her Involvement with Klingons:

I was one of the founding members of a local Klingon group called The Imperial Klingon Battle Fleet (IKBF). My Klingon name is qItahjoSa Tosh, and I held a position on the High Council within the group for the duration. At our peak, we had about 80 members on the books from Maryland, Virginia, and Pennsylvania with about 50 members that would dress in full Klingon. We required that members dress in uniform complete with headpiece and be active in our group. If you were really interested, we would make an appointment to have a partial life cast made of your head from just below the nose to just past the crown. Using your finished life cast, you could then design your own headpiece in clay. We took care of getting it to the appliance-with-wig stage. This process weeded out those who just wanted to be in a Klingon group from those who were serious. For example, we had two young males who wanted to join our group. They came to their first meeting, and we started to talk to them about headpieces and makeup. The one male was appalled at the thought of wearing makeup. I explained to him that it is like wearing theatrical makeup. He said something like "No, no, no. I was just going to wear the uniform and just say I was a human raised by Klingons." I pointed out that Michael Dorn wears makeup and that any male actor that you see on TV or in the movies wears makeup of some sort. It didn't wash with him, and he never returned. In my opinion, we were the best-looking Klingon group on the east coast, though some would beg to differ. Even on our worst days, we still looked good. We took great pride in our appearance and presentation to the public.

It was at Shore Leave in 1992 when we first showed up in full Klingon uniforms complete with headpieces, and we took the con by storm. From then on, we were a very active group. The jail was a novel way for us to raise money for charity since everyone wanted to have their picture taken with Klingons. You could find the jail on the lower level near the ballroom at the Hunt Valley Inn. We were loud, we were bold, and we were not afraid to go to anywhere in the hotel to arrest someone and maybe embarrass them all in the name of charity. For $5 you could be arrested, placed in our jail, "tortured," and get your picture taken with your jailers. There is a certain Star Fleet member who was arrested 19 times on his 21st birthday and spent most of his day in our jail. That poor victim was Dean Rogers, who was tortured way too many times by my son and the Barney song that day.

The Klingon Stick routines came about after several of us attended the Pennsylvania Renaissance Fair one year. These routines eventually led to the Klingon Feasts. In order to get more Klingon guests, we held a feast and provided entertainment for the guest. We really loved entertaining the guests, and there were a bunch of people who attended each feast. We performed everything from sea shanties to show tunes to Hotel California—all changed to suit the Klingon world, of course. Much to everyone's surprise, we sang well. We had five singers among us, two of whom played bodhrán while my husband played the guitar. We had some great harmonies. As we developed our show, we used karaoke music but put our own spin on the lyrics. Some of our songs included IKBF (YMCA), "Weapons Are a Girl's Best Friend" (thank you, Rachel), "Klingon Lady Marmalade," and "Gulag Rura Penthe" (Hotel California), just to name a few. The feasts were held in Frankie & Vinnie's at the Hunt Valley Inn. Where else could you get a meal, meet a Klingon guest, and have Klingon entertainment?

After being in a Klingon group for over 12 years, there are some stories to tell. In our heyday, we worked many MDA and Hopkins Telethons, and we were always on between midnight and 2 a.m. Where did we go when we left there? To the Imperial House of Pancakes, of course! The expressions on the drunks' faces when they walked in and saw us was hilarious! It was really fun to watch as they tried to figure out if what they were seeing was real. As they stood there swaying slightly, realization finally dawned on them. They pointed at us and said, "*Star Wars*!" We simply shook our heads and kindly told them that *Star Wars* is another universe and we are *Star Trek*, but by then they had wandered off to be seated at their table in another part of the restaurant. On another occasion, everyone in our group had been served their meal except for one. They had ordered mozzarella sticks, which we all know is the easiest of orders. Ten minutes pass and still no order. Burad, one of our senior members, walked over to the kitchen opening at IHOP, puts his fists on his hips and after he has gotten their attention states very loudly, "Cheese sticks!" He then turned around and then walked back to our table and sat. The waitress arrived not long after with the order of mozzarella sticks.

On Raising a Son in Fandom:

My son was born in October of 1999, and I entered him in a Masquerade the following July. For the entry, I was dressed as a Klingon and sang "Sesame Street" to him in Klingon. Bringing him into fandom was an easy fit. It was part of who we were as a family. He went with us everywhere, even when we dressed as Klingons. I remember attending a Balticon and using the harness to carry him while in my Klingon costume. It wasn't easy to change a diaper while dressed as a Klingon either. Duncan had—and still has—his own interests in fandom, which, of course, were not like mom and dad's. When he was a baby, I put him in the swing so that he could go to sleep, and I could get some things done. At that time one of the *Star Wars* movies was on TV. One of us decided to change the channel, but Duncan started crying. As soon as we went back to the channel with *Star Wars*, he stopped.

As a parent, you hope that you are doing everything right for your child. There were times that I would worry about what other kids in his class thought of him because of fandom. Yet, the more I thought about it, the less I worried. At a young age, Duncan was confident around groups of people. He was also confident in appearing on stage in front of a large audience and act out his current character in Masquerade. Compared to Duncan, the other kids in his class were stuck in their own little worlds and knew only what they were told.

On Her Favorite Con Activities:

One of my favorite activities at a con is participating in some sort of costuming panel. It gives me a chance to share ideas on costuming. Another wonderful activity is simply getting together with friends and having a couple of drinks. Some of these friends I see only once or twice a year. There were numerous times when we came up with an idea for the next con's Masquerade.

On Con Memories:

The first time I dressed as a Klingon brought some interesting reactions. The tunic I wore was borrowed from another member of our group. It was a dark green leather tunic that was captured at the bust by two safety pins. It was a very form fitting top since the original owner was not as well-endowed as I. The outfit also included black spandex pants and black over the knee suede boots. This reveal was at Shore Leave in 1992. I was with Bill (before we were married) and Susan, from whom I'd borrowed the tunic. We exited the elevator and walked past the lobby on our way to the dealer's room. According to my husband, male heads turned to Look. At. My. Cleavage. Finally, they would look at the rest of me, including my face. All hope was lost for them once they would speak with me and see the scowl on my face. They then became frightened. Little did they know that the real reason for the scowl was that I am very nearsighted and did not have my glasses on. This was before I began wearing contact lenses. I have always felt that unless the glasses are part of the character, you shouldn't wear them.

Another fun time was when Denise Crosby had a film crew at a con to film people for *Trekkies*. They asked permission to attend our feast, and we approved, of course. Everyone had to sign release forms. They filmed some of the feast and interviewed everyone that was dressed for the event. I was approached while standing in line to get food with Duncan on my hip. The question put to me was "What aspects of Klingon do you apply to your everyday life?" Without missing a beat, I answered, "I just do this for the costuming." They thanked me and walked away. Apparently, they were looking for over-zealous fans and I was way too normal for them.

On Guest Stars:

Of all the guests we have seen, my favorites were Michael Ansara and his wife, Beverly Kushida. They were our guests at the first feast we held. Our dinner conversation was not about *Star Trek*. Instead, we spoke about Gettysburg because it was a place they had visited prior to this particular convention and my husband and I had gone there for our honeymoon. They were wonderful guests.

On Maryland Cons:

I attend Maryland conventions because they are close and affordable. We don't stay at the hotel since we live only about 20 minutes away, depending on traffic. I also attend because I know that all of my convention friends will be there, and it's a great time to see them!

On Her Unknown Condition:

Something that most convention friends and acquaintances don't know about me is that I have a thyroid condition called Hashimoto's Disease. Just taking a pill is not the answer because there are many medical issues that have to be conquered to get better. There are many components, and it's challenging to get my family on board with meals, but they are starting to understand.

The Masquerade

Thomas G. Atkinson

On His Job in Real Life:

I'm a toymaker. I work with a local artist designing puzzles and games. I operate two amazing computer-controlled laser cutting machines. I like to say I have a very "science-fictional" job—I program robots to shoot things with lasers.

On His Personal History:

I was born in 1964 in Baltimore, MD to a Registered Nurse and a sea captain. At one time, my father captained what was then the largest oil tanker in the world, although I'm sure it would be dwarfed by today's vessels. I was the youngest of two sons. We moved a few times while I was growing up, but settled in suburban Baltimore. I moved in with my husband, science-fiction author Don Sakers, in 1987 (although we couldn't get legally married until more than a decade later).

On His Introduction to Fandom:

I was a nerdy kid. I enjoyed *Star Trek, My Favorite Martian, Doctor Who*, and plenty of sf/f tv in the 1960s and '70s. I read the *Tom Swift, Jr.* adventures and later more classic sci-fi, mostly checked out from the local library—Isaac Asimov, Ray Bradbury, Arthur C. Clarke, and so on. My older brother gave me the *Starfleet Technical Manual* and a boxed set of *The Hobbit* and *Lord of the Rings* paperbacks, all of which I still have.

On His Introduction to Conventions:

I became aware of *Star Trek* conventions in the mid-1970s. My brother, who was 11 years older than I, took me to the Boston *Star Trek* Convention over Easter weekend in 1976. We attended two of the four days, but didn't need a hotel room since he was living in Boston at the time. I got to shake James Doohan's hand. In the dealer's room, I bought a model kit of Space Station K-7 and marveled at exquisite replicas of *Star Trek* phasers, with lights and sounds and a price tag of $75, which might as well have been a million dollars to me back then. I wanted to enter the costume competition, but the notion of a "Young Fan" category was as yet unknown to the convention organizers, so I and my hastily-thrown-together outfit were turned away.

On His Years in Fandom:

About 40 years, depending on how you count it. In high school, I met some other fans. I do not remember how high school kids in the pre-internet days found out about *Star Trek* conventions in the Baltimore area, but somehow we did, and attended Starbase Baltimore, Shore Leave II, Balticon 15, and more as the years went on.

On *Star Wars*:

Star Wars changed my life. The movie was released just a few weeks before my 13th birthday, but didn't open in Towson, MD (where I first saw it) until a week after. My best friend at the time saw it before me and said, "You have to see this movie. It's funny." The notion of a funny science-fiction movie was new to us. We went one afternoon (we didn't have to wait in line) and sat through it twice. I had been a nerd before, but this was the movie I had been waiting all my life to see. That faraway galaxy seemed so real, and I wanted to go live there. I went to see the movie a dozen more times that summer—if I couldn't live in that galaxy, I wanted to visit it as often as possible. Plus, it was a good way for my parents to get rid of me for an afternoon.

On His *Star Wars* Toys Museum:

After *Star Wars* changed my life, I began hunting for souvenirs from that galaxy to take home with me. I bought some posters, T-shirts, and the soundtrack album on two long-playing vinyl discs. The movie merchandising machine was something else that *Star Wars* changed forever, and it wasn't until almost a year later that the toys and action figures finally appeared on store shelves. My older brother was already an experienced comic book collector at that point, and he advised, "If you're going to collect these things, buy two—one to play with and one to keep in the package." I wasn't able to do that with everything, but I've mostly kept that tradition with action figures. I simply kept all my old toys and continued collecting. I currently have more than 14,000 items. Over the years, my friends and I often joked about "the Museum," until we eventually said, "why not?" So as of 1998, our home is officially The Star Toys Museum and we welcome visitors by appointment. In 2007, the (now-defunct) Geppi's Entertainment Museum in Baltimore borrowed a boatload of my toys for their *Star Wars* 30th Anniversary exhibit, and that gave me the idea for what I call my "Traveling Collection," a subset of vintage *Star Wars* toys that I can take to events at public libraries, baseball games, town festivals, and anyplace people might like to see a temporary display of *Star Wars* toys. I've had enormous fun doing that, and many more people have seen the toys than I could ever hope to have visit my little Museum at home.

On His Current Connection to Cons and Fandom:

I have been the Masquerade Director at Shore Leave since 2007. I have been in charge of the Con Suite at Chessiecon since 2014. I am looking forward to my 15th season selling games and puzzles at the Maryland Renaissance Festival. I have been wearing costumes since I tied a towel around my neck as a cape when I was five years old and have expanded my costuming skills somewhat since then. I take advantage of any excuse to wear a costume and attend as many conventions as I can afford.

On Being a Masquerade Chairman:

I've always loved costumes and organizing events for people to show off their costumes has been a blast. I've worked with some great crews because putting together a costume competition that's satisfying for both the audience and participants is truly a team effort. I've been able to design the trophies that we give out—a new one every year—and I'm very proud of those. I feel like I could delegate some responsibilities better since the day of the Masquerade is often very stressful for me. And, of course, I don't get to present my costumes on the Shore Leave stage.

On Various Con Jobs:

I mentioned Chessiecon's Con Suite. I haven't held any other regular positions, but I've been a Masquerade Judge for both stage and workmanship at various cons and have volunteered to help backstage in other capacities. For example, at the San Jose Worldcon in 2002, I decided I was going to be the personal assistant to the Masquerade Directors (the husband and wife team of Sandy and Pierre Pettinger), and that was the right decision. There were a few times during the night when I was available to run and get something or deliver a message. I'm proud of that.

On Influential Media:

Oh, so many, including people who are no longer with us such as Marty Gear, Amanda Allen, Deborah Feaster Sears, and fantasy author Lisa Barnett, who was a great friend. I mentioned the *Lord of the Rings* and *The Starfleet Technical Manual* (and the author's daughter, Karen Schnaubelt, is a fan, costumer, and friend of many years), but also Ursula K. Le Guin's *The Lathe of Heaven*, *The Dispossessed*, and *The Left Hand of Darkness*, Marion Zimmer Bradley's *The Catch Trap*, and Anne McCaffrey's *Dragonriders of Pern* series. Arthur C. Clarke's *Imperial Earth* featured pentominoes, a geometrical puzzle that inspired my employer to go into business selling geometrical puzzles—which led to my job—and to my selling puzzles at the Maryland Renaissance Festival. So, there's quite a web of causality there. Alexander Key's *The Forgotten Door* sparked a lifelong love of alien cultures who are so advanced that they start to look primitive, living in harmony with nature (which *Star Trek*'s Organians, *Stargate*'s Nox, and many others have also touched on). I remember seeing George Pal's movie of *The Time Machine*, the Disney movie of *20,000 Leagues Under the Sea*, and *Forbidden Planet* when I was very young (at least two of them in cinemas, even though they wouldn't have been new movies at the time). Favorite TV shows include the usual suspects—*Star Trek, Doctor Who, Space: 1999*—but also many short-lived sci-fi shows that came and went in the 1970s. The original *Sealab 2020* fascinated me, *Land of the Lost* and *The Fantastic Journey* sparked a lifelong fascination with, and suspicion of, glowing crystal gemstones. *Quark, Red Dwarf,* and *Futurama* carried funny sci-fi forward.

On Costuming:

When I first became involved in fandom, original costume designs seemed to be held in higher regard than movie and TV re-creations, but I think that's changed. I've enjoyed being Luke Skywalker, a Starfleet officer, and Spaceman Spiff from the comic strip *Calvin and Hobbes*. The latter was a fun costume to wear. Among my best outfits is one inspired by a Gene Roddenberry TV pilot called *Genesis II*, as well as my *Blackadder*, based on the BBC series, and my Jedi robes. Back in the mid-1980s, I soft-sculpted a suit of Imperial Stormtrooper armor, which won no awards whatsoever, because Masquerade judges were tired of *Star Wars* costumes at that point, or so they told me. So, I shifted my competition focus from attempting to win awards, to just trying to entertain the audience and have fun. As it turned out, this led to winning awards. My magnum opus was our 2001 Worldcon (the Millennium Philcon) costume, entitled "Fridays at Ten," a 12-person, rocking tribute to the original *Twilight Zone*. All of our costumes were in shades of grey, including our hair and makeup, to simulate black & white TV. We used The Manhattan Transfer's "Twilight Tone" (their musical tribute to the original *Twilight Zone*) and rehearsed our choreography for months. The audience went wild and we won Best in Show (in a masquerade that included two giant, animatronic dragons). I haven't had any better ideas since then, and don't expect to.

On His Favorite Con Activities:

I like going to panels, and just talking about fannish things with folks. I enjoy filksongs and the occasional musician just jamming in a hotel lobby or someplace. Shopping in the dealers' room is always fun. But mostly just being around other fans with the opportunity to have a really good conversation, or run into a media guest, artist, or scientist from whom I can learn.

On His Favorite Recollection:

At one *Darkover* Grand Council—back when it was in Wilmington, DE—a bunch of us sat down in the hotel lobby on Sunday afternoon and had a conversation. It was particularly scintillating, and everyone had something to contribute. It lasted for several hours, with people filtering in and out as some finished up their last panels or volunteer responsibilities and joined in, while others had to leave for home. I remember very few details after all these years, but we all agreed it had been a brilliant example of conversation as a social and intellectual pursuit.

On His Favorite Convention Guest:

Artist Roger Dean was a guest at Arisia a few years ago, and I was surprised by my reaction to him. I don't draw or paint, apart from costume sketches, but I was absolutely fascinated and attended every panel and talk he gave. He's done some amazing sci-fi and fantasy art over the years, and I realized that his work played a major role in my visual perception of '70s sci-fi.

On Why He Attends Maryland Cons:

Well, Maryland is home, and they're a short drive. I'd like to think that I'd go out of my way for Chessiecon if I lived somewhere else. It (and its predecessor, *Darkover* Grand Council) is my favorite convention—a celebration of sci-fi, fantasy, history, music, and art in all its forms—in a cozy little venue of less than 1,000 people.

On His Favorite Person He Met at a Con:

That would have to be my husband, the aforementioned author Don Sakers. We met at Balticon in 1982 and moved in together in 1987. It's been a grand adventure.

On Something People Don't Know About Him:

I'm pretty open about most things, but people have been surprised to learn that I really like *Star Wars: The Phantom Menace* and *Star Trek: The Motion Picture*, two movies that are unfairly maligned, in my opinion. People have also been surprised to learn that I'm gay. I don't know why I expected them to know. Does that makes sense?

Stephen Lesnik

On His Real-Life Job:

My "real-life" jobs have ranged over my life. Mostly, I've worked in the computing field. I've been a programmer, administrator, security engineer, and program manager developing computing systems and applications for a range of industries and the government.

On His Personal History:

Throughout my youth, my family moved frequently as my father worked to build pharmaceutical plants for a number of companies. So before attending the University of Delaware at 16, I'd lived in Michigan, New Jersey, Puerto Rico, Pennsylvania, and Delaware. During my time at U of D, I also spent four months living in London. After some more time living in NJ and attending graduate school, I moved to Maryland to marry my wife, a talented artist and graphic designer.

I've had many hobbies over the years. Several have persisted to varying levels of obsession. I've always been an amateur astronomer, probably because one of my earliest clear memories is of Apollo 11 moon landing. I've attended many science fiction and gaming conventions over the past 35 years, including Philcon, Lunacon, Shore Leave, Atlanticon, DragonCon, Origins, and *Doctor Who* conventions. Attendance grew into volunteering and committee work, which I've now been doing for about 25 years. Board games and video games have been part of my life since college, where I found people with similar interests at my local gaming store. Another of my main hobbies is photography. I've had some great opportunities to photograph people, costumes, places, weddings, and movie sets over the years.

On His Introduction to Fandom:

Depends on your definition of fandom. If it's that moment of personal discovery that science fiction and fantasy are always going to be part of your life, then I'd have to say it started in Puerto Rico. I lived there between ages six and ten. There was little on television, but they did have *UFO*. Although the show was in Spanish and the title was pronounced as "oof-oh!" I still loved it, and it shaped my future. If being introduced to fandom was when I began to interact with other fans, it was probably when I started a UFO club in sixth grade. Although the purpose of the club was to study Ufology, we mostly talked about cool stuff like *Star Trek,* UFOs, astronomy, and Tolkien. It was a formative time that led to *Logan's Run, Buck Rogers, Battlestar Galactica, Thomas Covenant, Star Wars, Doctor Who,* and every other science fiction and fantasy book, television show, or movie I could get my hands on. I've been a proud geek ever since.

On His Introductions to Conventions:

I think I was like a lot of other people who found fandom and with it a sense of having "found my people." While I was in undergraduate school, the local PBS station showed *Doctor Who* on Saturday afternoons. I found my people when a large group of us descended on the common room, which had the TV, and forced the football fans to vacate in favor of The Doctor for an hour or so. In this group, there was someone who mentioned going to Philly for a convention to see a Doctor in person. I can't remember which one exactly, but I think it was Jon Pertwee. I'd never been to a convention, but I had read about the burgeoning *Star Trek* conventions, probably through articles in *Starlog*. It took a few years before I got to another sci-fi convention and in between were number of gaming conventions. The cons that really sparked my interest in running conventions were the one-off shows run by groups around the public television appearances of *Doctor Who* guests who were brought to the US. Sylvester McCoy and Sophie Aldred's appearance in New York pushed me to begin helping with small conventions and the nascent Creation Conventions.

On His Years in Fandom:

I've been a fan since I was six and started interacting with others at ten. I began attending fannish gatherings regularly at 18, so 47 years, or 43, or 35. Essentially, my whole life.

On His Connections to Cons:

I'm currently only supporting two conventions: Farpoint and Shore Leave. These days, I am a member of the Farpoint Convention committee serving as the Author Track manager and assisting with the Costuming Track and Masquerade (providing staff support to contest registration and as the Judge's Clerk). In addition to committee work, I attend a number of other conventions over the year promoting Farpoint.

At Shore Leave, I've been assisting with the Meet the Pros Party on Friday evenings, and on rare occasions, acting as a backup Judge's Clerk or Photo Stage manager when the Masquerade Director needs a hand.

I do provide moral support to my wife's committee work with a small gaming and relaxacon held in Virginia over Labor Day.

On Influential Media:

There's not enough time to write about all my influences. So, to keep it to a very non-inclusive list:

People:

- Richard Lesnik – My father encouraged my early interests in science fiction by providing numerous anthologies with stories from all the great early authors. Without those *Galaxies*, *Orbits*, and others, I would have missed so many of the great authors of the genre.

- Gene Roddenberry – *Star Trek* was formative in my life and seeing his name on every episode of *Star Trek* had a profound impact. As I grew up, I found that his vision of a future of tolerance, equality, plenty, and idealism was very much my own internal vision of what I thought people and society could be.

- Marion McChesney – Her conventions showed me how wonderful a con could be for bringing fans together.
- Isaac Asimov – I heard him talk at a Philcon, and his work ethic and range of knowledge fascinated me. I'm still waiting for a Hari Seldon to come along and give a plan to help us out of our current issues. "The Bicentennial Man" was an incredibly impactful short story to me.
- George Gamow – His popular science books didn't just teach me about the reality of the universe, but also opened my mind to what the great science fiction writers of the world were playing with.

Books:

- *The Lord of the Rings* and *The Hobbit* – Nothing else needs to be said.
- *The Chronicles of Prydain* – My first fantasy novels. I read them at an early age, and they gave my young brain a jolt that has remained with me through my entire life.
- *Ender's Game* – A book that always makes me think.
- So many more…

Movies and TV Shows:

- *UFO* – I'd never seen anything like it when I first watched it. It left a lifelong image in my mind.
- *Star Trek* – The show and vision through which most of my view of what is possible was conceived.
- *Star Wars* (some of the episodes) – Aside from *Star Trek*, the *Star Wars* universe was the next greatest influence on my fannish life. It also was the main feature of my first date. I went to see *A New Hope* with a girl I liked, and it was formative.
- *Doctor Who* – I saw my first episode, "The Claws of Axos," when I was ten. I've never been the same since.

- *Blake's 7* – The cast and crew of this show were the first ones I got to know as people in my fan life. It showed me that our guests are people, warts and all.

On Con Jobs:

For the last 30 years or so, I've been helping run conventions. I've had small roles like watching a door for badges and larger roles like co-directing the Masquerade at WorldCon. I tried to count the number of conventions and positions over the years but cannot come close to remembering them all. My favorite job among these has been the Judge's Clerk position. It has provided a lot of opportunities to work with our guests and see them off stage. Some of them have been fun people to talk with and get to know.

On the Farpoint Short Story Contest:

The Farpoint Short Story contest came about during an end-of-convention conversation with one my sister and of our author guests, Heather Hutsell. We talked about the usual variety of things and some photos were shown. Heather was intrigued by several of the images, and I was still trying to work out ways to improve the face-time of writers at the convention. So, I asked if she would be interested in a contest that was keyed off of a shared image. She thought it was a good idea and that she'd participate if we did it. With at least one writer onboard I put together some rules and documented the usage rights agreement, which I ran by a couple of our regular Farpoint author guests, Aaron Rosenberg and Robert Greenberger. Everyone was on the same page, and as a result, we wound up with one-third of our invited guests participating in the contest. Although this sounded good, it did have unintended consequences, and with the rules I'd worked out with the writers, it turned out we had too much of a good thing and not enough time for our attendees to read all the stories and vote. Although we did get enough votes to make the contest legitimate, we'll be making some significant changes to get better participation for year two.

On Being a Judge's Clerk for Masquerade:

The job of being the Judge's Clerk has been the most fun of all the stuff I've done over the years. Aside from those few occasions where either the Masquerade Director or the judges made me crazy by either having too many judges or being smart alecks and giving me weird judging responses, it has been a great privilege to get to work with our guest actors, costumers, and writers behind the scenes. I think this is the one job at a convention where you get to see the guests with their "on stage" guises turned off. It's hard to be "on" when discussing the authenticity of the bat'leth used in an entry with a writer or actor who has held one.

There have been enlightening moments along the years. On more than one occasion, my job seemed to be more about rousing drunks from the bar than clerking. Needless to say, most of those guest judges are hard to find on the convention circuit today. On other occasions, I've been absolutely gobsmacked at the intelligence, engagement, and insight some of our guests have shown our little contests. One awesome Geek Goddess and a TV vamp had a detailed and nuanced discussion of the entries from a particularly good masquerade. It was a tough set of choices and these two and the rest of the judges held a clinic in good and observant discussion about the entries. It was certainly the best time I had moderating and helping them come to decisions.

There have been several occasions over the years where we have had guests take their participation seriously, which made the job easier. I took tremendous joy in getting to see the people behind the character on the screen or the words in the books.

Some of the actor and writer judges I've enjoyed meeting most over these years have been Felicia Day, Sam Witwer, Erin Gray, JG Hertzler, Neil Gaiman, Alan Dean Foster, Melissa McBride, Robert Greenberger, and Michael Jan Friedman.

On His Own Costuming:

I have done some costuming over the years as the Internet so embarrassingly shows, but I've only done one costume for competition.

For Costume-Con 11 in Pittsburgh, my wife and I won Best Recreation Novice for our *Cloak and Dagger* (from the comic books) entry. Ever since, it's all been her game. Around 1987, I built a Chinese Dragon-style K-9 costume for a small *Doctor Who* convention in New Jersey.

On Creative Costumes:

One year we had Marc Okrand as a guest judge for the Masquerade. Rachel Wyman, one of our prolific and original costumers, entered as Patsy K'Line, a Klingon warrior who sang Patsy Cline's "Crazy" in the original Klingon to Marc. He nearly melted in his seat as she sang. It was a wonderful moment of a costumer and fan connecting with a creator. Another fantastic costume was a group entry from the Greater Columbia Fantasy Costumer's Guild at the Millennium Philcon—the 59th WorldCon—called "Fridays at Ten." It was a tribute to the show *Twilight Zone*, and was an unforgettable display of costuming talent and team work. On a less grand scale, I've encountered a few costumers that were insanely good at crafting clever, low-budget and tech costumes. The one that comes to mind most immediately was Garth Vader. Ian Bonds had decided to enter the Masquerade very late, and in a matter of an hour or so, came up with an entry that brought the house down with laughter.

Over the years there have been many more that still stick in my mind. We've had armored troopers, sexy warriors, dancers, and quite a number of Snow Queens.

On His Favorite Con Activities:

Masquerade, hanging out with friends, attending panels, listening to interesting guests, gaming, and building that sense of camaraderie among fans. The times I cherish most have been those late-night talks with friends in an empty room or at a table off to the side in a quiet area. I think the glue of fannish identity are these moments of shared conversations about the things we all love.

On Con Recollections:

In 2003, a blizzard extended Farpoint for two extra days. We called it alternatively SnowCon or DonnerCon depending on if we were worried about the food in the restaurant running out. During that extended convention, I had two of my most memorable con experiences. The first was having dinner with Armin Shimerman. He was standing in line waiting to get into the hotel restaurant like the rest of us, so I invited him to join our group. He seemed happy to have the company, and with the inclusion of Marc Okrand and others, we had an amazing dinner that included getting to know what Armin's real passions were in the industry, writing, and a decent helping of insider gossip about working with other people in Hollywood. It was a great time that is impossible to plan, but amazing when it happens.

The second great memory I have of that con was a hilarious moment that occurred in the Game Room. Most of the convention space was not available, but we were able to keep the Game Room space open. As such, we had a number of visitors that would never typically be in there. Sitting a table next to three well-known *Star Trek* tie-in writers playing Trivial Pursuit, I overheard the question in play, "How long does it take for light from the sun to reach the earth?" I waited for these luminaries of *Star Trek* fiction to laugh and immediately provide the answer. Instead, they all were befuddled. I turned to them and said, "Really guys? How do you not know the answer? You're all science fiction writers." Without a pause one of them turned to me and explained, "We don't write science fiction, we write *Star Trek*." That explained so much.

Another convention that held several special moments was a professional "Hollywood-run" convention for *Highlander* that was being held at the Hunt Valley Marriott. It was an event that showed how Marty Gear and I could create a costume contest out of thin air. We were wandering around when one of the few staff members we knew told us how the convention runners hadn't planned for the costume contest at all and expected her to just do something. Marty and I kicked into gear (pun intended), and in twenty minutes, we had a registration table in place, limited tech identified, judges set, and costumers signing up. It was a great little Masquerade, with the side amusement that when we tried to take the judges back stage to a sitting area to decide the winners, their "professional" body guards tried to divert them and separate myself and Marty from the group. It took one of the actors to scold the "professional" before they backed off, and we had an enthusiastic discussion. It was possibly the most fun I've had organizing a Masquerade. The last good memory of that night was dancing with actress Elizabeth Gracen at the follow-on concert given by one of the actors.

Overall, my years in fandom and supporting conventions has given me too many great memories to discuss. They range from truly silly fannish events like the Pajama Party in the bar at a *Blake's Seven* con to monumental moments like the final applause at the end of the 1998 WorldCon Masquerade.

On Con Guests:

Felicia Day is probably my favorite guest. In my mind, she is one of the few celebrities who has lived up to or exceeded the hype. She is brilliantly intelligent, attractive, and willing to be engaged in the events of the convention. Another favorite guest was Michael Welch. The first time I met him he was just 16. He seemed much older in how he handled the adoration of the crowd and really was a nice guy. We met again about ten years later, and he was still a great guy. Many other celebrities I've met over the years have been wonderful people, great convention guests, and fun to work with. I believe it's the personal encounters that I have through working the conventions that give me the best memories of meeting great actors, writers, and fans.

On the Reason Why He Attends Maryland Cons:

Maryland is home.

About What People May Not Know About Him:

I'm an open book. I'm pretty sure there isn't anything about me they don't know except perhaps my astronomy work as a teenager.

Brian Sarcinelli

On His Real-Life Job:

I've been involved in IT Support in one way or another for 25+ years. Currently, I'm an IT Asset Management Analyst for a large, well known, non-profit organization in the Education sector. My team is in charge of tracking all IT related equipment (PCs, monitors, printers, keyboards, servers, etc.) and software in the organization from purchase to disposal.

On a Brief Personal History:

I grew up in the boonies of Northeastern Pennsylvania, on a section of my grandparent's farm between I-81 and Lackawanna State Park. (Told you!) Mainly I tell people I'm from Scranton, PA (Yes, the Scranton of *The Office* fame) because no one knows where North Abington Township is. After graduating high school, I attended RIT (Rochester Institute of Technology) for a year where I made a bunch of amazing friends who shared the fandom genes. After that, I moved back home for a year before migrating to Northern Virginia. I've lived in Manassas, VA for the past 6 years or so.

I've always been "that kid" who checks the science and sci-fi books out of the library over and over again. Not to mention spending hours reading the encyclopedia. We had a set of *World Book*, and I'd bounce between articles following any interesting thread I'd pick up on. Getting sucked down the wikihole is NOT a new phenomenon!

As for hobbies, I can't even count the number I've cycled through over the years including astronomy, model rocketry, model building in general, reading, computers/electronics, movies… more that I can't think of. Books and movies have stuck with me and I've added photography and costuming.

On His Introduction to Fandom:

I started off reading general science fiction (I remember some of the story elements, but not the actual authors or titles) and moved on to more well-known authors such as Isaac Asimov, Arthur C. Clarke, Carl Sagan, etc.), TV shows, and movies. I was a huge fan of the "standard" Saturday and after school cartoons: *Thundercats, Transformers, SilverHawks, Voltron* (*Lion Force* FTW! *Voltron Vehicle Force* was less than stellar.), *Thundarr, M.A.S.K.*, etc. Then the local PBS station started running two episodes of *Star Trek* on Saturday nights at 11:00 p.m. (Much to my parents' irritation! Who needs sleep?) It progressed from there. I watched just about everything sci-fi related—*Alien Nation, Buck Rogers, Greatest American Hero, Max Headroom, Time Trax, V, War of the Worlds*. You name it, I probably watched at least part of it.

With access to conventions being limited early on, and only to Creation Conventions at that, my ability to truly interact with fandom didn't kick in until I was 18 and able to jump into my own car and travel to more fandom-rich areas.

On His Introduction to Conventions:

I was about 13 years old when my family and I were out running errands one day in downtown Scranton and I saw a sign for a *Star Trek convention* outside the Masonic Temple. They agreed (after an appropriate amount of "Can I go? Can I go? Can I go?") to drop me off for a few hours. Even though it was a super small convention, Leonard Nimoy (Mr. Spock himself!) was the main guest. My biggest fandom regret is not getting his autograph that day. The addiction took hold immediately. Since then I've attended conventions up and down the east coast, Canada, and even one in the UK.

On His Years in Fandom:

That depends on how you define "been in fandom." I've been a huge sci-fi geek my entire life (much to the confusion of my parents since they certainly aren't). If you count my first actual interaction with the fandom community (i.e. conventions), I'd say about 30 years.

On His Fame or Connection to Cons:

I don't consider myself "famous," but since I like to work the Farpoint publicity table at other conventions, I would like to be known locally as one of the Faces of Farpoint.

Most of my involvement across the board is behind the scenes. Even though I'm a costumer, I don't compete in contests, so I'm not "out there" being seen. (except for hall costumes). Even in other fandom projects, I'm more interested in supporting than being front and center. For example, when we made our fan film, *Star Wars: Revelations* a few years ago, I was a PA, craft services (food) monkey, driver, photographer, costumer, and more. OK, technically I had two on-screen parts, Boba Fett (the bounty hunter no longer appears in this film due to editing requirements) and the Dead Senator, but I mostly worked behind the scenes.

I'll share with you a funny story about being "a big name in fandom." Sarah [Yaworsky] and I attended the UK Discworld Convention in 2006. A friend of ours was on the committee, and we had planned to spend the weekend at the convention, then take the following week and a half to tour England with her and her husband. We didn't have details, only that they had an itinerary for us. The only two people we knew were Jen & Gideon, but when we arrived, *everyone* knew who we were and what the rest of our trip was going to be! We're talking about a few hundred people from all over Europe, plus two fabulous older ladies from Texas and Dot & Tommy (the Perky Goths!) from Arizona. After the first few hours of meeting people and having them say, "Oh! Jen's friends! You must be big names in fandom!" we had to pull Jen aside and grill her as to what she had said about us. We never did get a straight answer from her, but since she was Head of Registration, she managed to talk to just about everyone beforehand.

On Producing the Farpoint Program Book:

It's a lot like herding cats (with a generous allotment of "hurry up and wait!"). Sarah and I work closely with the programming team throughout the year as we put together each Farpoint. We gather guest and panelist bios, panel descriptions, schedules, special announcements, etc. Then we double and triple check all this against multiple sources. We also coordinate with other conventions and events for advertising in our program book.

So, for the first few months of planning, we pull together information at a leisurely pace. Then we hit November and things kick into high gear. Then December hits *us* and it really gets serious. Even though the convention "isn't until February," we lose a significant amount of December to the holidays, and since our printer requires at least two business weeks to produce the program book, we only have the beginning of January for final information collection, proof reading, last second changes, etc. There's always some piece of info (a guest bio, photo, advertisement, etc.) that didn't come in, so we have to track it down. Plus, the programming team is still working out the schedule up to the last second. There's a saying, "The convention schedule isn't locked until the day *after* the convention ends." Thus, Sarah and I are constantly tweaking the program book until the last possible moment before sending the document to the printer.

Additionally, page space is always at a premium. We do our best to squeeze as much raw content and information into the least number of pages possible. We can't just add one page if needed... pages need to be added in groups of four because of the way printers and staples work, and every four pages adds to our cost.

Then, once the book is locked and sent to the printer, we continue to work with the programming team to produce the updates insert. This covers any changes (panels, guests, schedules, etc.) that are made in the two to three weeks before the convention. This gets printed *right* before the con and inserted into the book when the registration bags are assembled.

I have to say, Sarah and I might be a pain in the butt to the programming team right at the end, but I think we (the entire team) run a tight ship.

A few years ago, we explored on-line guide options and rolled out our version of Konopas (a free, open source, web-based scheduling app specifically designed for conventions). As we compile the physical program book, we also update Konopas on a nearly real-time basis to provide the most up-to-date information possible.

The best part of putting together the book is, even though it's a really work intensive job, it's all done *before* the convention, so there's almost nothing to worry about *during* the convention.

On Influential People and Media:

Star Wars, Star Trek (Not including the reboots… not going there), Isaac Asimov, Carl Sagan, J.R.R. Tolkien/Middle Earth, J.K. Rowling/ *Harry Potter*, Arthur C. Clarke, James Doohan, just to name a few of well-known ones who set up universes to explore.

Locally and more personal, people like Marty Gear, Sharon Van Blarcom, Sandy Zier-Tietler, and others who provide the opportunities to explore those universes.

Of course, my mom, Barb, who—while never quite understanding my geekdom—made my first costumes, drove me to my first conventions, and even *attended* a convention or two.

On His Previous Con Jobs:

Now that I think about it, I've held quite a few, and with several different conventions.

At Balticon, I worked under Marty Gear on the Masquerade staff for several years. My main jobs were manning the Masquerade Registration table, Green Room Assistant (a.k.a. Den Daddy), Assistant Judge's Clerk, and Photo Stage Manager.

When Costume Con 27 was organizing, I volunteered to help with on-line pre-registration for the various events held at the con. Through a series of events, my role transformed from on-line pre-reg assistant to on-line pre-reg lead then to on-site registration manager for *all* events and contests at the convention that year.

I even volunteered for convention security at the 2006 Discworld Convention in Hinkley, England. That was supposed to be a "work-free" convention, but once we got there and settled in, it felt weird not helping!

For Farpoint, I started with a bang. One day, I asked if there was anything I could do to help, since I had been attending for a few years and really enjoyed the convention. The response was, "Hi! We need someone to run the Science Programming! Welcome to the Committee!" (Not "Want to badge check?" or "We could use someone to help at Registration!") Since then I've run the Live Events programming, helped in the Masquerade Green Room, judged Workmanship in the Masquerade, co-ran the charity auctions, put together FarpointTV, and co-produced the program book. In 2018, I ran the Costuming/Cosplay programming while still put together FarpointTV and co-produced the program book.

I'm sure there are others that I'm forgetting. I can't help it... if the convention is fun and well organized, I like to help where I can.

On His Own Favorite Costumes:

Again, too many! Since I have to choose, I'd have to say:

Wizengamot robes (from *Harry Potter*) – Before the movies came out, the Wizengamot robes were only described in one line of the book. "Purple robes with an embroidered silver 'W'" or something to that effect. As a group costume, several friends and I all made our own interpretations. We wore them to several conventions and made quite the impression. We don't speak about the test robe we made out of white muslin that our friend Dawn tried on. It looked fantastic until she pulled up the hood and turned into the wrong type of Grand Wizard!

V (from *V for Vendetta*) – This was one of the more basic costumes I've made and worn, but it was a LOT of fun to walk around in. Especially right after Valentine's Day when roses go on super cheap clearance sales because sometimes props make all the difference.

Boba Fett – Try finding consistent reference pictures of this costume! There are none! Every single picture taken is slightly different. We eventually chose one good front and one good back photo as our references. This is also the costume where we discovered that details make all the difference. We were almost done, and it was looking great, but there was still something off. We had not yet attached the cape. If you ever watch any of those bridal shows on TLC like *Say Yes to the Dress* where the bride or bridal party is waffling over the decision and the consultants "jack them up" with the veil and bling… The cape was the "Jack Up" moment.

Professor Quirrell (from *Harry Potter*) – As part of a larger group costuming effort (we also made Professor McGonagall and Professor Sprout costumes) I made a Quirrell costume. We wore these things everywhere! At DragonCon, I was asked to walk in the parade for the first time with the *Potter* group. We also participated in a midnight book release party at one of the book stores in Columbia MD. As it turned out, between the four of us in costume (Quirrell, Sprout, McGonagall, and Sinestra), we had representatives from all four houses. Plus, Marty Gear dressed as Dumbledore. The local paper ran a great article and a lot of people thought we were professionals. More recently, I dug it out of the closet when a local ice cream shop held a *Harry Potter* event.

As for awards, I never competed in anything individually, but have been part of three Best in Show group entries at Farpoint and Shore Leave. I moved on from competing in the contests to running them.

On Performing with Luna-C:

I've only performed one role so far and that was Mal Reynolds, Captain of the Serenity from the TV series, *Firefly*. I'd love to be more involved, but the timing never works out well.

On His Favorite Con Activities:

I'd have to start with people watching. I love seeing people in costumes and enjoying themselves—all types of people in all types of costumes. I've also met some of the most interesting people you can imagine.

There are so many things I love about cons. Attending panels, wearing costumes, meeting people, hanging with friends, and much more.

On His Favorite Con Stories:

At Discworld Con 2006, Peter Morwood and I had a shared stalker experience. There was one particular attendee who, shall we say, had less than well-developed interpersonal skills. He apparently latched on to anyone who interacted with him for more than a few minutes at more than a casual level. After chatting with him about something for a while, I drifted over to another conversation, and he followed... and to another... and another. Eventually, I excused myself to use the restroom... and again he followed. A friend on the committee intercepted him and ran interference. Later, I was talking to some friends and was introduced to Diane Duane and Peter Morwood. Somehow, the conversation turned to strange people, and it came up that Peter had had the same experience with the same person. We bonded over the stalker.

Several years ago, I think it was at Shore Leave, Nichelle Nichols was a guest. I managed to take several good photos of her during one of her talks and had one printed for her to sign later. When I presented it to her for her autograph, she looked at it funny and asked where I had gotten it since she had never seen this particular image before and she really liked it. When I told her that I had taken it the day before, she asked if she could have a copy. Of course, I gave her that printout along with a copy of the digital file. (I had another printout for her to sign as well) That picture was up on her web site for quite a while.

Then there was the time I was attacked while cosplaying as Professor Quirrell at Farpoint. I was helping in the Masquerade Green Room, escorting entrants back and forth to the Workmanship Judges, when I felt a tug on the back of my robes. I turned around and this little girl, who couldn't have been more than a few years old, was yelling "Hello, Professor Quirrell! Hello, Professor Quirrell!" I bent down to say hello and all of a sudden—*WHAP!*—she started hitting me with her lunch box! I don't remember exactly what she said, but it was apparent that she didn't like the Professor.

On His Favorite Con Guest:

I honestly can't answer this one. I don't have a favorite. I don't even know if I can narrow down the list to any sort of manageable number. There are the people who everyone knows and loves: Nichelle Nichols, George Takei, James Doohan, but I've had absolutely amazing experiences with people I had never heard of or seen on screen. For example, recently, at an extremely small convention in Frederick MD, I was completely unfamiliar with the guests. Since the convention was so small, the guests were wandering around chatting with the vendors. One in particular, Harry Judge (Tellarite Admiral Gorch on *Star Trek: Discovery*), stopped by the Farpoint table and had a complete fanboy moment when he saw that we had Peter David booked as a guest. We ended up talking to Harry for several hours over the weekend and had a terrific time.

Another was Nora McLellan. I had never seen any of her shows, but she was an amazing guest. Engaged, fun, appreciative, and a great person to chat with. It's always a wonderful experience when a guest really enjoys his or her fans.

Who would I love to see? Anyone who enjoys interacting with his or her fans. I've seen guests who were, shall we say, less than enthusiastic about interacting and only wanted to sit, sign autographs, and collect their appearance fee. Not the best experience.

On Why He Attends Conventions:

Not to be too sappy, but stripping away everything down to its core, I have to say family and community. I have a large extended biological family, but it pales in comparison to my convention family. You know that saying "You can't choose family?" Well, my convention family is one that I *do* choose to be a part of.

A convention is not only a vacation from work and other life issues, it's an opportunity to spend time with other people who get you, and that you get.

All the fantastic, geeky, nerdy friends I've made all over the world are always there for each other. Even though I haven't seen some of them in over 20 years, and we're on different continents, there's *always* an instant reconnection over some shared fandom.

Cindy Shockey

On Her Real-Life Job:

In real life, I am the Director of Estate Agency for the Department of Human Services in the Child Support Division. I work with 24 counties on fiscal issues, and I have been with the state for 22 years.

I was brought up in Arbutus, Maryland. My father was into SF and *Star Trek* and, when I was ten, introduced me to the genre through reruns of *Star Trek* and other shows like *Battlestar Galactica* and the *Star Wars* movie. I was in the Air Force for six and a half years in the 80's in the Intelligence Dept. I loved the Air Force. Everyone should have a chance to experience the military life. I met a lot of like-minded fans, like the D&D group in my squadron. However, when my mother became ill, I took a discharge from the Air Force.

On Being a Fan:

I have been a fan for 40 years. In 1977, when I was ten years old, my dad took me to my first con after seeing an ad on Channel 45 for a *Star Trek* convention in New York City. He took the whole family to see the entire *Star Trek* cast. I saw them as characters on the television show so to see them in person was unbelievable. I was amazed by the costumes and the props people had at the convention.

An incredible story came out of that trip to the New York con. My dad, a friendly and outgoing man, went to the hotel bar that evening while my mother and I remained in our hotel room. My father later walked into the room and said that he had a surprise for my birthday. Jimmy Doohan followed him in, sang Happy Birthday, and gave me a hug and a kiss. I was totally blown away and kept saying, "I met Scotty!" for the rest of the night.

On Starlog Magazine:

When I was younger, *Starlog* fed my hunger for SF news and I excitedly waited for each monthly issue. It was my window to fandom. I enjoyed the pen pal listings in the magazine and wrote to other fans listed there.

On Costuming:

My mother taught me to sew, and eventually I made an original *Star Trek* uniform. Over time I made the uniform in different colors. I learned techniques by reading articles by Bill Theiss about the original costumes, and I ordered emblems from Majel Barrett's company.

I went to Maryland cons and watched the costume calls to revel in the amazing costumes of individuals like Angelique Trouvere. In my late teens, I competed in a costume contest at Balticon. I worked with fellow fan and costumer, Wendy Ross, dressing as the Dark Paladin to Wendy's centaur. At a costume con held in Maryland, I became interested in the behind the scenes workings of masquerades. When Sue Fine from Shore Leave asked me if I would take over the masquerade, I said yes and never looked back.

On Being a Masquerade Director:

I stepped into the position of Masquerade Director without any training. I initially let the masquerades continue as they had been previously run but made changes over time. I took the judges off the stage during the show and placed them down at the foot of the stage facing the costumers. I wanted the attention to be focused on the costumers. Moving the judges off the stage allowed large group presentations to fit more comfortably and safely—and safety is a big issue. I've seen people fall off the stage and one costumer who attempted to blow himself up on stage. Moving the judges to the floor provided a much-needed element of safety.

Providing a separate room, a Green Room, for the costumers gave them a place to relax and calm their nerves. My respect for the costumers inspired me to provide snacks, drinks, make up, and fix-it kits for those last-minute emergencies such as wardrobe malfunctions. I continued the practice of den mothers and den dads who assisted their assigned groups of costumers in the Green Room and who ultimately rooted for their dens.

It's critical to put together a good team. My team members included Anne and Steve Lesnik, Cheryl Koblinsky, the Conventional Magic tech crew, and the runners who ushered costumers off stage and took them to the photo area. Everyone had input and could step in where needed. I always made a point of thanking my team. I've also been grateful for the Stage Ninjas who were there to be stage props or helped a costumer off the stage.

Many costumers stand out in my memory, but I absolutely loved the little Batman in the Children's Category who came onstage and began running in a circle... and running... and running. Before long, one parent and two stage ninjas were running in a circle behind the Batman... and running... and running. The audience and the judges were weeping with laughter, and the little superhero stole the show.

I was also impressed with the child who came onstage as a chemistry tube with a graduation cap—he was a graduated cylinder!

In all the years I've been involved in the masquerades—at Shore Leave, Farpoint, Balticon, FanOut and a few others—I have seen thousands of costumers and feel that all of them had something unique and wonderful to contribute to the masquerade. In 2018, I took a hiatus after 20 years of directing masquerades or managing Green Rooms. I want to give special mention to my mentors, Marty and Bobbie Gear, now both deceased and missed terribly by fandom. They offered me sage advice whenever and wherever it was needed.

On Con Activities:

Besides the masquerade, I enjoy going to panels and the art show, socializing with friends, and attending the game room. My husband, Chris Shockey, has run game rooms at the cons for 14 years. I also enjoy visiting the dealers' room where there are incredible items that can't be found anywhere else. I recently found onesies for my granddaughter, Layla, including a *Star Trek* one that reads, "I Just Boldly Went" and an Admiral Ackbar one that reads, "It's a Crap." I've performed in various fan plays and in *The Arbiter Chronicles*. I've acted in fan films, including *K'Thelma and K'Louise* in which I played K'Thelma, and Cindy Woods was K'Louise.

On Con Memories:

I fondly recall the Farpoint when it snowed so much that many fans were stranded at the Hunt Valley Inn. The extended con was relaxed and very social. There was no programming per se, but the stars who were also stranded made themselves available to the fans, including Gil Gerard, Erin Gray, and Armin Shimerman. The fans pulled together to help one another obtain needed medications, food, or money. Even before the snow storm, people standing in a long autograph line demonstrated their generosity by contributing selflessly to the fundraising efforts of my daughter, Courtney, for the Baltimore Zoo.

On Guest Stars:

My favorite guest at a con was Melissa McBride from *The Walking Dead*. I had a chance to talk with Melissa since she was a judge during a masquerade. Melissa is a sweet person who is very good with the fans. I also admired Laurie Holden (Andrea from *The Walking Dead*) who wanted to hold my grandson at a convention.

On Maryland Cons:

They're a family reunion. I enjoy seeing people from out-of-state, spending the weekend hanging out with friends, and going to the con suite to eat and relax. I've had the support of friends, such as Ethan and Christian Wilson, who have helped to babysit my granddaughter, Layla, during the con, giving me a chance to attend some functions. I like that I know everybody at the cons and that I can trust other fans to give me a hand with Layla.

On Being Thankful:

I want to express how thankful I am for the friendships and support I've received as a department head. When things get crazy, you call on friends to help. Mine are there when I need them, and I am grateful. I couldn't do my job without the committee behind me to support me with changes. It makes a difference.

Sarah Yaworsky

On Her Real-Life Job:

I'm currently unemployed due to ill health. I've done a variety of retail jobs (the customer is *not* always right!), been the security supervisor for a big box store, and was a financial analyst for a government contractor.

On Her Personal History:

After a childhood spent in upstate New York, Seattle, and central Texas, I moved to Northern Virginia when I was 17. I'm a voracious reader with failing eyesight so yay for e-readers. I'm a bit of a history buff with a little bit of knowledge about a lot of subjects and a knack for sounding as if I'm much more adept than I really am. I haven't travelled nearly as much as I'd like. My favorite experience was a solitary walk atop the ancient walls encircling the city of York and touching 2000 plus years of history. In my 20s, I started cross-stitching and eventually stumbled into sewing and costuming. I think the internet is the best thing to ever happen to hobbyists and DIYers of every kind.

On Her Introduction to Fandom:

That was a combination of things! I was born in '66, so I don't ever remember *Star Trek* **not** being on in reruns and I went to a (single screen!) theater for a friend's 11th birthday party to see *Star Wars* in 1977. I read Isaac Asimov and Anne McCaffrey and everything in between, including, eventually, comics. But I'd say my real awareness of "fandom"—as something to be shared with other people—came when I read *Star Trek Lives!* and *The Making of the Trek Conventions* (about early *Trek* fandom including the campaigns to keep the show on the air, philosophical reasons for the show's appeal, fanfiction, the *Star Trek* Welcommittee, and the first conventions) and David Gerrold's two behind-the-scenes books (*The World of Star Trek* and *The Trouble with Tribbles*) around 1980 or so. That's when I realized that "fan" was something to be *and* something to do.

On Her Introduction to Conventions:

Technically, my first con was helping to run UtherCon 5, a gaming convention, as part of the University of Texas Gaming Society during my brief college career. I'm only an occasional gamer and don't really count it as part of my fandom existence, but it was fun and a way to socialize. However, as far as what I count as my first con, I'd have to go with a Creation Con in Crystal City, Virginia in 1991. Bill Shatner was the main guest and the dealers' room was a revelation—phasers! tribbles! art! fanzines like I had read about in those books! Eventually, though I needed a bigger, better fannish fix than Cretin (ahem!) Cons could offer and discovered OctoberTrek (a predecessor of Farpoint) and Shore Leave and went to my first fan-run, stay-at-the-hotel con. These were the full-body, immersive con experience, if you will. I was hooked.

On Her Years in Fandom:

I've been a fan all my life. I've been involved in organized fandom since that first con in 1991, over 27 of my 51 years. Yeah....

On Her Connections to Conventions:

My biggest personal claim to fame is my involvement with the *Star Wars* fan film *Revelations*. It's a 47-minute movie released in 2005 after three years of work by hundreds of people, all volunteers, from around the world. I co-wrote the script, did costuming, acted as site crew, production assistant, craft services, continuity supervisor, and even directed a scene! It was a marvelous experience and really stretched the fan film boundaries for its time. We premiered it a month before *Star Wars Episode III* came out and garnered much positive national and international attention, including a nice review in *Entertainment Weekly*! The film—and a very cool collection of making of videos—

can be viewed on YouTube at: https://www.youtube.com/channel/UCR_WcaiSI0LyOJhNbICp97A

I've been going to cons in the Virginia/Maryland/DC area consistently since 1991 (OctoberTrek, Farpoint, Shore Leave, Balticon) and branching out sometimes as my interest is piqued. I fondly remember Big E Con down in Norfolk, Virgina one Halloween weekend where I toured the USS *Enterprise* CVN-65 aircraft carrier then in port. It makes a nice match to the time I got to tour the USS *Enterprise* OV-101 space shuttle as a child in Seattle. I've also been to half-a-dozen DragonCons, which are a bizarre hybrid of like fifteen fan-run cons and three mega-commercial corporate comic cons all jammed into five hotels at the same time that shouldn't work but somehow continues to thrive.

On Convention Program Books:

It's a game of hurry up and wait! The bulk of the book is dependent on input from other people. We ask every invited guest to provide a brief biography and a photo. However, not everyone feels the urgency that I do as our December 31st deadline nears. Darn those pesky holidays! We also list every single panel and event occurring at the con, complete with a descriptive write-up that includes date, time, and location. Since our Programming committee is juggling to fill a three-day schedule while tracking guests' availability, suitability, needs for rest and food (how dare they!), and desire to attend other panels, this information continues to change until... well, until the con is actually over. But by December 31st, they typically have a good idea of how it's going to look. So Brian Sarcinelli and I have about two weeks to concatenate this input, edit it, format it, proof it, track down anything missing, list all the necessary rules and regulations, put in ads for all the other cons who are getting space in exchange for our ads in *their* books, and squeeze in any advertising we managed to sell, all while trying to use as few pages as possible since every four additional pages increases the printing cost. Did I mention that it also has to be readable? If we were allowed to use 4-pt. font, we'd spend a lot less but only ants would be happy reading it. Ta da! Finished book!

On Influential Media and People:

Swing a bat and hit the usual suspects—*Star Trek, Star Wars,* Marvel, DC, *X-Files, Buffy the Vampire Slayer, Harry Potter.* Was it a genre television show? I've probably heard of it. In some, my knowledge is deep, in others, it's more of a passing but happy familiarity. I like the idea of fandom itself as much as any specific source material.

Personally, I'd have to cite my brother, Thomas Yaworsky, who's the kind of fan who owns dozens of copies of Tolkien's work because he likes different editions for different reasons. He made a Hobbit costume when he was 11 (remember, this was 1979!), and has raised four children who can discuss Morgoth's theft of the Simarils. Now, let's move on to his love of comics... on second thought, let's not. There's isn't enough time. Needless to say, I read and saw a lot of things because he insisted on how great it was. Conversely, I didn't read or see an equal number because he insisted on how great it was and by god, I don't have time for this, Tom, go bother someone else! He was with me every step of the way for almost two decades of con attendance before married life changed his schedule.

And I can't forget Dawn Cowings, my partner in crime in learning to sew because we wanted to make pretty dresses. Her love of *Star Wars* is massive, as is her energy. At Farpoint 1997, we walked past the Masquerade table with its display of trophies and she said, "I want one." So, we got her boyfriend into the Han Solo costume she'd made for him (for a forever unfinished—and hopefully forever lost—first attempt at a fan film long before we had any idea what we were doing) and sent him out on stage. He won her a trophy, and we were on our way. Dawn and I and various friends entered four Masquerades in a row and won four Best in Shows. Then we stopped competing and—while marriages, babies, home purchases, and job changes hit everybody—we made *Star Wars: Revelations.* It was an amazing experience and I truly treasure it. I'd never have had the guts to attempt such a massive undertaking on my own, and I'm so glad she took me along for the ride.

On Her Con Jobs:

Currently, I'm on the committee of Farpoint, a fan-run convention in Hunt Valley, MD. In 2012, my friend Brian Sarcinelli and I began programming Farpoint TV, a collection of song vids, archival con footage, humor shorts, fan films, and satiric commentary broadcast in the con's lounge area and (when allowed by the hotel) into guest rooms. In 2014, we added the task of producing the Farpoint program book to our duties, which lists bios of all invited guests and complete schedule of panels and events accompanied by an interactive online guide.

We also ran the Charity Auction for the last five years, raising over $15,000 for Farpoint's charities, including The Julien Fleming Memorial Fund and Art Way Alliance. That's going to be someone else's baby from now on as we gave up that department in 2018 so we could take on the Cosplay/Costuming track, Brian as track manager and me as his lieutenant. Frankly, I'm not sure what's going to take up my time at the next Farpoint since FTV is programmed in advance, the book is finished before the start of the con, and most of my on-site track duties are concentrated around the Masquerade costume contest on Saturday. That leaves most of my Thursday, Friday, and Sunday relatively free (the charity silent auction room set-up, the live auction prep, and the room break-down are all very labor intensive and on-going during the con). Perhaps I'll actually attend some panels!

On Con Panels:

Most that I've been involved in as a panelist, rather than just an audience member, have been about either the making of *Star Wars: Revelations* or costuming.

During the making of the movie, the core production group attended many cons up and down the east coast to increase awareness of our project and recruit volunteers. We'd discuss everything from the business of filmmaking (even an amateur, non-profit group should think about insurance. When you're using a borrowed crane and directing 50 people in expensive storm trooper armor through a working quarry for 10 hours, it's good to know that one freak accident won't financially destroy the rest of your life!) to how to use your state's film bureau to find free locations and extras, to how to feed those 50, 100, even 200 people on a budget. At the cons, we showed off new costumes, performed stunt demos, and previewed screen-finished special effect shots. It was a great education in public speaking, public relations, and the importance of always having something new to share. The audience doesn't want the same old stuff every time. It was also a great motivator to keep working on the film even when we got discouraged. Got to have something new for the next con!

It was also fun, after the movie came out, when Dawn and I were part of a fan film panel at DragonCon. We were the only women on the panel, most of the other films were humor shorts rather than dramatic adventures, and we'd had a cast and crew of more than one hundred. Our behind-the-scenes stories were epic and the other filmmakers' reactions were extremely satisfying.

On the costuming side, I usually speak on the ins and outs of workmanship judging, educating costumers as to what different kinds of con judges they might encounter (International Costumers Guild events are different from comic cons are different from Farpoint/fan-run cons etc.) and what they can do to present their work in the best light. I've also participated in panels on steampunk, costuming on a budget, and what "cosplay" and "costuming" mean to different people. I also do a critique panel every Farpoint the day after the Masquerade, reviewing each contest entry and offering constructive criticism to participants and insight into the judges' decision process.

An intersection of these two strains of participation came at the DragonCon where I was asked to be a judge at the *Star Wars* track's costume contest. The awards I presented to Workmanship winners were modeled after the ones Princess Leia awarded to Han and Luke at the end of the original movie!

On Costuming:

My favorite costumes that I've made are two that I crafted for friends who wanted Sweeney Todd and Mrs. Lovett's swim costumes from the short scene in the Tim Burton movie. There were only a few shots of them, they were sitting down, and the only other homemade version I found online was for a tiny, little slip of a girl in Japan with no construction information. But I was able to find a modern vintage bathing suit pattern for her and a modern vintage underclothes pattern for him that I could modify. I was so pleased with the way they turned out.

His fabric was an off-white with a black stripe reminiscent of a prison uniform and when my seams lined up the stripes so perfectly, I did a little dance and made everybody admire it. Her outfit had a lot of embellishments, with piping and ruffles and bows. I had to carefully create a striped fabric from two solids that I could fold to have one color peeking out from inside each pleat. There was a lot of precise placement, sharp corners, and careful stitching. Both of them looked amazing, and I have to laugh every time I see the photos another friend took of them. They're sitting down, recreating the movie scene and Sweeney is sitting with his knees splayed out, the soles of his feet touching. The stripes of his pants come together at his crotch, making a striking X pattern. Go, me!

Of things I've made for myself, I love my "cowmono," a 100% unauthentic kimono made with a delightful black and off-white cowhide patterned fabric. It's lined with red cotton because cows are red on the inside. Whenever I wear this onstage, I get mooed. When I wore it while judging at Balticon, I also wore a large green rosette ribbon like all the other judges. I told everyone that I'd won First Place at the State Fair.

I have an unusually high ratio of entering to winning because I haven't actually entered that many competitions! As I mentioned before, my first Masquerade experience was when Dawn Cowings' boyfriend won an award at Farpoint. I helped create his presentation (which won Best Presentation). Dawn and I, already addicted to winning, soon came up with another idea. Much like the men in *The Full Monty* staged a strip show to earn money when unemployed, surely the Imperial officers from *Star Wars* would find something to do after the Death Star was destroyed. So was born the Men of the Empire (Dawn's boyfriend Shane, our friend Brian Sarcinelli, and another friend), who would strip to "You Can Leave Your Hat On" for the Farpoint audience.

Being inexperienced, we solved most of our sewing problems by reinventing the wheel. Badly. Need to make pants? Make the wearer lie down on the fabric and trace around him! We also didn't realize the complexity of making three full tear-away costumes that would survive a dance routine. Ignorance is bliss and you can do a lot if you don't know it's impossible. Eventually, we made it to the con (after re-working the choreography at the last minute because one move from the film was just impossible without multiple shots with costume adjustments between them) and were told by the Masquerade director that our carefully worked out routine and edited music was too long according to the rules (seems we'd found an incorrect list during planning). Also, we'd probably bore the audience and lose their attention before it was halfway over and when not if, that occurred, the Masquerade reserved the right to turn off the music and escort the guys off the stage.

Tensions in our group were already high as Dawn and I were getting cranky about finishing the costumes and nit-picking the guys during rehearsals. We were so bad that they threw us out of a rehearsal at the hotel and we went off to sulk in a corner. Now this! Crying and clutching at each other, we vowed to continue anyway. A last-minute disaster was averted—one pair of pants ripped from one thigh up to the waist, across, then down to the other thigh when the Velcro used to reinforce the snaps holding side seams closed proved to be a little bit too strong when the final tearaway was tested. Did you know that Velcro pulling apart really does sound exactly like tearing fabric? I do now 'cuz I've heard them both.

Grimly, we proceeded with repairs. Less grimly, we reported to the Masquerade. Fairly cheerfully, we waited for the guys to hit the stage. Contrary to the warnings and far exceeding our wildest hopes, the audience went wild. The judges went crazy. The hotel liaison waved dollar bills. The ballroom took forever to settle down.

Two entries went on after the Men of the Empire. Let's just say that it was hard for them to engage the crowd. Anyway, we were euphoric. We sent the guys out to collect a Workmanship award and one in the Science Fiction category. Rather than try to sort out all the costume pieces they'd ripped off and flung about, we'd put them in bathrobes, boots, and of course, they'd left their hats on. They were definitely crowd favorites.

Then came the major awards. Dawn and I sat in the audience as Most Humorous went to someone else. Most Original. Best Presentation. We were bewildered and quite honestly crushed. We thought the guys had nailed it. What had gone wrong? Why did the judges hate us?

Somehow, both of us had completely forgotten the award called Best in Show. The judges hadn't. I don't think any of us came down all night. There was a bar at the Ten Forward party afterwards, but it wasn't necessary. The endorphins were amazing.

Did I say we were addicted before? We did a huge six-person presentation at the next Shore Leave (Dawn and me taking the stage from now on), singing an "Oklahoma" parody called "Tatooine". The Masquerade director (Steve Lesnik, same as at Farpoint and now a good friend— hi, Steve!) had learned his lesson and put us on last to bring the show to a rousing close. Again we took Best in Show plus Best Workmanship.

The next Farpoint, just something simple and easy, as Dawn and Shane were getting married. Nothing complex, just six people parodying "Summer Nights" from *Grease* as "Naboo Fights" with S-Lords, Pink Padawans, Danny Maul, and Sandi-Wan Kenobi. Yet again we went last, closing the Masquerade, and yet again took Best in Show.

At the *next* Farpoint, we had a bit of a dilemma. We couldn't figure out a good group presentation. Ideas were discussed, started, discarded. Finally, we ended up with a five-person, all-female group, all from different fandoms. I was Buttercup, a life-sized plush *PowerPuff* Girl in a giant, sensory-dampening costume. Everyone else was a normal human, the lucky ducks. Again, we were all-singing, all-dancing, though we hadn't had to record our own music this time. Instead we used "Larger than Life"—a pop meditation on fame and an artist's relation to the audience—and danced like a boy band.

I love the smell of Best in Show in the evening!

After that, as a group, we mostly concentrated on making *Revelations*, which ate up most of our energy and creativity for several years. Since then, I've entered the odd show or two, winning a construction award at Costume-Con 27's Single Pattern Competition and a Second Place with my steampunk *Star Trek* doctor at StarQuest in 2016. But mostly, I've been making things for my four nieces and nephews (school projects, Halloween, Ren Faire), friends, and myself. Most of my con attendance these days is centered on manning the Farpoint table and promoting the con, so I don't show up to a lot of events just to go to them.

On Being a Workmanship Judge:

Workmanship judging is my secret treasure. I get to see costumes up close and study them. I can poke and prod and ask all the questions I want. I get mini classes in problem solving, upcycling, and just plain faking it. I'm introduced to new materials and techniques I've never seen before. I also get to meet new, enthusiastic people who like the things I like, reconnect with familiar faces, and see novice costumers as they grow in experience. Children grow, too. It's disconcerting when a kid you've seen several times in the Young Fan category is suddenly competing with the adults. Where did the time go?

On Her Favorite Con Activities:

Obviously, I love Masquerade and all things related to costuming. I like DIY panels and demos where people share new ideas and techniques. I love "what-if" panels for current fandoms where we discuss what might happen next. The social events, like karaoke on Friday night and Ten Forward on Saturday, are events where I can be silly and catch up with out-of-town friends that I only see at cons. My bed's only an elevator ride away, so why not stay another few minutes?

That sense of being among my people, where I don't have to explain a reference or defend an interest, is what drew me to conventions in the first place. Now that fandom is more mainstream, it's not the refuge it was before. And that's fine. It's still where I can forget the rest of my life for a weekend and just be with friends. It's an outlet for creativity and drive, whether I'm working to make the con successful or just enjoying other people's hard work.

On Con Guests:

I can't name a favorite. I've had nice, quiet moments with so many (a perk of interacting with them as part of the Charity Auctions and Masquerade judging) and listened to stories that had me in stitches. I've met people who I've never seen perform (and sometimes still can't remember their names!) but who held an audience absolutely rapt and eager to see them the next day. I don't have one favorite. I have too many.

On the Reasons for Attending Maryland Cons:

Originally, because they were local. Then because they became my "home" conventions, the ones where I saw friends and knew the routine. Now I feel loyal because not only do I help run a Maryland convention, but I recognize that this area has been vital to keeping fandom, the kind of fandom that I love and want to others to experience, alive and well.

On Something People Don't Know About Her:

I'm shy. But shhhh! It's a secret.

THE SUPERFANS

Diane Lee Baron

On Her Real-Life Job:

I'm a Teacher of the Visually Impaired for Montgomery County Public Schools in Maryland. I'm currently working with blind and low vision kindergarten students. It's a challenge and a delight!

On Her Personal History:

I was born and raised in Pittsburgh, PA and later moved to West Hartford, CT with my family. I attended the University of Connecticut and graduated with a BA in Liberal Arts with an English major (and we all know where a Liberal Arts degree gets you). I volunteered at, and then worked for, Southbury Training School, a facility for the mentally challenged. I was there for ten years before heading to the bright lights and big city of New York. I lasted there for another ten years or so, doing work with the blind and managing to get my master's degree paid for in full by my job (nice if you can get it!). I became a runner, and even raced in some Corporate Challenges. The cement was terribly hard on the feet. After working full time and getting a Special Education degree from Hunter's College, I decided to try living in Maryland. I liked it! I have made so many friends here, mostly in the fandom family. I've been married and divorced twice—they just didn't take. My hobbies include swimming year-round, reading voraciously, and writing books like this one!

On Her Intro to Fandom and Conventions:

I was a *Star Trek* addict. When I lived in Connecticut, the reruns played at 6:00 p.m. nightly—the same time my mother served dinner. I bolted down my food and managed to see at least half of every show. I bought every James Blish book that came out. In fact, I learned of cons from a woman named Shonna, who I met at the local bookstore in West Hartford. She, too, was picking up the latest Blish book and told me all about a con that was soon going to be held in downtown Hartford. I was thrilled about this because I had just learned about New York conventions from a special source—James Blish's son! I worked on a high school project with the boy, and while at his house in my neighborhood, I learned who his father was and got to fondle a pair of Spock ears that the kid had purchased at a NY con.

Later, at the Hartford con, I mistook a man for William Shatner. It turned out to be Bill Hickey, a fun guy who got himself on the set of the first *Star Trek* movie through his sheer will, determination, and boyish charm. He was a dealer of *Star Trek* uniforms and actually attended many of the early Shore Leaves. After the Hartford con, New York cons beckoned. I went on my own and met two people in the audience who became very good friends. Bill Hickey was at that con, too, and we laughingly decided he needed his own fan club since he was so charismatic on the stage with his descriptions of the first *Star Trek* movie.

Bonnie LeRoy, Sue Doelling, and I got to work with the help of another gal, Pam Trelli, and we produced quite a few fan newsletters/magazines. We started printing stories, con reports, and essays all about *Star Trek*. This went on for several years, giving Bill Hickey an inflated ego and us a fun hobby. We all went down to the New York cons, the Townsley ones, which were pretty horrible. It was all about the dealer's room and a few guests. We stayed in the hotel to have a party with various folks we met along the way. Bill introduced us to George Takei and Walter Koenig who often came to our parties, or we went to theirs! Eventually, we put on our own one-day convention in Connecticut called Conn-Mini-Con. Over 30 years have passed since then and I still meet people who attended that con. Unfortunately, Bonnie, Pam, and Bill have all passed away, but my memories of those times still make me smile.

On Her Connection to Fandom:

I'm the type of person who enjoys meeting the folks that make the magic happen. I loved meeting writers of the *Trek* books and the various TV series. After attending the disappointing New York cons, I managed to go to Shore Leave V with my friends. We were enthralled!

At the first few cons, I met the Boogie Knights guys, Dave Keefer and Lance Woods. I met *Star Trek* writers Howie Weinstein and Michael Jan Friedman. I got to be friends with the convention committee members like Marilyn Mann and Sharon Van Blarcom. And over time, the amount and intensity of the friendships grew and grew.

I began to make costumes, and I actually won awards for some. Trekkercise was a hit, as well as Treknado. My forte was in the presentation with comedy leading the way. I started entering Art Shows with various projects such as Royal Bears, clay gnomes and mushrooms, and Art Boxes. Then I decided to create a game show. My first one was so silly and fun with various stunts and contests, but the surrounding rooms complained of our noise. So, I was eventually moved to the big stage, and the focus of the games slowly changed to trivia questions. Recently, I found something new to present at the cons, so keep an eye on your program books! I'm so grateful to the con staff of Farpoint, Shore Leave, and Clippercon who have allowed me to play in their big sandboxes. I proudly wear my Guest badge at the cons, and I never take that honor for granted.

On Writing:

Not many people know this, but I have an unpublished book called *False Pretenses*. It's a romance novel, and I really should do something with it. It is loosely based on a romantic connection that I had with a certain *Star Trek* producer. I kid you not!

When I was made aware that a second *Batman* movie had been made by Adam West and Burt Ward, I went a little nuts. After watching the movie, I was determined to meet Mr. West in person. And so I did, many times! I even became a producer on the documentary that Adam's son-in-law made to campaign for Adam to get a star on the Hollywood Walk of Fame. I decided to write a novel loosely based on my experiences of getting to know Adam, and *Gal Wonder*, published by Firebringer Press, was born. Adam supported the idea of the book, which took me years to write due many personal issues like divorce, moving in and out of states, and changing jobs. Fortunately, Adam read *Gal Wonder* two months before he passed away last year. It was a dream come true to finally hold a published book in my hands. I liked the feeling, so I decided to write more. *The Fandom Fifty* came about after I read an issue of *Time Magazine* about 100 of the richest or most popular people (or something to that effect) in America. I wanted to highlight 50 fans who make our convention experiences unique and wonderful. And believe me, 50 was more than enough. Often, it felt like herding Hortas to get everyone to submit their finished interviews or photos by the deadline.

I'm currently writing a science fiction novel called *When the Skies Fell* about a creepy alien invasion. It should be done in 2020. After that, who knows?

On Favorite Media:

Of course, I have always loved the original *Star Trek* series. I also became quite passionate about *The Next Generation*. I lost interest in the subsequent *Star Trek* series' as they came along. *Star Wars* became another passion, and I enjoyed all three of the original movies. *Blade Runner* was certainly a frontrunner in my list of favorite films. The fangirl in me loved *Ladyhawke* because of the hotness of Rutger Hauer.

I have one truly favorite book, *Dandelion Wine* by Ray Bradbury. If you haven't read it, please consider giving it a try. It is magical in the way that the best books always are. It captures the imagination and takes it soaring.

On Guest Stars:

I have had the fortune and the gumption to meet several guest stars and develop friendships outside of the cons. I tend to be gregarious at the cons, and as I've noted, I want to know the people who make the movies or TV shows happen. I met Michael O'Hare from *Babylon 5* at I-CON at Stonybrook University in New York. He was a guest even before the show had aired. My brother had been geeking out on J. Michael Straczynski's blogs about the new show and wanted to meet the actor and perhaps other B5 guests at the con. My brother pointed Michael O'Hare out to me then left to do something else. I walked over to the handsome actor who stood alone on a balcony smoking a cigarette. I said, "Hi! How does it feel to know that you're going to be the next Most Sexy Actor on the cover of *People Magazine*?" Seriously, I can be very bold at times. Anyway, Michael laughed and shook my hand. We introduced ourselves and talked for quite a while. Imagine my brother's shock when he returned to find me chatting up Michael. Michael and I remained in touch, and I recall his excited phone call when he told me that B5 had been picked up for more episodes. Once my brother and I went to his apartment in NYC and watched a B5 episode with him. I loved Saturday mornings when he would wake me up with a phone call and would start reciting the opening monologue from B5. "It was the dawn of the third age of mankind…" He knew it would make me swoon! Things went downhill quickly for Michael near the end of the first season. I won't go into details, but he pulled away from friendships and eventually moved to London.

I developed a similar friendship with Bruce Hyde who portrayed Lt. Kevin Riley in the original *Star Trek* series. He would meet my group of friends for lunch in New York, even when he wasn't a guest at a con.

Bruce and I developed a letter correspondence, since at that time I lived in Connecticut. I had been in a debate with myself over whether I should move down to NYC and try a life there. Bruce wrote me a one-line letter saying, "Just do it!" So, I did. What was the point of debating? Bruce ended up moving to California and we lost track of each other. But it had been fun watching him in off-Broadway musicals in New Jersey and drinking plum wine at a favored Asian restaurant.

Another cool experience was having dinner with Colin Ferguson. At the Friday night Farpoint banquet, he asked if he could join De Baisch and I for dinner. That turned out to be a fun time.

Meeting director and producer Nicholas Meyer and having an hour to spend alone with him was beyond the moon. De Baisch and I bid on the hour during a con auction, and it was worth every penny and more.

On Inspirational People:

The one person who has proven to be a good friend and supporter is author Howie Weinstein. We met decades ago at one of the first Shore Leaves and have managed to maintain a friendship based on our mutual love of writing. Of course, Howie is more prolific and famous than I ever will be. He's a real writer whereas I've been a dabbler. But Howie pushed me to keep at my writing, and I finally have dedicated myself to this pursuit with all the seriousness and time it deserves. I have to thank Howie for his long-standing belief that I could indeed write a novel. I'm sure that he is as surprised as I am that I'm in the process of writing two more books at this time. Further, Howie encouraged me to put a dog in my first book. Now in Howie's honor, I have a dog in my next novel, too. It's a bulldog named Satchmo, and Howie, you're going to love him!

On Her Favorite Con Activities:

It has always been the same for me. I attend cons to meet people and hang out with my friends. Sometimes, I go to hear the guest stars or to listen to an interesting panel. But mostly, you'll find me sitting in a lounge or lobby gabbing away with friends. I have to mention that I met one of my longest-standing friends, Jon Eigen, at an early Shore Leave while he was in college and I lived in NYC. I eventually met all his wonderful friends, about six other young guys, and we all hung out at Ten Forwards. Over time, all the boys got married and moved away, but Jon stayed in the area and married wonderful Anna. She has become a dear friend and, god bless her, she seems to enjoy the cons, too. Jon and Anna have a daughter, Thalia, who is in her early twenties and now comes to cons with her friends. Jon is one of those friends who never lets you drop the lines of communication. But that's how fandom works. You meet a person, then you meet their people and they meet your people and the next thing you know there is an explosion of friendship of all ages and interests.

Oh, and yes, I enjoy karaoke, Ten Forward, Dean Rogers's game shows, Luna-C, and the Boogie Knights. I also enjoy meeting prospective dating partners at the cons. Well, goodness, it's no secret that many of us are doing that!

On Maryland Cons:

I can't say enough about the Maryland conventions. Farpoint and Shore Leave have been my escapes for decades. I can't imagine my life without these cons. The people are my extended family. I can be myself with them and no one judges me. When I was younger, I felt like a belle at the ball at every con. People paid attention to me, laughed with me, and danced beside me. Now that I am older, I am an elder statesman at the gathering, no less a part, just a bit quieter and more focused on others. I am thankful to all of the people who have worked to make these conventions happen. I love you all.

T.A. (Alan) Chafin

On His Real-Life Job:

I work at Charles Town Races in West Virginia. I was born in Groton, Connecticut to a Navy family. I've lived around the world, in places like Connecticut, Hawaii, Washington, D.C., Hong Kong, and Northern Virginia.

On His Introduction to Science Fiction:

My initial introduction to science fiction occurred at age eight. While flipping through channels, I observed a guy with pointed ears saying to a man lying on a hospital bed that this could cure or this could kill him. And Kirk, the man on the hospital bed replied, "I'm going to die anyway." I thought this scene was idiotic and turned the channel. Flash forward to living in the United States while in junior high school, and I gave *Star Trek* another chance, wondering where this had been all my life. I've been hooked on *Star Trek* ever since.

On His Introduction to Conventions:

My introduction to conventions was an August Party in 1975 at the University of Maryland, College Park. My claim to fame is that I was the first attendee of the first *Star Trek* con ever held outside of New York. My time at the August Party convention showed me that I wasn't alone in my interests. When I mentioned things related to *Star Trek*, people understood.

Shortly after, I went into the military for four years as an airman in the Air Force stationed at Offutt Air Force Base in Omaha, Nebraska. I attended the first science fiction con held in Omaha, called Technicon. Jesco Van Puttkamer was the guest at this small one-day con and only 22 people attended.

I eventually moved to Maryland where I attended the local conventions. I have been to over 200 cons in my fandom life that began in 1975.

On the Maryland Conventions:

I've attended cons on both coasts and from north to south, and Maryland conventions are the warmest, friendliest, and most organized. Guest accessibility is almost unparalleled in fandom. At other cons you can barely say hello to guests. I once met Karen Gillian from *Dr. Who* and *The Avengers* at a Shore Leave and talked to her for five minutes. There's a willingness to let you get involved. If they like what you have to offer, they accept you.

On Costuming:

I don't sew, and I'm not creative that way. I'm great on concept and originality. My presentations at conventions have brought down the house, much to the consternation of the Costuming Guild who felt my entries ran counter to their specifications of costuming. In fact, I had an article published in *Starlog Magazine* on costuming. My strength relies on the three-edged sword of quality, originality, and presentation. My Chocolate-Covered Riker will go down in the history books of masquerades. I recreated the scene from the *ST:TNG* episode "Skin of Evil" where Riker becomes engulfed by the Sludge Monster—by having a girl in a bathing suit pour a gallon of Hersey's chocolate syrup over his head on stage. There was a tarp to catch the runoff, sparing the stage from damage, and I walked away with two awards that evening: Most Humorous and Most Original. The best part of the experience was that Jonathan Frakes was a judge that evening and was a witness to the fun.

I'm also proud of my costume of Yarment the Peasant. I wore a filthy, smelly costume and appeared very physically ill with maladies. While I was onstage, a voice from the heavens said Yarment would be cured if he could get a kiss from Marina Sirtis (who just happened to be judging the masquerade that evening.) Marina almost gave me that kiss until the Voice of God said, "Oops, I made a mistake. What you need is a kiss from an editor of DC comics." Bob Greenberger just happened to be sitting at the judges table. I looked up to God and then Bob three times, and then walked off stage, shaking my head. The audience loved it, and I received a workmanship special award in the hopes that I never again build a costume soaked in a gallon of used motor oil that reeked to high heaven.

I believe that anybody can costume. Do not allow yourself to be intimidated by what other people are doing. From my own experiences, I know that when you give it your best, you'll be interesting in some fashion. Unfortunately, I don't get the chance to costume as much as I did in my earlier years in fandom.

On *Star Wars*:

Star Wars has been a big part of my life since August 1977 when I first watched the original movie. When I noticed a mistake in the movie—a stormtrooper banging his head on the door of the control room in the docking bay of the Death Star—I became hooked on bloopers. I wrote the *Unauthorized Nitpickers Guide to the SW Saga* in 2006 with co-author Polly Luttrull.

I'm known at Maryland cons for my *Star Wars* panels. The panels encompass much more than *Star Wars* topics, and I often show clips of interesting science fiction shows or movies. I admit that it's getting tougher to do *Star Wars* talks since so much information is accessible on the internet.

On Why He Attends Conventions:

I enjoy attending conventions and catching up with old friends. I'm always on the lookout for new or old genres that I haven't been exposed to. In spite of the internet, a convention is a warmer and more personal hub of SF and fandom knowledge.

On Reading Science Fiction:

I read SF 'in excess' with my favorites being Heinlein and Spider Robinson, and I loved the movie, *The Martian*.

On Something People May Not Know About Him:

I've discovered the older I've become, the more susceptible I have become to stage fright. I have to psych myself up for talks. I don't want to be the center of attention.

One other thing fans may not know about me is that I attended Space Camp four times and was part of the first adult space camp ever. I got to be part of the team that designed the ten-day space camp that people can now get college credit for. I've also taken rides on the Vomit Comet and experienced zero-g. My experiences were documented in an article in *Analog Magazine*.

June Swords and Dan Corcoran

On June's Brief History:

I was raised in Lawrenceville, NJ. I never went to college; didn't even bother to take any of the SATs. Right after high school, I took a job at a local farm and orchard that had a little store on the property. We grew fruits and vegetables and made apple cider. I did a little of everything in the 14 years I was there, from managing the store, to baking pies and frying donuts, to taking care of the animals, and working in the fields. Much of my heart is still back at that farm.

I was the sixth of seven siblings. I naturally watched a lot of what my older brothers and sisters watched. In the late '60s and early '70s, that included *Star Trek, Time Tunnel, Lost in Space, Lost Saucer, Twilight Zone,* and *Night Gallery*. I won't list every weird show that was airing at the time, but we watched them all. We watched a *lot* of TV. I think the days had more hours in them when I was growing up.

I learned sewing, stitching, and crafting from my mother. I pestered her constantly. "Mom, I want to make something!" and magically, she would produce supplies. I learned "car stuff" and "fixing stuff" from my dad. He would bring home old radios and TVs that we could take apart or put together. I loved to read, mostly science fiction and fantasy and random books from my dad's bookshelf. I have a surprising amount of knowledge about WWII submarine warfare because of that.

On Her Con Experiences:

I attended my first SF convention in January 1983—my senior year in high school—courtesy of my friend Louise St. Romaine, who had been attending them for years. Until then, I had no idea they existed.

We went to Philcon '82.1 (it should have been held in November 1982, but they couldn't get the hotel). It was a revelation.

I'm sure my "first con" experience was like most people's. Suddenly, there was an entire community of people who enjoyed all the science fiction and fantasy stuff that I did, and many of them were far more invested than I ever was. The dealers' room was full of books and collectibles. I had no idea there were so many. The halls were full of costumes. I was smitten. Louise and I moved into an apartment together. I started attending cons up and down the East coast including Philcon, Lunacon, Boskone, Disclave, and Arisia.

My first several years of attending were consumed with costuming. I fell in love with, and married, a fellow fan. He was thin and tall, willing to walk the halls in costume, and compete on stage in the masquerade wearing costumes I made. So many costumes. I specialized in re-creation. I really liked to do characters that looked interesting and amazing to the viewer, even if they knew nothing about the source. Some example included *Star Blazers, Macross*, most of the cast of *Lupin III*, Peace the assassin from *Wizards*, Jack Skellington and Sally, Nausicaa, the Blue Meanie, Worzel from *Lensmen*, and Arthur from *The Tick*. I did some originals as well. I made some super wings and did a couple of sword wielding angels.

The Angels were very popular. On New Year's Day in 1994, my friend, Thom Truelove, and I donned the costumes and marched in the Philadelphia Mummer's Parade. We won a trophy for "Best Couple." I brought it home proudly but was aware of an unfortunate irony. My marriage was deteriorating. It dragged on for a few more years and when it finally ended, I was in a deep depression, both mentally and financially.

I still managed to attend Philcon yearly, with financial help from Louise, and emotional help from Thom. In 1997, Thom introduced me to a group of fans from Maryland. I distinctly remember, with strange clarity, going to a room and being introduced to a guy in a white sweatshirt in bed reading a comic.

"June, this is Renfield."

On Renfield's Brief History:

I grew up in Laurel, Maryland and I'm rather put out that I never made it further afield. Life was so dull and drab growing up that I promised myself I would travel constantly when I became old enough, or move to the mountains, or to Australia, or to that promised moon base. I guess Baltimore is far enough. As a child, I was a voracious reader, devouring every fantasy and science fiction book I could get my hands on, and then discovered comic books as I got older.

On His Convention Experiences:

One day when I was sixteen, my cousin Mary called and asked if I wanted to go to a science fiction convention that weekend. I said, "Yeah!" True story. We went to Balticon 20 at the Sheraton in downtown Baltimore. I enjoyed it immensely. I had heard of science fiction conventions but knew nothing about them. Then I was at the hotel, immersed in an entirely new and interesting world—people strolling about in different costumes, people lying in the hall playing D&D, and everyone uttering SF and fantasy references that made sense. When I said similar things, they understood what I was talking about. Suddenly, there were people I could relate to. It was absolutely magical. I took a lot of pictures that weekend and as I went through them years later, it was heartening to note that almost all were people that I am currently friends with.

I stayed overnight in the hotel with my cousin and her friends. I felt bad because I ditched her almost instantly. I didn't mean to, but there was so much to see and do everywhere that I kept moving from the moment we arrived. It worked out, though, since she hit it off with some filk guy she met there named Dave Keefer (currently her husband, and founder of the Boogie Knights.)

I ran into a guy throwing a party for his convention (Rivercon) and hung out with him and his friends. One guy a few years older than I had to drive home to Arlington on Saturday, and I went with him. I have no idea who he was. I went to his house, had a few drinks, watched the Five Doctors episode of *Doctor Who* all while the con was going on so many miles away. (It was only when I related this story for this interview that it was pointed out to me what I considered the magic of my first convention could be construed as disturbing when viewed a certain way. I was a minor who traveled across state lines with a stranger, after all.)

We returned to the con and wandered around. I poked my head into the ballroom and noticed a couple of aliens moving across the stage (it was later explained to me the concept of a masquerade). I do recall that the next day, I went to my Arlington friend's room to say "hi," but he was busy showering with a woman and having a grand old time.

On the Origin of His Name:

After that first con, I went with Mary to Shore Leaves and other local conventions. At those cons, I met other friends who brought me into their circle of friends. Some of them invited me to the New Orleans WorldCon in 1987, where I was introduced to the Costumers Guild. There was one woman I met who kept getting my name wrong or forgetting it entirely. At one point I wound up wearing someone else's badge named Richard or something, and he had terrible handwriting. My friend asked, "What does that say? Renfield?" So, when the woman entered the room and forgot my name again, everyone told her it was Renfield and it stuck.

On His Performing with Cheap Treks:

Dave Keefer not only fronted the Boogie Knights (the Weird Al Yankovics of the filk world), he was also a driving force behind the comedy troupe Cheap Treks, known for *Star Trek* comedy plays performed at the local cons. The first one I saw, "Star Trek 4: The Voyage the Hell Home" was performed at a Clippercon. I wasn't in that play, but you can hear me laughing in the audience on the videotape! June says it's unmistakable.

When they performed the *ST:TNG* inspired "Hard Day's Light Year," they needed a Wesley Crusher who was going to get shot early in the show. Mary, who had never warmed to my fan name, had to explain to people, "We cast my cousin Dan as Wesley. We're going to shoot him." To the looks of confusion, she begrudgingly added, "You know him as Renfield." Then the person said, "Excellent choice!"

I was in several more shows with small, but memorable, roles (I did several shows in a row where I wound up in my underwear on stage.) The roles grew larger due to experience and attrition. The Cheap Treks name was retired as different groups and subsets started producing plays under various other names. Eventually, Steve Wilson created The Usual Suspects as one banner to include everyone. When June moved to Maryland, we were cast in the plays together, both stage and radio (Prometheus Radio Theater.) By that point, I was writing shows myself, including "Harry Potter and the Giant Robot from Planet Krazny" and "Have Browncoat Will Travel."

On the Meeting of Renfield and June, as Told by Ren:

In 1997, a friend of mine from the plays named Andrew Bergstrom invited me to join him at Philcon and while there, he introduced me to his friend Thom Truelove and Thom's friend, June Swords. She caught my eye immediately, as she was smart, funny, pretty, and single. I was at a point in my life where I was beginning to think the perfect fem fan did not exist and suddenly in walks a unicorn. One incident from that weekend has always stayed with me. The whole group of us went to a nearby comic book and game store to browse and shop, and while we were heading back to the car, June asked to go into a shoe store we were passing. I rolled my eyes, but figured it was only fair as the guys had just spent an hour looking at comic books. She walked up to the counter, pointed at a pair of Chuck Taylors and asked, "Do you have those in purple?" When the salesperson replied in the negative, June said, "Thank you," and left. I was impressed that there was not a single stereotype that could be applied to her. Andrew asked us both to perform in a play at the following Balticon in 1998. We grew interested in each other at the rehearsals and after the play we threw ourselves at each other.

At that time, I was living at the Star Toys Museum with Thomas Atkinson and Don Sakers. When June came to the house for the first time, I introduced her to my roommates before we went out on our date. As we were leaving, they saw us out with the Princess Bride quote, "Have fun storming the castle. Think it will work?"

June replied, "It will take a miracle."

The next day, my roommates told me in no uncertain terms that they would not allow me to date anyone else, and if we broke up, they were keeping her.

It should be noted that when June and I started dating, I was prepared to leave my fan name behind as part of my effort to distance myself from my wild carefree bachelor days and clean up my act in pursuit of The One. But we did meet at a convention, and Renfield was the only name she knew me by. And she has a large family. So, when I finally met her parents, and all six of her siblings, and their families, they all already knew my name was Renfield. So now I have several nieces and nephews who know me as Uncle Renfield, and the name on my driver's license has been relegated to a nom de plume.

On June's Move to Maryland, as Written by June:

When I started dating Renfield, I spent many months driving back and forth to Maryland. Not an ideal way to live. Finally, I said my goodbyes to NJ and moved to Baltimore. This was Part Two, a new life. Another wonderful benefit of leaving NJ and moving to Baltimore (other than the love of my life) was that I instantly joined an enormous circle of friends. Some had overlap with Philadelphia fandom, most were new, but between Farpoint, Balticon, Shore Leave, and the Costumer's Guild, *everyone knew everyone*. And suddenly, I was part of that group.

On June & Ren Together, as Written by June:

We've done a lot more together than we'd ever dreamed of doing on our own. We've climbed the Sydney Harbor Bridge in Australia, fished in Colorado, saw the total eclipse in Oregon. We enjoy puzzles and escape rooms. June still sews and "makes stuff." Ren writes and has a couple of published stories.

When we were still involved with the stage plays at cons, our house became a favorite rehearsal spot. It was a selling point for other houses in the neighborhood. The neighbors enjoyed watching the theatrical troupe rehearsing in the driveway.

Aside from an occasional group entry, June left competitive costuming behind in New Jersey but was a costume workmanship judge at the Maryland cons. She often volunteers in the Masquerade green room.

Renfield was called on to do more and more emcee work and charity auctioneering, but we do everything together. If Ren runs masquerade, June is working the table. If Ren is emcee, June is in the Green Room. Whatever one is doing, the other is helping. In our quest to do a little of everything, June has also been emcee for a couple of masquerades and has sold a few pieces in the Farpoint Art Show.

We prefer not having official roles. For the Farpoint Art Show, all materials are stored in our garage because we have the room. Every year we help with set up, but we're not official art show staff. We are not on the volunteer list, but if someone needs help, we're always carrying things.

On The Marriage Proposal:

A friend asked us to be in his group masquerade presentation at the 1998 Philcon. It was a re-creation of a scene from a book that the guest writer had coming out. The presentation was extremely elaborate, with many people involved. It included a magic trick and at the end, a banner would unfurl with a bad in-joke.

However, instead of the punch line, the banner read: *June, will you marry me?*

The entire presentation was carefully created to keep June from guessing what was actually going to happen, and all our friends were willing conspirators. There were a lot of people and costumes involved with hours spent on choreography and practice. A giant monster was created and transported to the convention, but never made it to the stage. There was a giant box built inside which June would be brought onto the stage, thinking she would slip out the back. As soon as she entered the box, though, everyone on stage took their positions so that June could be led out and read the banner. June had worked with the decoy banner for the presentation (before it was switched backstage.) Ren told the masquerade director and even the con's guest of honor knew. The author didn't have a book coming out; it was a complete fabrication. The only people who didn't know were June, the audience, and June's best friend (everyone knew that he couldn't keep a secret). As June stated, "I have so many good friends, and they are all such accomplished liars."

When the (real) banner unfurled June said, "You ass. Yes." Then she really let Ren have it with a string of blue language that would have made a sailor blush. She unleashed death threats on everyone. "You're dead. You're dead. And you're dead," can be clearly heard on the masquerade tape. She made Ren promise that he would never interfere with a masquerade presentation again.

On May 4, 2001 – A Wedding Odyssey, as Written by Ren:

We wanted to have a science fiction-themed wedding but couldn't decide on a date until the obvious one presented itself. We mailed out the invitations with the wording: Formal dress from any time, place, or planet is encouraged but not required. A few days after the invitations were mailed, I received a phone call from my mother.

"Hi, I received your wedding invitation."

"Great, mom."

"Do you know where I can buy butterfly wings?"

"...Yes...Who is this?"

Taking my mother to Hot Topic is a story unto itself, but our wedding was just as happy and fun as we wanted. We were married by a Jedi. A Klingon was our photographer. June's dress and my jacket both included star fields. June's Man of Honor (Thom Truelove) wore a steampunk tuxedo. My Best Man (Mary Keefer) wore a tuxedo dress. We were married in front of a giant poster of the Earth as seen from the moon. Our wedding cake was a stack of Twinkies topped by two astronauts. Our guests came dressed as bikers, holograms, lounge lizards, Civil War soldiers, Starfleet officers, Kennedys, Brad and Janet, Ming the Merciless, and riverboat gamblers. Some wore kimonos, others wore saris, and many others joined us to celebrate.

June's father, however, was told in no uncertain terms by her mother that he was to wear his good blue suit to his daughter's wedding, which he did. During the reception, though, an astronaut with a big silver helmet entered the room and made the rounds, stopping at every table. He had a tape recorder with a recorded message to "talk" to people. Burning with curiosity, I finally scanned everyone in the room to see if I could determine if anyone was missing, and just as I realized who it was, June's father removed the helmet. June's oldest brother helped her father rent the costume and helped him sneak away to change so he could surprise us. Her mother wasn't pleased, but it was a lot of fun.

Pat Duff

On His Real-Life Job:

I've been an architect since graduating college in 1988.

On His Personal History:

I was born and raised in the college town of Columbia, Missouri. I am an identical twin. My parents were both raised on farms. My mom was born in the house she lived in with her parents on 160 acres until she got married just shy of age 20. My dad enlisted in the navy when he turned 18 (in January) and finished high school after being discharged.

My brother and I were both percussionists from 5th grade through high school and loved marching band.

I attended the University of Kansas School of Architecture. I spent a semester abroad in Denmark immediately following six weeks in Tokyo (with John Irvin).

I interned at an architecture firm in the D.C. metropolitan area in 1987, and then lived in Arlington, Virginia from 1988 to 1993. I volunteer as a tour guide at the Pope-Leighey house near Mount Vernon, Virginia. It was designed by Frank Lloyd Wright from 1987-1993

On His Introduction to Fandom and Conventions:

My brother and I started watching the animated *Star Trek* series when it premiered in 1973 (we were in 4th grade) and began watching the live action series a few months later (maybe early 1974). It was being shown at 10:15 p.m. on Saturday nights after the 15-minute local news. The first episode we saw was "Wolf in the Fold." The episodes were being aired completely uncut in production order. It required staying up past our traditional bedtime. Fortunately, it was Saturday, so that was possible. We began attending a weekly *Star Trek* club with grade school friends who'd told us about the live action version of the show. One of their older sisters had written a fan script and the plan was to eventually shoot it on 8-millimeter film.

Gene Roddenberry visited the University of Missouri in the spring of 1975 and spoke to a mostly college audience which also included myself and my brother at age 11. Roddenberry brought the blooper reels with him and finished his talk by introducing his black and white copy of "The Cage" (he said he couldn't afford a color one because he had to pay for it himself). His talk was very similar to what you would hear on the audio album *Inside Star Trek*. It was just over a year and half from when we started watching the show, and we'd seen its creator in person.

In 1976, a flyer was posted in our junior high announcing a *Star Trek* fan club meeting at the Columbia Public library. It was on September 7 or 9th, 1976 (either way, it missed the show's tenth anniversary by one day). The meeting was organized by a ninth-grade student in our junior high (we were in 7th grade) who we had never met before. His name was John Irvin.

In 1977, at the age of 12 (a month from turning 13), my brother and I attended a *Star Trek* convention in Kansas City, Missouri (a two-hour drive away!) with James Doohan, Nichelle Nichols and Jesco von Puttkamer. We'd told our parents we were going, so they drove us up and we stayed at our aunt's house. Our dad dropped us off in the morning and picked us up at night—we were unsupervised all day each day! There was supposed to be a full-size replica of the bridge which didn't quite materialize. Instead, there was only the captain's chair, helm, and railing. The movie theatre attached to the convention hotel was showing *Star Wars*.

On His Current Connection to Maryland Cons:

There may be witnesses to those occasions when my brother and I appeared as Data and Lore at Hunt Valley conventions in the early '90s when Brent was a guest, then sometime in the early 2000s, and again in 2013. After that, we officially retired the Data makeup.

In 2014, we attended Farragut Fest in Kingsland, Georgia and visited the replicated sets of the original *Star Trek* series. It was a completely mind-blowing experience and a life-long dream come true. I'd never really considered where the rooms really were in relation to each other. I obviously knew there was one corridor, but it never occurred to me that you could tell which set was behind something by the color of the door or which hallway configuration you were passing. I will always be eternally grateful to Starship Farragut, John Broughton, and Michael Bednar for that experience.

On Influential Media:

Dark Shadows, Star Trek, The Six Million Dollar Man, Man from Atlantis, Star Wars, Bosom Buddies, 21 Jump Street.

When *Dark Shadows* was cancelled, my brother and I wrote our local television station and received a letter back. We were 6 years old.

I remember as a young child being told that my mother used to write to Hollywood stars to get their autographs on postcards. Most were signed while some were reproduced. I don't remember ever seeing them and I thought they were lost to time or adulthood. I never thought about it during all my years of fandom, then I discovered them in 2016 after my mother passed. Somehow, it makes me feel that some level of fandom is hardwired in my DNA.

On His Time in Fandom:

45 years.

On *Star Trek* Outside of the Cons:

We met Richard Arnold through his mother at conventions in Missouri and visited the standing sets in the '80s. In the '90s, I hung out with Richard during a trip to Los Angeles while he was Gene's assistant. For a few hours, I answered the phone which meant picking it up and saying, "*Star Trek.*" The business of making television and movies always fascinated me.

We also visited several *Star Trek* filming locations from the series and movies. I went to an amazing park in Vancouver, Canada that I would have never seen unless it had appeared in *Star Trek Beyond.*

In February 2014, I went to Oklahoma City to be an extra in a fan film crossover of Starship *Valiant* and Starship *Ajax* called *Infinite Moon*. The film has never been released. I had visited their sets a couple years earlier when the bridge was completely stripped of viewscreens and buttons to be refinished. Even in its unfinished state, it was still an emotional experience to walk onto the bridge of a starship along with my mother and my ten-year-old son. I think my mom thought I was crazy when we drove up to a perceivably abandoned warehouse in Oklahoma City on the way back from Dallas and walked onto the bridge of the Starship *Enterprise*. In its darkened unlit state, it felt like walking onto the bridge of the *Defiant* in "The Tholian Web." We'd gone to Dallas to see Southfork, which my mom really enjoyed. They'd actually been shooting the new *Dallas* television show the day before we were there, so the exteriors were all dressed, and everything looked great.

In January 2016, my brother and I travelled to Kingsland, Georgia to be extras in Starship Farragut's *Homecoming* (long story) which premiered at Farpoint 2018.

On His Favorite Con Activities:

Nowadays, my favorite activity is seeing old friends.

On His Costuming Experiences:

As my brother and I are identical twins, Data and Lore from *Star Trek: The Next Generation* made obvious choices early in the run of that show, along with some reasonable resemblance of facial structure. We stood in the lobby of the Hunt Valley Inn all day at Shore Leave in 2013 dressed as Data and Lore.

On His Favorite Con Story:

I could probably go on forever, but seeing Brent Spiner when we were dressed as Data and Lore (twice, once in the early '90s and again in 2013) is a highlight. Other memorable experiences include riding an elevator with Patrick Stewart in Denver in 1988, John de Lancie's first convention at the Twin Bridge Marriott in D.C., Brent's first ever convention in New York in 1990, dinner with Mark Lenard, and dinner with Siddig el Fadil in St. Louis in 1994.

The emotional resonance of Hunt Valley now spans decades. I remember thinking, *Shore Leave X, these guys have been around forever.* Now, it has been over 40 years.

Seeing Walter Koenig and Grace Lee Whitney in Joplin, Missouri in 1978 straight from the set of *The Motion Picture* was memorable. They were making *Star Trek* again! A first in our time in fandom.

I loved seeing the trailer for *Star Trek II* in St. Louis in April 1982 before the movie came out in June.

Seeing Zachary Quinto in Denver with half his eyebrows shaved off in 2008 made you think that that is what it would have been like if you'd met Nimoy 1966-1969.

Ten years into attending conventions, I never thought I would get to see Mark Lenard. I finally saw him for the first time ever in Washington, D.C. in 1987, then several more times at cons in Baltimore, Maryland and Jefferson City, Missouri. He would always start his stage talk with a few corny jokes.

In February 2018, I went to St. Louis to see James Frain, who plays Sarek in *Discovery*. I decided it was my duty to pass Mark Lenard's jokes on to him. From memory, my brother and I jotted down a few of Mark's jokes. I printed them on a card and gave them to James Frain in the autograph line along with an explanation of their significance. James opened his talk that day with Mark Lenard's jokes. I'd felt I'd done my part in passing the torch of Mark Lenard and Sarek's legacies.

On His Favorite Person to Meet at a Con:

Marc Okrand, a friend for life.

Mark Lenard, Siddig El Fadil (a.k.a. Alexander Siddig), Colm Meaney, J.G. Hertzler. So many convention guests have been amazing down-to-earth people.

On His Favorite Con Guests:

There have been so many great ones. Will Wheaton is always amazing. Going to Baltimore and meeting people like Dennis Bailey,

Howard Weinstein, and Ann Crispin was unbelievable. Even more unbelievable was that they made meaningful contributions to *Star Trek* and would recognize my brother and I as we continued to attend conventions there. I never developed a fan network in Kansas City, even though I've been here for 24 years. Baltimore/D.C. is fan home base.

On Why He Attends Conventions:

I got to meet my heroes and listen to what they had to say about the shows. After seeing the primary casts, I always loved seeing the behind-the-scenes people.

On What People Don't Know About Him:

Hmmm. I'm a bit of a space buff (probably not a surprise), and I've seen many astronauts speak in person.

My son and I watched the original *Star Trek* series from start to finish after the 2009 film came out. He was seven then, and he's 16 now. He seemingly has some appreciation for this. I've never been prouder than when my son started marching band in high school. Aside from stirring up nearly 40-year-old memories of my own band experiences, he is unbelievably talented.

Phil Duff

On Elementary School:

I started watching the animated *Star Trek* series in 1973. Based on my fellow fourth graders saying at recess that you had to stay up late Saturday night to see the real actors, I started watching The Original Series (TOS) soon thereafter.

On Trek at Work:

People learn I'm a *Star Trek* fan. In a previous job, my coworker Shannon said "Phil, did you hear that? Travis has a question." Travis from IT jumped in and said, "Which is better, *Star Trek* or *Star Wars*?" I responded, "Look you guys, this is easy. I love *Star Wars*, but I *live my life* according to *Star Trek*."

On His Fan Friends:

In the early 1990s, Dennis Bailey generated the "How sick does this make us?" analysis of the things people in fandom do—like the partial bridge reconstruction in Dennis's basement, the number of phaser props someone owned, a sandwich bag full of wood chips from the original starship *Enterprise* filming model at the Smithsonian (saved from the early 90s restoration), or how far you would travel to an event. Most memorable was Dennis's post-mortem of a WHFS comedy club event where you could win a "You Klingon Bastard…" t-shirt. My brother and I drove for over an hour in pouring rain, and when we entered, Dennis and his group were already there. Dennis declared us 'sicker' because the comedy club was only five minutes from his house.

On His Job in Real Life:

I am an architect. I live in Seattle, Washington and work in Portland, Oregon three days each week. I work on primarily health care facilities including a new headquarters for Chase Brexton Health Services in Baltimore, Maryland. Chase Brexton was used as the filming location for "Slugline" on *House of Cards*. Last year, I recruited the 1977 president of the Columbia (Missouri) Star Trek Fan Club from Fort Meyers, Florida to be the CFO for the company I work for. *Star Trek* connections run deep.

On His Personal History:

I grew up in Columbia, Missouri. I am an identical twin. I have lived in Seattle for 19 years. *Star Trek* is my hobby.

On His Introduction to Fandom and Conventions:

The Columbia Star Trek Fan Club was founded in fall of 1976, with 3 goals—screen episodes, one I've forgotten, and attend conventions.

The club planned a trip to Star Trekkon '77 in Kansas City—120 miles away. Carpools were arranged for the weekend. Even at 12 years old, I recruited parents to drive and chaperone, assigning the members in four cars (cars were larger in the '70s) and calculating gas expenses per head. Another mom volunteered to drive at the last minute and busted our gas cost calculations. (We already had enough cars. Life lesson learned young: Plan all you want, life intervenes.) Everyone else stayed at the Rodeway Inn while my brother, my parents, and I stayed at our aunt and uncle's house to save the hotel cost.

It seems crazy now to think that my parents would drop two 12-year-olds off at a hotel convention center for an entire day. Most memorable for me were the older die-hard fans who adopted us and brought us in their fold, including Kay Johnson, Anna Hreha, Denny Arnold, and a dealer named Harry Friedenberg, to name a few. (Anna was the president of the Jimmy Doohan International Fan Club, and for a membership fee of $10, you could join a private party with Jimmy. Kay let us both join for the one fee.)

On His Times Spent with Marc Okrand:

While meeting Marc Okrand at the Hunt Valley in the late 80s, we determined my office on upper Connecticut Avenue in D.C. was within walking distance of his home, and his office at National Captioning Institute was close to the condo I shared with my brother in Arlington. As such, we established our respective residences as each other's snow emergency plans. We never invoked a snow emergency, but there were numerous happy hours and dinners based on whether something more interesting was happening in D.C. or Virginia. We had Monday night watch parties for the airings of *Star Trek: The Next Generation* on Channel 20. Marc would try to decipher the "Klingon." (TNG was known for pulling words out of the dictionary with less regard for grammar and pronunciation as the films for which Marc continues to develop the language.)

When Marc updated the Klingon Dictionary, Pat Duff listed all the TNG episodes that used Klingon words so Marc could include them, irrespective of how incorrectly they may have been used. In the update, Marc made up a word that is a combination of our first names with Klingon pronunciation that is spoken in *Star Trek VI* and a recent episode of *Discovery*. Hearing it on *Discovery*, 26 years after *Star Trek VI*, was crazy.

Marc also shares a story at conventions about the Vulcan in *Star Trek V* for "Is it you?" Apparently, screenwriter David Loughery approached Marc on the set and asked how "Qual es tu?" sounded as Vulcan for "Is it you?" On the spot, Marc said it was a little too Latin, and perhaps use "Qual se tu?" which is in the film. However, at conventions, Marc has noted that "dw" is a prominent sound in the Vulcan language and the phrase ideally should have been "Dwal se tu?" If you know the film, the phrase is spoken between brothers and to a god. Amongst a small group of die-hard fans (How sick does this make us?) we greet each other with "Dwal se tu?" under the retcon that "Qual" is a formal variant only used when addressing a brother or a god.

On Rightful Heir:

I met Jim Brooks at a New York convention through Richard Arnold and we became lifelong friends. At the time, Jim said he was working on his writing. My brother and I read a few of his draft scripts and told him he needed to go ahead and send something in to TNG. He did, and the reader loved it, but it was too similar to a story in production. Jim got invited to several pitch meetings and made the one TNG sale—"Rightful Heir" [Credited as James E. Brooks.] Similar story for Tim DeHaas's TNG sale "Identity Crisis."

On Doomsday:

The fun thing about hanging out with writers is they will write stuff. One day, Jim Brooks was on a tear about how so many scripts, shows, and fan productions wanted to revisit a *Star Trek* episode and the results were marginal at best. I said I'd like to see the hour of television before "The Doomsday Machine," and Jim said, "Man, I'd write that." The prequel script turned out to be amazing because Jim is an amazing writer. He has several fantastic unproduced TNG scripts and just finished a spot-on spec script for *The Orville*.

A year or so later, in the spring of 2016, I got off a plane in St. Louis and called a diehard *Trek* friend to let him know I was in the state. He told me he was in Kansas City (four hours away) because he was driving to Oklahoma City the next morning (5 more hours) to shoot test footage on the bridge set there. I asked *what* he was shooting, and he said they were just doing test set ups. I told him I'd meet him in the morning (after driving 4 hours) to jump in his car, and I'd have a script with me—"Doomsday." We shot the teaser that day on no notice, and he edited it in the next few days, including looping dialogue due to bad in-camera sound.

On Media that has Been Influential to His Life in Fandom:

The Original Series.

The Making of *Star Trek*, *The Starfleet Technical Manual*, and *The Enterprise Blueprints* by Franz Joseph (which I'm sure is related to my being an architect today).

The AMT model kit of the *Enterprise*. It had all the decals of the original Constitution class starships, but seriously, who was going to ever put anything but "NCC-1701" and "Enterprise" on that model? Later in college, my brother and I got a Missouri personalized license plate "1701-D" (TNG had just aired and my last name is **D**uff.)

Spock influenced my life.

By 7th grade, I had a commercially available *Star Trek* uniform top from a store at the mall called Golde's (like a Macy's). It was blue with the insignia and black knit color. It had no braid, and erroneously also had black knit cuffs. I wore it to junior high school on the first Thursday of every month (the day of the Columbia *Star Trek* Fan Club meetings).

At the Missouri Conventions in the late '70s, Denny Arnold changed my life when she introduced me to her son, Richard Arnold, who was Gene's assistant on the Paramount lot.

I toured the sets of *Star Trek* several times, starting in 1985 after *Star Trek III* was filmed, then again during the shooting of the courtroom scene in *Star Trek IV* in 1986. During one of my visits to the TNG sets in 1988, I watched the filming of the episode "Conspiracy."

Of the *Star Trek* novels, I enjoyed *The Entropy Effect*, *Black Fire*, and *Yesterday's Son*

On His Years in Fandom:

45 years

On Starship Farragut:

In August of 2015, John Broughton of Starship Farragut posted on Facebook that they were looking for a location in the metro D.C. area to serve as the home of the captain's mother in their final episode "Homecoming." Although I've lived in Seattle for 16 years, I was once a Northern Virginia resident, and as an architect, I racked my brain to think of something significant and posted a photo of a Frank Lloyd Wright house in Northern Virginia for which I had worked as a volunteer guide 22 years earlier. From there, several weeks of negotiations ensued. The director didn't think he could work under the restrictions set by the National Trust for Historic Preservation, and the Trust (at least initially) didn't see the value of letting a film crew use the house. I appealed to everyone as a fan of *Star Trek* and an architect that the shoot and the architectural significance were complementary. Farragut shot at the house for two days that fall, and as a result, my brother and I traveled to Kingsland, Georgia in January 2016 to serve as background extras for the scenes shot on the starship sets. Another dream come true.

Subsequently, I spent a weekend in May 2017 as an extra in *Walking Bear, Running Wolf* shot at Dogpatch USA (also a dream come true) in a Farragut tunic and pants.

On His Desire to Direct:

Starting in 2011, a group called 'Hello Earth' started producing *Outdoor Trek* in an amphitheater each summer in Seattle—an original series episode adapted for the stage. They could tell I was a fan because I kept coming back and the next year, I played a hoe-wielding colonist in "This Side of Paradise."

In 2016, their director wanted to take a break, and I stepped in and directed "Space Seed" in celebration of the 50th anniversary of *Star Trek*. The actors for Kirk and Spock are the same every year and have it down, but we cast Khan and Marla. They were both new to the production, and it was a blast working with them on the episode.

There's a particular scene in the TV episode that I've always loved, where Kirk leans up on the rail by Spock's station. Nicholas Meyer replicates it for a scene in *Star Trek II*. However, in the amphitheater, we didn't have the railing, so we pulled off a *West Wing* walk and talk. Instead of the corridors of the White House, Kirk and Spock circulated through the audience.

We gave Marla a *Star Trek II* style belt buckle to setup Khan's neck medallion in the 1982 film. We also dropped in scenes from the shooting script that had never aired until the release of "The Roddenberry Vault" DVD a few months later. Anton Yelchin had just died, and we dragged out a chair for the navigator in every single bridge scene in the episode but left it empty. R.I.P., Anton. I still hope to produce "Doomsday" in that amphitheater.

On His Favorite Con Activities:

I enjoy seeing guests become truly engaged with the audience during their talks.

On His Favorite Question:

This is related to a Zach Quinto appearance in Denver in 2008. I mentioned that *Time* magazine had run an article listing the ten unintended beneficiaries of the writers' strike, and Zach said, "Was I number one?" Unfortunately, he wasn't mentioned, but Zach went on to tell the story that in order to do *Star Trek* (2009), he had to negotiate out of *Heroes*. Due to the writers' strike, his last episode of *Heroes* ended up being *the* last episode shot that season so he did not miss any episodes of *Heroes*.

On His Costuming Experiences:

Data and Lore brought the house down in Atlanta, and my brother and I were invited to ride in a NewsChopper over Stone Mountain. After retiring Data, and later acquiring a Starship Farragut screen-worn sciences uniform, I was coerced by Jim Brooks to go to Duran's in LA to get measured for 2 pairs of custom authentic boots. Duran's made boots for the original series. They are still there today, and they take enough measurements to fit you with a bionic limb, including tracing your foot. Why two pairs? Because some things just happen that way when you are an identical twin. The sequel to "How sick does this make us?" is when your fandom friends drag you into stuff you would *never* have done yourself. I don't need authentic boots, but if Jim Brooks says I do, apparently, I do.

On His Favorite Con Story:

Sleeping with Grace Lee Whitney.

Just kidding, but Grace Lee was *crazy*. We saw her in 1978 in Joplin, Missouri and again at Star Trekkon '80 in Kansas City just short of our 16th birthday. On stage, with a microphone, Grace Lee said "The twins are here! Hi, guys." Then she looked at the audience and said, "They're getting to be about the right age." We were naïve midwestern boys, but to have Grace Lee remember you at a convention from one year to the next was just nuts.

On His Favorite Guests to Meet at Cons:

Most recently, Nick Meyer was a blast. In the mid-90s, Siddig El Fadil. In the late 80s, Bill Theiss was wonderful. Mark Lenard was sublime in Jefferson City, Missouri in the 90s. Connor Trineer killed it in Portland when his family showed up. Patrick Stewart commanded the room in Denver in 1988. After less than a full season of shooting, he mentioned that when he read each script, his reaction was, "Relva VII? Haven't we been there before?"

DeForest Kelly was amazing. Specifically, when on stage, he would note that McCoy entered Starfleet after a bitter divorce. Harve Bennett was amazing, too. Ralph Winter talked about interviewing "Oingo Boingo" for *Star Trek IV* but went with the Yellowjackets for the jazz riff. [Translation: Ralph *almost* hired Danny Elfman to do film work before *anyone else did*.] Bob Justman was great.

On Why He Attends Conventions:

Live your life according to *Star Trek*.

There's a story about my current coffee shop. People kept telling me I should check out this geeky coffee shop less than a block away from where I was buying coffee. For a couple of years, I deflected these requests, but when my coffee shop temporarily closed, I thought, *Aw, hell. I guess I'm going up the street.*

I walked in and on their chalkboard menu, there's a drawing of the *Enterprise*. I took a photo and posted it to Facebook with the caption, "Things are looking up."

Flash forward to a clip of Mike Sussman on *The Roddenberry Vault* release a few years later. He shows a little doodle on lined paper of the mighty starship, like we all drew a thousand times on notebook paper in grade school, and comments, "The *Enterprise* is here, things are looking up." It's true. The *Enterprise* spreads hope.

The feeling you get from a *Star Trek* rich environment is like no other. Dwal se tu?

On What People May Not Know About Him:

I'm an open book. That said, it's probably how much time I spend with my 12-year-old daughter, who doesn't actually watch the show. I gotta work on that.

I got married at Yosemite because of *Star Trek V: The Final Frontier*. My wife is from California, so the second she suggested Yosemite, I pounced. John Irvin and Pat Duff were groomsmen, as well as Marc Okrand. My wife's brother could not make the wedding because of a work commitment, so Marc filled in for him and read a letter from my brother-in-law to my wife while standing on a chair. (They are nowhere near the same height.) I have never seen Marc so nervous than when he was reading someone else's words, and he did a fantastic job. People littered the reception hall with tribbles.

In the early 2000s, my father platted a subdivision. There are now people living on a street in Holts Summit, Missouri with an address on "Kirk Drive."

Lisa Sponaugle

On Her Real-Life Job and Personal History:

I work as a full-time professional actor for commercials, film, and TV. I also do lifestyle modeling. Previously, I was a medical news editor and reporter. I live in Germantown, MD and have been married to Patrick Sponaugle for 19 years. We have one daughter, Grace, who is a senior in high school, and we all spend a lot of time taking care of two dogs, two cats, and a guinea pig. My hobbies include reading, yoga, cooking, and spending inordinate amounts of time watching TV.

On Her Introduction to Fandom and Conventions:

I was introduced to fandom by finding several science fiction books in the library when I was 13, as well as *The World of Star Trek* by David Gerrold. Mr. Gerrold's book prompted me to write my first fan letter. He kindly replied with a form letter listing upcoming conventions, which is how I learned about the 1974 Worldcon in Washington, D.C. It was the first con I ever attended and I've been a fan ever since. That was 44 years ago. During that time, I have been connected to conventions in many ways. I've been a guest, a panelist, a costumer, a committee member, acted in several plays at Balticon, Farpoint and Shore Leave, and was chair of a science fiction convention at the University of Maryland.

On Co-Writing a Star Trek Script:

In 1989, I worked on a script—together with lead writers Dennis Russell Bailey and David Bischoff—for *Star Trek: The Next Generation*. The episode was entitled "Tin Man." Being involved with that show was a joyful experience, particularly as we were invited to visit the set while our episode was filmed and even got the chance to see some dailies screened in Gene Roddenberry's office! I have always enjoyed sharing my experience working on the show on panels at conventions, but also in later panels about a variety of topics, most recently about *Game of Thrones* and how to get started in the local film and TV industry.

On Acting in Convention Plays:

Regarding my favorite roles in the convention plays, two stand out—Lisa Douglas/Deanna Troi in Klingon Acres, which was a play I collaborated on and performed in with my favorite acting partner, Pat, who played the part of Oliver Douglas/Worf. My other favorite was Boomer, in the *Battlestar Galactica* parody, Battlestar Gargleblaster.

On Influential Media and People:

I have several influences in fandom, and chief among them are Harlan Ellison and Gene Roddenberry, both of whom I was fortunate to meet in person and see speak several times. I admired Harlan because of his honesty, ferocity in defending right vs. wrong, and his eloquent creativity. Gene is a big influence due to his visionary strength in depicting a beautiful, tolerant future at a time when it was nearly illegal to do so. Of all the science fiction shows I love, *Star Trek* has been most influential in my life, sparking my interest in writing, performing, and creating. The ideals of the original series have helped me form a core philosophy of tolerance and appreciation of diversity that has guided my whole life.

On Raising Her Daughter in Fandom:

Raising our daughter to love science fiction has been mostly successful though her interests somewhat diverge from mine, as she is drawn to superhero movies more than hard science fiction. She shares her father's appreciation of fantasy, enjoying *Game of Thrones* and the *Lord of the Rings* movies. When she was very young, conventions were always a safe, entertaining space for her, which I really appreciated.

On Her Favorite Con Activities:

My favorite convention activities locally usually involve socializing with people I rarely get to see on a regular basis, so local conventions tend to be more like a party! In general, I love seeing the main speakers talk, watching costume contests, and looking for more merchandise (as if my house isn't already bursting with it).

On Her Favorite Con Story:

My favorite convention story is the time I interviewed Michael Dorn for Majel Barrett's *Star Trek* newsletter. She was publishing it through Lincoln Enterprises, the company that she and Gene created to sell *Trek* related merchandise. I interviewed Michael at a small convention in Arlington, and he was delightful and kind. The interview was conducted early during the filming of the second season of *ST: TNG*. I was fortunate enough a month later to be invited by a friend who worked with the production to visit the set. While I was there, I reconnected with Michael and he invited me to his trailer while his Worf makeup was applied (he was bored and needed company). I declined because in those pre-cell phone days, I had no way to reach my friend who was somewhere else on the lot. I still regret turning down the invite!

On Her Favorite Convention Guest:

When selecting a favorite convention guest, it's impossible to come up with one. I have to say my two favorites were at my first convention, the Worldcon in Washington, D.C. in 1974—Harlan Ellison and Isaac Asimov. They had a joint speech/insult contest that may have been the wildest thing I'd witnessed at that point. The lightning quick humor and timing they both possessed then is reminiscent of Robin Williams in his prime.

On Something People May Not Know About Her:

One thing that only a very few convention friends or acquaintances know or remember is that in 1975, I asked Gene Roddenberry an unexpected question. I was part of a small group from the University of Maryland *Star Trek* club, meeting with him after his talk about *Star Trek*. He pulled out a tape recorder and asked us what we would like to see in a new *Star Trek* film. I inquired whether it would be possible to include a black Vulcan character. This was four years before *Star Trek: Motion Picture* was released and twenty years before the first black Vulcan appeared on television in *Star Trek: Voyager*.

Patrick Sponaugle

On His Real-Life Job

I'm basically a code monkey. I graduated with a bachelor's degree in computer science, which launched me on a software engineering career.

On His Personal History

I grew up in Virginia and moved to Maryland right after college. I'm married and have lived in my current residence in Germantown, MD for nearly 20 years. My wife Lisa (also a science fiction fan) and I have a lovely daughter and are currently blessed with two cats and two dogs. (Our daughter also has a guinea pig.)

I think my most active hobby at the moment is either walking our youngest dog or supporting my wife's acting career by helping her memorize lines and being her cameraman for taped auditions. When I'm not doing that, I try to write. Maybe one day I'll write a book, but at the moment, I'm either writing for my pretentious blog or feature articles for Watchers on the Wall fan site (which is focused on HBO's *Game of Thrones* television show.)

I used to practice martial arts, but to be honest, I haven't been active like that in nearly two decades.

On His Introduction to Fandom:

This is a complicated question, because I'm not sure what fandom really means. I didn't attend my first science fiction convention until I was 22, but I was a fan of the genre before that. I didn't necessarily engage with other people about science fiction or fantasy novels, unless you include playing tabletop role-playing games in high school (when Dungeons & Dragons made its way into the national consciousness.)

It could be said that my introduction to fandom on a personal level occurred when I saw the original *Star Wars* in 1977 (when Han Solo shot Greedo first. Believe it.), but that doesn't seem sufficient, I guess? I became a *Star Wars* fan, but I don't think that puts me in *Star Wars* fandom. I suppose that didn't happen until ten years later when I became friends with people who regularly went to science fiction conventions and participated in many fandom-related activities. That's probably my true introduction to fandom—meeting to a group of fans who embraced it as a lifestyle. This is my personal definition, other people's mileage and definition may vary, and their perspective is valid as well. Vive la différence!

On His Introduction to Conventions:

In high school, I read science fiction novels, and at some point, I picked up the Illustrated Roger Zelazny paperback, which included some of Zelazny's short stories—illustrated—along with artwork inspired by his epic Amber books. This sparked my interest in reading the first Amber book, *Nine Princes in Amber*, and eventually I tracked down all five books in the series. (Zelazny went on to write a second five-book series in the *Amber* universe, but the original chronicles are the best.)

At the end of college, I heard that Roger Zelazny was going to be the guest of honor at Balticon, a science fiction convention in Baltimore. A friend of a friend from Baltimore was going to the convention and I was invited into the group. It was my first exposure to a big (to me) convention hotel experience.

On His Years in Fandom:

Even though *Star Wars* made a big impression on me in 1977, it wasn't until 1987 when I went to my first Balticon, and made friends with the convention crowd. So if we do the math from then until this writing, it would be 31 years.

On His Current Fame/Connection to Fandom:

Fame is kind of a strong word. At the local conventions, I'm known for supporting the costume masquerade as a ninja, someone who is available to help out contestants in various ways—sometimes wrangling their props before or after their presentation, sometimes making sure they can safely exit the stage if their costumes limit their vision (the masquerades have people in place at the front of the stage who ensure this. They're the real support for this.). Since my frequent co-ninja, Dan, and I dress as ninja, we're often asked to represent a generic villainous opponent in a costume presentation, which requires us to die on stage, dramatically. So, I guess I'm known for loudly falling down.

Otherwise, people like my *Game of Thrones* essays, and that secured me an invitation to present at the 2017 Con of Thrones in Nashville, and then again in 2018 at Con of Thrones in Dallas. I've been invited to talk *Game of Thrones* on podcasts and have garnered a small following thanks to my blog.

On His Fandom Influences:

My seventh grade English teacher, Mister Shaw, alerted me that this movie called *Star Wars* was coming out in the summer and that I should probably see it. (I'd written a science fiction story for class. I don't remember much of the plot, but I know that it wasn't worth remembering.) *Star Wars* had a big impact on my impressionable brain. Inspired, I started reading science fiction books, notably *Ringworld* and *Dune*. I hadn't watched much of the original *Star Trek* television series, but I'd read all of the James Blish novelizations.

In college, my friend Steve loaned me all of his Roger Zelazny books to read, since he saw me with Zelazny's *Amber* books. (The Virginia Tech bookstore had a fair science fiction paperback section, and it picked up the last two books in Zelazny's first *Amber* chronicles.) Since Zelazny being a guest of honor at Balticon was one of the reasons I went, I credit Steve for helping nurture my interest in this author and my interest in science fiction fandom.

On His Con Jobs:

Being a costume ninja is probably the closest thing to a real convention job. I've never worked with planning, security, guest relations, public relations, information, or set up. However, back when the Sunday Showcase was a thing at Farpoint and Shore Leave, I remember sticking around to help break down the main stage.

On the Stage Ninja Origin Story:

I might not recall the full details correctly. Nowadays, the stage ninja are an expected part of the masquerade at Shore Leave and Farpoint, but it wasn't always that way. Yes, there were always support personnel for wrangling props or helping people off stage. But around twenty years ago—I can't remember at which convention this first took place—there was pressure to combat a trend in people putting on extremely long presentations. The costume contest rules usually specified a time limit on individual presentations, but for several years in a row, people were performing well over the time limit, which extended the masquerade and didn't benefit the presenters. I think points were automatically deducted for going over to encourage tight, focused presentations.

In a nod to the Gong Show, the costume contest entrants were warned that if their presentations went overlong, the stage ninja would deal with it—and we did. Dan and I, dressed like ninja, would come out and stand in front of the presentation as a passive indication that the costumers were being given the old Vaudeville hook procedure. This might not have been the most sensitive way to address the issue, but it worked. On successive masquerades, the amount of overlong presentations dropped dramatically. We've not had to intervene in a presentation in probably fifteen years, thankfully. These days, the stage ninja's role is to support the costumers.

On Cheap Treks Shows:

Earlier, I mentioned the Sunday Showcase, where the final hours of the convention were typically filled with a humorous parody of our favorite science fiction shows (we did a lot of *Trek* parodies.) One group that perpetuated that tradition was called Cheap Treks, and I was fortunate enough to be a part of many of the early performances. My favorite roles were typically ones where I didn't have many spoken lines but was required to fall down often. I'm not really a good actor, but I'm appropriately affected by gravity. My favorite role was probably the Klingon version of Aunt Bea from *The Andy Griffith Show*. No other context will be provided.

On His Blog and the Game of Thrones:

I originally hadn't planned on blogging about *Game of Thrones* when I started. Back in 2013, I started writing long movie reviews on Facebook. I think I just had way too much time on my hands one weekend. A buddy of mine complained that the long reviews were blowing up the Facebook app on his phone. He suggested that if I was going to be so long-winded, I should do so on WordPress, because it's free and I could bloviate to my heart's content. So, I did. I wrote a few movie reviews and a post about Ned Stark (if you don't know who that is, Ned was a character on *Game of Thrones*, played by Sean Bean.) I didn't know that millions of people were writing about *Game of Thrones* on Reddit, but I was making friends via WordPress with people who were writing about *Game of Thrones*, or who liked what I'd written. So I took it as a blogging challenge to write an essay or feature every 1 to 2 weeks about the show. (It was mostly as therapy in-between seasons.)

Over the years, I've been exposed to more and more people who have solid foundations and a following based on their *Game of Thrones* analysis on Reddit or YouTube or their own blogs that were better marketed than mine (I was not really smart on that). It's been gratifying to be treated like a peer based on my body of work.

On Introducing His Daughter to Fandom:

Fandom wasn't something that I wanted to push on her, because I didn't want it to be something that she rebelled against. "No father, I won't see the next *Avengers* movie!" So Lisa and I were deliberately low-key in our influence. We've been lucky that the Marvel movies were so fun and fortunate that *The Force Awakens* provided the character of Rey as a protagonist. My daughter identified with her the way I (as a whiny teen) identified with Luke Skywalker and his penchant for staring at the sunset with longing. But we let her find the things she wants to interact with. She's old enough now to know what she likes and doesn't like.

On the Fandom Person Who Has Changed His Life:

I met my wife, Lisa, via our group of convention friends. That feels sufficiently life-changing.

On His Favorite Con Activities:

When I was younger, I went to the panels. Now, I mostly hang out in the public spaces to mingle with friends and acquaintances. Conventions nowadays are all about re-uniting with people that I haven't seen in a while.

On His Favorite Con Story:

One year, Lisa and I brought our infant daughter to a Farpoint along with our friends' two sons, Jason and Alex. They were both either tweens or low teens, and we were playing the part of quasi-aunt and uncle in taking them to a convention. They were going to help babysit our daughter. During that weekend, it snowed so heavily that the highways were shut down. No one was escaping the hotel, including the celebrity guests. On Monday, there was another day of programming and the stars of *Alien Nation* hosted an impromptu panel for the convention goers. I don't think they were compensated, and of course they didn't have to do that.

On His Favorite Con Guest:

Felicia Day, at another Farpoint. She was incredibly sweet to our daughter (that would be my daughter with Lisa - I don't have a daughter with Felicia Day) and told her to listen to Lisa when it came to Lisa wanting our daughter to practice music lessons, or whatever.

On Why He Attends Conventions:

I had a fantastic time at the very first convention I attended. Everyone I met was engaged and accepting. It was transformative and showed that there were a lot of people who shared my interests, which provided a sense of community. Attending conventions rekindles that feeling of community.

Ariel Vitali

On His Real-Life Job:

I'm a board-certified psychiatrist, with sub-specialty training in Child and Adolescent Psychiatry.

On His Personal History:

I was born in Puerto Rico, but my dad brought our family to the Los Angeles area when I was a toddler. I'm very much an Orange County kid and still put direct articles in front of highway numbers. I could probably navigate the Los Angeles freeway system blindfolded, but that would not be a safe thing to do.

I've lived in various parts of the country over the years, mostly in California, but also eight years in New England and many years in the mid-Atlantic. I also spent some time in Texas. I'm tired of moving and I like being in Maryland.

I live southwest of Baltimore with my wife Terry. We've been together since 2001 and were married in 2006. We've both been married previously. I have two daughters from my first marriage, both adults now. Anya is pursuing a doctorate degree, and Sarah is going to graduate college very soon. They're both in New England with their mother.

On the side, I love tinkering with computers. I'm a big Apple fan, so I work mostly with Macs. I am also an amateur musician, playing trombone for a local concert band. I've become an avid player of board games since moving to Maryland (nerdy ones like Splendor, Catan and of course, Cards Against Humanity), and have been a mouse-and-keyboard gamer for decades. I play mostly Western-style RPGs such as Guild Wars and Diablo 3. I used to play World of Warcraft on a regular basis, but there's no time for that. It would be nice to get back into playing pen-and-paper RPGs. I enjoy science-fiction and some high fantasy and I tend toward media-oriented material. My favorites include *Star Trek, Star Wars,* Wizarding World (*Harry Potter*), *Battlestar Galactica, Middle-Earth, The Expanse,* and *A Song of Ice and Fire/Game of Thrones.*

Even though I'm pushing 50, I still read comic books. I read exclusively DC, but I do like the Marvel movies. My favorite superheroes are Green Lantern (both Hal Jordan and Jessica Cruz), The Flash (Barry Allen), Wonder Woman, and Spider-Man (Peter Parker, I'm not too familiar with Miles Morales). Terry eventually turned me around to Aquaman, her favorite. I'm also very much into the *Supergirl* TV series. Maybe one of the convention committees could invite Melissa Benoist or Chyler Leigh (hint!).

I am also a lifelong baseball fan. Except for a brief flirtation with the New York Mets, I've remained a True Blue Fan of the Los Angeles Dodgers. I won't hesitate to root for the Los Angeles Angels of Anaheim—given that they are sort of the hometown team—but it's still the Dodgers all the way for me, even though they haven't won a World Series since 1988. Maybe this year. Shortly after we started dating, Terry got me into watching professional football again and while I remain a Los Angeles Chargers fan at heart, the Philadelphia Eagles rule the roost at our home. I enjoy college football more, but it's very hard to find a televised Ivy League or UCLA football game where I live. Even a Temple game is hard to find.

I enjoy many things Disney and have a love/fear relationship with them. The Mouse pervades culture and politics where I grew up, but fear because have you seen how much it costs to go to a Disney park these days? Disneyland was just there for the visiting (which I've done countless times) and there would be very little doubt we would be regulars there. I specify "Disneyland" as my point of reference even though I'm an East Coaster now. I've been to Walt Disney World no more than four or five times.

On His Introduction to Fandom:

With regard to organized fandom, I didn't get into it until my early 30s. I had moved to a strange city and wanted to make friends. I got word of a *Star Trek* fan club that was recruiting members and became curious since it would be easy to make friends based on common interests. Before 2000, I believed going to cons or joining a fan club was "crossing a line," whatever that "line" was, but life is short and social contact is and was important. If I didn't like it, I could always quit.

On His Introduction to Conventions:

I had high school friends who attended cons in the late 80s/early 90s, but I didn't give any thought to joining them, again thinking and fearing I was going to cross the line into moving from "fan" to "fanatic." How about I blame that on the SNL "Get a Life!" skit that Shatner did way back when?

Shortly after joining the USS Northstar, that *Trek* club I referred to earlier, some friends on the ship took me to the New York Comic-Con, which I enjoyed very much. I think my second con was Grand Slam in Pasadena, California. This was a huge *Star Trek* convention that I attended not long after moving back (for a brief time) to California. That is when I took a bigger step into a larger world.

On His Years in Fandom:

Since October 20, 2000. That was the day I joined the USS Northstar.

On His Medical Perspective of Cons:

It's a whole other world there. I'm one of no more than a handful of physicians (that I know of) in my con scene. The only connection to medicine is getting to meet a favorite TV doctor. There have been a couple of occasions over the years when I responded to some acute situation, but for the most part, I'm off the clock during conventions. There was one exception at a Farpoint, where a friend of mine needed to go to a local hospital because she was falling ill. My reaction to a possible medical situation is just part of my training. I can't and won't change that. It's what I do.

On His Current Connection to Cons:

I have my group of core friends and various acquaintances. I've befriended many of the authors who attend Farpoint and Shore Leave and am known by those cons' respective organizers.

I've started moderating panels over the past five or six years. I usually do something ad hoc, if SFI is hosting their panels. I've been pulled aside to participate in panels related to *Doctor Who, Deep Space Nine, TOS,* and possibly one or two about DC films. I've been one of the go-to *Star Trek: Discovery* people since that show came on. The one panel that people associate with me is the one I've done for several years, where I mash-up Jo Rowling's *Wizarding World* with my background in psychology. There's not much medically related in that universe, so I took another tack. I did this panel in my Ravenclaw-styled Hogwarts uniform. I've done this panel at Farpoint and PotterVerse and finally, at Shore Leave in 2018. It was a good send-off because I needed to find something new to talk about.

On Influential People and Media:

As far as *Star Trek,* I'm like many others reading this who watched it with a parent or two. I'm too young to have caught *TOS* in its first run, so I watched it with my dad when it was in syndication (I think it was on KTLA-TV, Channel Five, Los Angeles).

One movie that stands out is *The Empire Strikes Back* because I basically nagged my family into seeing it. We waited about three hours in line on opening weekend. I won't spoil what happened.

As far as other TV shows, the only show standing that I ever saw in its entire first run was the original *Battlestar Galactica.*

Regarding books, it took me three tries to finally get through *Dune.* I was 17 when it finally happened. That was a world that I envisioned in my head, and it looked nothing like what David Lynch put up on the screen.

On StarFleet:

I'm currently a member of the USS Richthofen, based in Glen Burnie, MD. I've been a member of that "ship" for almost three years. My wife and I met on the USS Angeles back in late 2001 and have been on quite a few ships and stations since we've been together. I've been Chief Medical Officer on the Northstar and Angeles and do some behind-the-scenes work for others at a Regional level, as well as assisting in moderating a STARFLEET-related Group on Facebook.

On Karaoke at the Cons:

Nerve-wracking. I have some stage experience, but those old nerves still show themselves. I can carry a tune, for sure, and I'm somewhat of a perfectionist. I want to get a song as right as possible. Once the nerves settle, I'm rolling—most of the time. I enjoy challenging myself on occasion. One of my friends called "Despacito" the "Mount Everest of karaoke," but that's only if you don't understand or speak Spanish. I climbed that summit—twice so far—and lived to tell the tale. I do my best to stay within my range. It doesn't go so well at times.

On His Favorite Con Activities:

Well, there's karaoke. And for me, especially the past six or so years, cons have been more about being with friends who I don't get to see the rest of the year. It's a feeling of "old home week." I'm not really into collecting autographs, but there's usually one or two people who compel me to wait in line. Waiting in long lines is something I do not enjoy at all. I'm too impatient for that.

I'd like to do more cosplay because it's fun just being in costume outside of Halloween. I just haven't gotten around to doing more outfits. One of these days, I'll get my Jedi robes.

On His Con Recollections:

There are so many, but three specific events stand out, and all of them involve Shore Leave.

One time, I saw two young women cosplaying Anna and Elsa from *Frozen*, and they nailed it. I saw them walking down the corridor at one point during the second day and right behind the Queen and the Princess was this little girl, about four years old. She was just staring in awe at Anna and Elsa, as if they had just jumped out of the screen to be with this little fan. It struck a chord with me, seeing how incredibly cute it was and how this little girl was just lost in joy. And the two women just got into the roles and made this child's month. I've seen similar such moments at Disneyland, but there was something about this occasion that put a smile on my face.

The second event happened at Shore Leave 32 in 2010. It was the first time I met cast members from the *Battlestar Galactica* reimagining. That year, we had Edward James Olmos (Admiral William Adama) and Katee Sackhoff (Kara "Starbuck" Thrace, the Harbinger of Doom). Not only was Mr. Olmos surprised that I remembered him from an early stage performance, but later that weekend, I sat in the hotel bar with them. A small crowd had gathered to watch World Cup football. I sat on the side rooting for Germany while Katee and Eddie were rooting for Uruguay. We just started chatting about life in general, life in Southern California. I also told myself, *do not talk Battlestar right now. Just make small talk.* There was some mild smack back and forth related to football, but we all had fun in the end—and Germany beat Uruguay.

The third, ironically, occurred at a Shore Leave that I wasn't able to attend. Terry and I had to cancel at the last minute because I was admitted to the hospital for an inflamed gall bladder. I was recovering from my cholecystectomy over Shore Leave weekend and was upset because I would not be able to see my friends—or see Marina Sirtis, who I'd met once at a con in New Jersey. About six days after my surgery, our friend Zan Rosin came to our home to deliver a huge get-well card signed by our friends, acquaintances, and maybe a couple of actors. She also brought "Flat Terriel" (Terriel has been our joint nickname since the Angeles days) and showed us pictures with those at the con. That was a thoughtful consolation for not being able to participate in Shore Leave shenanigans.

On Favorite Con Guests:

Well, it's always a treat to see those whom I call "the usual suspects." Those are the regular authors who appear at almost every con I attend, including Keith DeCandido, Bob Greenberger, Mike Friedman, Peter David, Glenn Hauman, Phil Giunta, Sue Reilly, and the rest of the crew. Sometimes even Dayton Ward and Kevin Dilmore will show their mugs, and that's a good thing. By the way, I *still* owe Dayton a drink.

Some of my favorite actors over the years include Katee Sackhoff, Tricia Helfer, and Edward James Olmos from *Battlestar Galactica*; Saul Rubinek, Eddie McClintock, and Allison Scagliotti from *Warehouse 13*; Rob Paulsen ("Pinky" from *Pinky and the Brain*); Neil Grayston from *Eureka*; Jane Wiedlin of The Go-Go's (high school crush); John Billingsley (Dr. Phlox from *Star Trek: Enterprise*) and his wonderful wife, Bonnie Friedericy; Mike and Denise Okuda; Jonathan Frakes and Marina Sirtis from *TNG*; Kate Mulgrew, aka the awesome Captain Janeway of the *USS Voyager*; Aron Eisenberg from *Deep Space Nine*; I could go on.

One guest whom I didn't expect to enjoy was Amanda Tapping. It's not that I didn't like her, which I do. I'm just not much of a *Stargate* fan. My wife knows her from *Sanctuary*. What a classy and kind person she was.

A note about John Billingsley and Bonnie Friedericy—they are two degrees removed from Terry and me. One of our Los Angeles friends works for them. He and his husband sometimes get together for dinner with John and Bonnie. I could imagine all of us having dinner every now and then, if we had stayed in California.

On Why He Attends Cons:

Conventions are one of my most important social outlets. My wife and I look forward to every Shore Leave and Farpoint. I pick out those two because those are just part of the seasons for us. We haven't gone together to PotterVerse yet, and we still have to get to Regeneration Who, Balticon and some of the ones like in Frederick. Neither of us is a fan of the larger cons. They're too crowded. For example, I attended Philly Wizard World once and that was enough for me. I went to NYCC when there were only still a few thousand attendees. I'll enjoy San Diego Comic-Con, BlizzCon, and DragonCon from the comfort of my social media feeds.

On Someone Who Has Made a Lasting Impression:

I'd have to say those in our con-related social circle. Just the fact that they rallied to do Flat Terriel is something I will never forget. I see con members often rallying to help sick friends or to memorialize those who passed away since the last gathering.

On Something People Don't Know About Him:

I used to surf and snowboard, but it has been a while since I did either one of those things. For those who remember where I went to school, I never expected to land there in a million years. I applied to Dartmouth (and Brown) for laughs, just to see if I would be accepted into one Ivy League medical school. I was too scared to even consider a place like Harvard or Cornell. I expected to end up somewhere like UCLA or UC Davis (near Sacramento), especially once UC Irvine rejected my application. I ended up getting into a few schools including UC Davis, University of Wisconsin-Madison—and Dartmouth. It was the tempting financial aid package that finally sealed my fate. That was a bitter pill, and no Mexican restaurants within almost three hours of where I was.

Martha Sayre

What do you do in real life?

I am a craft instructor for Michaels Stores.

Give a brief personal history

I am a former French teacher, and for 20 years, I was an HIV and STD counselor for Baltimore County, MD. I was born in Uniontown, PA, and moved to Hagerstown, MD when I was six years old. My father was in the hotel business, and I attended Frostburg State College (now Frostburg State University).

Junior year i studied in Rouen, France and lived with a French family. I graduated college, married my first husband and moved to Baltimore, MD. I have one son, Ian Bonds. I married Jan Sayre in 1996, and he passed away in 2003.

What else do I put? There's a lot of history!

Ian is a musician and an actor. I met Jan Sayre through fandom. My fandom friend Jan Davies knew him because he worked for her husband, and he had actually been doing security at Shore Leave. Jan [Davies]--the great matchmaker of fandom!

What was your introduction to science fiction and fandom?

My introduction to science fiction was *Star Trek*. I did not think of myself as a science fiction fan. I was not into science fiction growing up. I didn't even really watch *Star Trek* first run. I started watching it when I went to college, and it was stripped in the afternoon on channel WTTG-5 out of Washington. We would watch *Star Trek* in the dorm, downstairs in the TV room.

I did see an episode of Star Trek in first run. My friend Cindy came over one day. We had a little folk group--my first group, The Clique. We performed at the coffeehouse in town. We did Peter, Paul, and

Mary numbers and things like that. Anyway, at rehearsal that day, Cindy said, "Well I *have* to see *Star Trek*!" So we watched it. It was "A Piece of the Action" that was my first episode. Spock was saying, "You are an excellent Starship Commander. As a taxi driver, you leave much to be desired." And I thought to myself, "Why don't they know how to drive a car?" Years later I got into it and it made sense.

I got into fandom because I read an article in the *TV Guide*. They used to do yellow pages in the back, newsworthy items, like one line. It mentioned the Star Trek convention in New York City. So my husband and I drove up to that. It was at the old Statler Hilton, and there was a huge line. I remember there was a little girl in front of me who was, like, twelve, and really excited to see DeForest Kelly.

And it was Shatner's first convention, as a matter of fact. I remember very well, he wore navy pants and a maroon sport coat, and he didn't know the episodes. People were very upset with him. I think he studied before he came to another con. We checked our coats in the coat check and went to the costume call, as they were called in the old days. In those days they would take all the seats out of the ballroom, and you would sit on the floor with aisles for the fire marshal.

It was great. Walter Koenig was there. Mason Reese, a child actor, was there. Harlan Ellison was there. I made a friend, and we exchanged addresses and started writing as pen pals. She was from Boston. That August, I went to the first August party, which was an all fan run convention. It was at the University of Maryland in College Park. We went all three days. We liked it so well, we drove back and forth. And they had the famous Gene Roddenberry telephone call. Listening to him on the phone, I choked up--The Great Bird! He was also at the con in New York in 1975, but this was so intimate. Also, one of the things they showed that weekend was the first episode of Space:1999.

[In addition to discovering fandom at conventions] I also had the books, *The Making of Star Trek* and *Star Trek Lives!* Oh, and *The World of Star Trek*. *Star Trek Lives!* talked about fanzines, and that's when I started writing. Writing fan fiction, I mean. I've written all my life. I wrote my first play in the second grade.

But I count my actually being in fandom from June, 1976, when I met Bev.

Beverly Volker and Nancy Kippax, it turned out, were at the [1975] New York convention too, but of course we didn't know each other. I met Bev and Nancy after I went to a convention in DC, and they had a program book that mentioned the Welcommittee and listed zines. That's where I first saw Beverly's name and address.

[Editor's Note: Martha most likely means the 1976 Washington D.C. Schuster Star Trek Convention, held July 9-11, 1976. But that convention occurred after her meeting with Bev Volker. It's most likely that the zine publisher info was also shared in a progress report. Prior to the advent of the Internet, nearly all cons sent out two or three printed progress reports to registered members in advance of the convention weekend.]

Right before July Fourth, I looked in the phone book and got her number and called her on the phone. I called a total stranger and said, "Hello," and I said, "I like Star Trek," and she goes, "Oh, God, they're coming out of the woodwork!" So she invited me over on Saturday night and the rest is history. 6/26/76. They had only been publishing their zine for a year. *Contact* #2 had just come out couple weeks before that, and my first story was in *Contact* #3. Bev and Nancy read my stuff, and, within a few weeks, they had me editing stuff. I was honored.

It was a landmark zine, the first zine devoted exclusively to the friendship between Kirk and Spock. We went to the second August Party, and all of us I walked around with *Contact* in our arms, selling it. We were itinerant zine sellers! It was fun in those days. I talk to a lot of younger fans, and I always say that I'm living proof you don't grow out of this. For some people it's a phase of life and for some people it's a *way* of life. As the saying goes, "FIAWOL: Fandom Is A Way Of Life."

On Working for Starlog Magazine

I think I interviewed everyone *except* William Shatner! *Starlog* sent me to the "Con of Wrath" in Texas. [Editor's Note: Martha is referring to the infamous "Ultimate Fantasy " con, actually the seventh and last Houstoncon, held June 19–20, 1982, at Houston's Summit Hotel.] Leonard [Nimoy] was not there. I interviewed everybody else including Merritt [Buttrick], and Kirstie [Alley], and Nichelle [Nichols] and George [Takei] and Harve [Bennett]. By the time I caught up with him, Shatner was leaving, and I heard him say, "Five minutes, *Starlog*," directed at me. And then he said, "What time is it? What time is it?" and somebody told him. I guess it was five minutes later than he thought. He looked at me and said, "Sorry, *Starlog*."

My friend Gina Godwin and I got to ride in a limo back-and-forth. The cast had a limo driver, because they had the convention hotel and then they had this giant arena where John Denver appeared the next week. It held thousands of people, and there were 200 of us. I don't know if the limo drivers ever got paid, but this limo driver took us back-and-forth too. We rode with Jimmy Doohan, George Takei and Walter Koenig, and the driver called them "Mister Walter," "Mister George," and "Mister Jimmy." This may or may not have made it into my article, but the whole weekend had gone wrong. The actors knew that the fans had paid and didn't get their money's worth. On the last day, we got to the hotel Jimmy and George had their luggage in the trunk. The limousine dilemma driver was going to drop us off at the hotel and head straight for the airport with Jimmy and George. George said, "What time is it?" Of course this was in the days when you didn't have to get to the airport two hours ahead. They said, "You know we don't *have* to be there for another hour. Let's go in to sign some more autographs." Because they wanted to be nice to the fans.

Everybody was so intense in Houston. Jimmy took me aside and said, "Please don't quote some of the things that I've said," and I said, "Jimmy, I'm a fan too. And the fans don't need to hear that and don't *want* to hear that."

Harve Bennett was great that weekend. There was supposed to be a press conference-- just the working press was allowed to be there. But, because of everything that was happening, they let fans in too. And the actors walked in, the press and fans were there, and Harve Bennett took the mike and he said, "As of 8:35 this evening, I am taking command of this ship!" Harve and the actors were like, "The outpouring of love is so great, we're not going to disappoint you guys."

That was the "Ultimate Fantasy" con--the ultimate convention horror story.

I did interview Leonard [Nimoy] one-on-one during that time period, at a St. Louis convention. I was in Leonard's hotel room--alone with him! He was a perfect gentleman of course. I watched him make a martini. He opened the bottle of vermouth over the martini glass, unscrewed the lid--I never saw any vermouth go into the glass--I think he let the aroma *waft* overtop of his martini glass. He liked a *very* dry martini!

They used to call me the human tape recorder. We would stand in line to meet someone or get an autograph after a play, and everybody was so excited they couldn't remember what was said. But I would always retain it all. Still, I did record my interviews. I wasn't videoing--we did not have phones in our pockets with cameras--I had one of those little tape recorders you use as a journalist.

I remember one particular time I interviewed [a Trek actor who shall remain nameless]. *Starlog* editor Dave McDonnell assigned me to do the interview. I asked, "What do you want me to talk to him about?" He just said, "For God's sake, try to make him *not* sound like too much of an idiot!"

On Filking with the Omicron Ceti III

One of my favorite things about my participation in Trek fandom was performing with my filk group, the Omicron Ceti III. I'd been playing guitar for years and started playing around with the John Denver tune "Take Me Home, Country Roads," coming up with some Trek-related lyrics that ended up becoming our signature song, "You're My Home, Enterprise." The original OC3 consisted of my now ex-husband, Rodney Bonds and my song writing partner and friend, Kathy Burns. We first performed on stage at the Bicentennial-10 Convention over Labor Day weekend of 1976 in New York City. We went on to compose many songs that we performed at cons from Baltimore to Philadelphia, to Cleveland, to Toronto to St. Louis. We recorded two albums that were reproduced on vinyl, plus an audio tape of some of our songs and those performed by other filk groups we were friends with. Eventually, the group expanded to include, at various times, Russ Volker, Sr., the late Carolyn Venino and others.

It was a wonderful journey for we fans who weren't professional musicians but developed a following, fellow fans who sang along with our songs when we performed, who awaited our attempts at making an album and who cheered us on every time we got up on a stage or sang late into the night while filking with other fans at various cons.

Nothing will ever equal standing on the New York con stage and seeing Issac Asimov, who was scheduled to follow us on stage that day, take a seat in the front row and start singing along to our funny song, "The Captain and Miss Piggy." We felt like real rock stars.

I wrote stories inspired by Star Trek, I did costumes and worked on cons and produced fanzines, but being able to express my love for Trek through music was one of my most fulfilling ways to be a fan--we sang our hearts out about Kirk and his love for Edith Keeler, about the old country doctor, McCoy and about the deep friendship between Kirk and Spock. All the hours of rehearsing, the awkward attempts at recording in a real studio, the stage nerves, the ups-and-downs--they were all worth it, and I treasure those memories as some of my best times as a hard-core Trek fan.

On your time in Fandom

I have been an organized fandom for 42 years. I count from June, 1976 when I met Bev.

On Influential media

Gateway was my first fanzine in Trek, and it was sort of influenced by *The Twilight Zone* and *The Outer Limits*. I guess you could say I *did* like science fiction [before *Star Trek*], because I was into those. *Starsky and Hutch* in the 80s. I usually spend five to ten years in a fandom, and I never really leave the old ones. I'm not even producing anymore, but I still have a love for it, because of the nostalgia and because of the family that's still there. And then I got into *Alien Nation*, which for me was kind of perfect, because it was cops *and* science fiction. And, for once, all of the Contact Crowd were into the same show again. It was so sad when it got canceled! I was into *The Sentinel*, which also was cops in science-fiction. I dabbled in *Highlander*. I was into *Person of Interest*. And I am currently into *The Walking Dead*. I've always had an interest in dystopian societies. One thing you can say about "Walking Dead," it's pretty dystopian!

As a first-generation Trek fan, what's your opinion on Star Trek vs. Star Wars?

I was there when *Star Wars* happened! I like *Star Wars*. I would not call myself a big *Star Wars* fan. I've not seen the most recent movies. I don't know them by heart. I only went once in the theater to see the original, and the reason for that is we were struggling and hoping to get a movie of *Star Trek* made. *Star Trek: The Motion Picture* came out in 1979. *Star Wars*--the first *Star Wars*--came out in 1977. And I very much resented it, because it took off like it did. There were fans, like costume people, who would enter every costume call in a Trek-inspired costume, suddenly doing all *Star Wars*. People started doing *Star Wars* zines. *Star Wars* and *Starsky and Hutch* were like the second big media fandoms that had a big zine presence. I had been a hardcore Trek fan for about twelve years. I really was bothered by the fact that *Star Wars* was so popular.

It was the first time our fandom had branched off. I understand it more now. I don't hate *Star Wars* because of that all these years later. At the time it bothered me.

You mentioned seeing the first *Star Wars* only once. Was that unusual?

We went to see the *Star Trek* films multiple times and our crowd would go to the premiere showing of every new Trek film. I once called Ian out of Catholic school, so that we could go to the theater for the new showing of the movie, up through First Contract. This is before they started doing the midnight shows, and now the 8 o'clock shows the night before the actual premiere.

We used to do displays at the movie theaters. We would take our memorabilia and they would display it. Then they would let us in to see the film for free. We went and did that for *Star Trek IV* at the theater on York Road--the Yorkridge I think it was called. While we were working on the display cases, the manager said, "We're starting to screen the film to check it for imperfections and things do you guys want to come in?" And we said, "No were still doing your displays."

And so we finished our work, and he came back out, and we said, "Okay we're ready to watch the film." He said, "I've already screened it. I'm running it again." We finally talked him into it; he was not happy with us. But he said from the moment that the Leonard Rosenman theme music started and the credits began and we all started applauding and jumping up and down, he was *so* glad he'd said yes. We were excisted to be seeing the film literally before the public.

Trek was just a big part of our lives. We don't have anything like that anymore it was considered a religious holiday in my family.

Were you a science fiction fan after Star Trek

In a way. For a while, it was just *Star Trek.* my husband had all of the original *Isaac Asimov's Science Fiction Magazines.* He was also a big fan of the *Lord of the Rings,* and, because he talked about them constantly, I refused to read them. I read some CJ Cherryh and some Marion Zimmer Bradley and that kind of thing. I started reading the science fiction that of the rest of our crowd was reading, and I started liking a lot of science fiction movies. Once you're in *Star Trek,* you're pretty much "into it."

Were you into the sequel series?

No I have not watched all of those other series--and I call myself a Star Trek fan!

I was also a into a lot of other fandoms beside *Star Trek* when those shows were airing. I got into *Starsky and Hutch* in a big way. I haven't watched "Discovery" yet.

What jobs have you held it conventions

Volunteers, registration, chairman--I've chaired a few conventions. My biggest regret about being on our convention committees is I never got to meet any actors! I very rarely got any perks. If a group when out to dinner with the actor the night before, well, that was with the actor liaisons. I was never on that part of the committee.

Who have you met a cons that made a lasting impression?

It's funny because I've been in fandom for years, and I often meet people who can't tell their close family or friends what they do. For me, everybody that I know, everybody that I'm close to, I know from fandom. Mary Mills and Michelle Holmes, the Wilsons... When I moved here in '73, I only had made a couple of friends locally. I had a job and I didn't socialize with other teachers. My first real social contacts were with the Contact Crowd. So, to this day everybody that I'm really close to knows that I'm in fandom.

If I were going to pick somebody who made a lasting impression I would say Gina Godwin. [Editor's Note: Gina was a longtime fan, known for her costuming and artwork, who was murdered in 1988] Her loss really informs my life for the last 30 years. I met her at the top of the escalators at the Hunt Valley Inn, and we were so very close. I remember one time Bob Greenberger and Gina and I were sitting at the Paddock bar about 2 o'clock in the morning, having a drink. Bob said he didn't understand K/S [fan fiction in which Kirk and Spock are depicted as lovers--one of the earliest examples of "slash" fiction], and he asked us about it. Gina said, "Well, I've read it. It's not really my thing." And I said, "Bob, you've seen porn films?" He said, "Yeah." I go, "How do like the scenes with the two girls?" Notice I didn't *ask* if there was a scene with two girls. And it was like I could see a light bulb appear above Bob Greenberger's head, and he went, "Ohhhhhh!"

So, let's talk about "Slash."

All of fan fiction, and all of fandom, is based on what wasn't on the screen. We wanted more *Star Trek*, so we wrote it ourselves. In the early days of slash in the 70s, Kirk/Spock was seen as a very equal relationship, rather than a male-female relationship which inherently had a power imbalance in many ways. In slash, you can take two equal partners and explore their relationship, and that's what dragged me into it

I was in an interesting position, being with the *Contact* group--the people who are into the Kirk/Spock friendship, or what might be called *bromance* today. Because we did *Contact*, we also knew the early slash writers. So I straddled that fence. I've been on the side going, "No, I don't see it that way! They're just friends! They have a very deep, abiding spiritual relationship." But then there were all those questions--"What if they were down on a planet and Spock was in *pon far*, and Kirk was the only one there..." Well I could see what they meant.

I also had really good friends who saw it as a definite slash relationship.

And then I got into *Starsky and Hutch,* and I saw the slash. I've often explained this to other people: once you see it, you can't *un*-see it. To this day I don't write K/S, because I don't write Trek anymore. I could've written K/S, because a lot of people would've lapped it up. But I only write what I believe. Once you see it, you can't un-see it, but I don't see it with every two guys.

That part of fandom life lead me to my career as an HIV counselor. Because of the *Star Trek* philosophy of *IDIC* and the openness and the diversity--and welcoming that I diversity--I felt open to that to having gay friends or working with people that were gay. This was 1985 when I started getting involved, and there was no medicine. I was still really heavy into fandom, and, because of that, I couldn't sit by and do nothing. I had to volunteer. I volunteered for H.E.R.O and answered the state hotline for two years. I literally painted the walls! That got me my job at the County for 20 years. You run a convention, you can do things in the private sector. I'm a good editor and writer because I did that for many years. I sell T-shirts now. I do decal work and dye sublimation, and people always ask, "How do you get the decal on the T-shirt straight?" I just eyeball it! I did a lot of layout. I can tell when something looks straight. It's just a thing I can do. I owe that to *Star Trek* fanzines. There was no desktop publishing. We made our fanzines with stone knives and bearskins!

Years ago, in the 90s, I was in a chat room when a girl asked, "What's the difference between print fanzines and online fanzines?" And I said, "Well print zines are *printed*, but there's no such thing as 'it's only good in fanzines and all online is crappy.'"

What is something conventions have given to you that is not available in everyday life?

Every aspect of my life relates to fandom. Conventions *are* my everyday life.

It gives you a sense of belonging, when you didn't belong, If you were a *geek* in those days, and you didn't fit in. Marion McChesney is an example. Marion didn't have much of a social life, but she found her niche in fandom. There are like-minded people at cons. It's the one place I've been when nobody ever judges you by how fat or thin you are, where you went to school, how rich or poor you are, what color you are, or what your education level is. I could be middle-aged and be close friends with somebody who's, 20 because we love the same show.

Also you get an intense friendship very quickly, because you don't talk about mundane things. You don't talk about sports. You don't talk about the weather. You talk about how the Vulcans felt about their planet being blown up. You may not know each other, but these really deep things you talk about get you close very quickly.

On a Favorite Con Memory

I remember meeting [Steve Wilson] on the train to New York to see Leonard Nimoy at a Creation Con. And Gina [Godwin] was on that trip too. And Ian was along. We got a Star Trek trivia game in the dealer's room, and we were playing *Star Trek* Trivial Pursuit, and when it was Ian's turn Gina would make up a question on the level of a five-year-old. She would make up a question so Ian could get the answer right. He thought he was so great! That was such a great trip, and I remember thinking, "That young boy Steve is really nice he's got a lot on the ball!"

What is something that your convention friends and acquaintances don't know about

I'm an open book. I found out in my late 40s that I have ADHD, and I realized that a lot of the stress of a convention for me is due to. that I've been to New York Comic-con as a dealer, but to go and see *The Walking Dead* actors in that kind of a mob scene--I don't think I could deal with that. There's 175,000 people there! God forbid you have to go to the ladies room!

THE INHERITORS

Thalia Eigen, Grace DeWitt, & Nellie Vinograd

(Thalia is the daughter of long-time fans Jonathan and Anna Eigen. The Eigens have brought both Grace and Nellie to conventions with their daughter for many years. All three girls are close friends who appreciate the diversity and unique flavor of conventions.)

On College:

Thalia: I studied Environmental Science and Psychology at the University of Maryland, College Park. I want to save the world! And perhaps get a Master's in Public Policy.

Grace: I studied Animal Science and Studio Art, also at UMD, CP. I want to do museum work.

Nellie: I went to Guilford College and studied Sociology and English. I want to write and help people.

On Growing Up in Fandom:

Thalia: My dad (Jonathan Eigen) didn't bring me along to these things until I was about nine, so it was cool to join this community as I got older and see the deep connections that my parents had made. The older I got actually the more I appreciated the opportunity.

Grace: It felt important. It taught me acceptance and interest in non-conformity. I got to see so many unique people over the years. It's something that spices up life.

Nellie: Discovering fandom felt like finally finding comfort in being a totally passionate person. To see people wholly and sincerely owning and celebrating what they love was foreign to me. It felt freeing to finally discover that as a teenager, I could release myself from insecurities.

On Reading Science Fiction:

Thalia: I'm more into fantasy, George R.R. Martin, and J.R.R. Tolkien.

Grace: I enjoyed young adult sci-fi, but I haven't found the genre as accessible as when I was a kid.

Nellie: I'm more a fan of speculative fiction such as Margaret Atwood and Matthew Tobin Anderson.

On Science Fiction in the Media:

Thalia: Funny enough, I don't think I'm necessarily that into the sci-fi genre. I have always loved the comic book movies and tv shows, and I don't think I get enough of them!

Grace: I gravitate more towards fantasy than sci-fi. I like *Black Mirror*.

Nellie: I watch *Stranger Things, West World, Supernatural, Daredevil* and *Black Mirror*.

On Describing a Convention to Someone Who's Never Been to One:

Thalia: You get together with your friends and spend a weekend listening to and participating in conversations about your favorite tv shows, movies and books that "normies" don't necessarily understand.

Grace: It's an overnight gathering of like-minded enthusiasts, generally celebrating entertainment media through costuming, panels, and conversations.

Nellie: It's a little overwhelming with tons of people, vendors, conversations and very, very friendly chatty people. It's a unique experience.

On the Most Fun Thing They've Done at a Con:

Thalia: I placed in a sword-fighting tourney of champions!

Grace: I placed in a miniature painting contest at GenCon.

Nellie: I met LeVar Burton! I was also an alien in a hilarious masquerade sketch about Old MacDonald.

On the Strangest Experience They've had at a Con:

Thalia: It was when Nellie and I got kicked out of a Geek Ball by pretending to beat up Grace.

Grace: There was bidding for a lunch date with Felicia Day that had gotten to $850. I screamed, "I could buy a refrigerator for that much!" And then the lunch date sold for $2,000.

Nellie: I've gotten into a lot of weird conversations with strangers because they just start talking to you.

On Enjoyable Con Activities:

Thalia: I love the masquerade; it's fun to see the costumes.

Grace: I enjoy perusing the dealers' hall and the art show. I love to support local artisans, and it's a great gift opportunity.

Nellie: I like walking through the book dealers and seeing the authors chattering. I also love the movie previews shown by Bob Greenberger.

On Favorite Con Guests:

Thalia: John Barrowman--he's hilarious and very real.

Grace: Felicia Day- I love when guests have fun and treat it as an opportunity to get to talk about all the crazy stuff that they like.

Nellie: LeVar Burton- He's an exquisite public speaker and seems so genuine and personable with the crowd. And he sang the *Reading Rainbow* theme song!

On the Con Person Who Made a Lasting Impression:

Thalia: Anthony Lemke-We had a great chat, and he was so supportive when I recognized him from his role in *Blue Mountain State*.

Grace: Irene the Tarot Card Reader. She changed my mind about Tarot. Seeing her working with people in such a vulnerable and intimate practice felt special. You could see that she was one of those inspirational people who could somehow fit many lives into her singular life.

Nellie: Marc Okrand. I often think about what an interesting approach he had to linguistics.

On Something People May Not Know About Them:

Thalia: I love to travel, and I am out of town and on the road a lot. However, I have a deep connection to and love living in Maryland, in the DC area, even when I've been gone for a long time.

Grace: One of my dreams is to ride the Trans-Siberian Express through Russia. New people and new places are the core to my creativity, and, therefore, help me to better know myself.

Nellie: I come off as very polite and friendly, but I actually think of myself as very shy and introverted. It takes a lot of energy for me to socialize and meet new people, even if it doesn't seem that way.

Llyssa Holmgren

On Her Real Life Job:

I have two jobs that I do in "real life." The first is what I call "the day job," which is working for a retailer for Verizon Wireless. The other is running my own face-painting business called "Oh My Face Painting." I've been doing that for about five years now, and it's the best job I've ever had. I am working on becoming a full-time face-painter again.

On Her Personal History:

My life began during a blizzard in early February. (I've actually had people *blame* me for the Farpoint "snow cons"--Farpoint is my birthday weekend and so it must snow.) I was born in Baltimore and moved to the Lower Eastern Shore when I was three, but I moved back to Baltimore two weeks after I graduated high school. Baltimore has always been my answer to "Where are you from?" or, "Where's home?" I have always been a bit eccentric, which I guess is mostly considered "normal" by our crowd, but I loved making my own clothes and costumes as a kid and a teen. I also learned to play D&D when I was ten and somehow was able to convince my mom to drive us kids up to a local gaming store every weekend, so I could play. Our family vacation was always planned around Shore Leave, which meant time with my closest friends.

On Her Introduction to Fandom and Conventions:

How was I introduced to fandom and conventions? I was born into it, literally. My father, Bill, was one of the founding members of STAT and Shore Leave (at only 17 years old!), and he and my mom met at a con. They had a wedding ceremony during Shore Leave 8, and my siblings, my daughter, and I were all baptized in the Temple of Trek during our first Shore Leave. So, I've literally been in fandom since I was born (1988).

On Her Convention Connection:

I sort of fell into becoming synonymous with local cons by accident. For the first 18 years of my life, the only convention I attended regularly was Shore Leave. After graduating high school and moving back to Baltimore, I decided I wanted to go to a few other cons I had heard about but was never able to attend. In that first year I went to Horrorfind, NostalgiaCon, Baltimore Comic-Con, MythicFaire, Farpoint, and Balticon. I had so much fun that I kept going, and now I attend between eight and eighteen conventions and festivals a year, depending on when they are and if I have time off from the day job. After a few years of this cycle, people who would see me at numerous events might forget my name but always refer to me with, "Hey, you're that convention girl aren't you?" I mentioned this one day during a STAT meeting, and our web guy said that would make a great online handle. Lo and behold it was available on every platform! My Facebook is closing in on 2K followers, and I'm slowly but surely building on Instagram and Twitter; I have started working on a few new YouTube series as well. I tend to staff most of the cons I go to, but I've been lucky enough to also be on a few panels as well, and I love it! I just submitted to be a guest at RavenCon, where I have never attended, but would love to be a panelist.

On *Star Trek*:

Star Trek has always had a huge influence on my life, both in and out of fandom. The phrase, "Everything I know in life I learned from *Star Trek*," is quite relevant to me. One thing that always stuck with me was being smart enough to trust the opinion of someone more knowledgeable than you. Janeway never hesitated to ask her crew for their thoughts on matters unfamiliar to her. Picard re-enforced the lesson of staying calm during a crisis until the crisis was over, something my Dad taught me.

On Con Jobs:

Oh, Lord! What jobs have I held? Let's see, of course I started out as a lowly gofer, but I've worked as the art show chair for Shore Leave. I was the volunteer coordinator for both the Maryland Faerie Festive and the Baltimore Faerie Faire for a number of years. At Balticon, I ran the staff den for a few years, and for four glorious years I worked with Onezumi Events for ReGeneration Who, Intervention, and PotterVerseCon, as personal assistant to Con Chair Oni Durant. Those were just jobs with official titles. I've also had my hand in with guest liaison, programming, logistics, and operations. In fact, the only department I haven't spent much time in is tech. I've been banned from working tech, however, as electronics tend to break down and stop working when I try to help out.

On Being a Younger Fan:

Being a younger person amongst older fans definitely had its challenges. Like I had mentioned earlier, I learned D&D when I was ten, because my dad would play several hours of it during Shore Leave; and I always wanted to be a part of whatever he was doing. He was also the youngest person in the group, at age 36, which meant that I was joining a party of much older men who had little patience for ten year-old me. Thankfully, my uncle Jim was running the game, so everyone put up with me, although it was rough. As far as friends my own age, there were seven of us "STAT kids" that kept a pretty tight clique, until we reached our teenage years. That's when I met the rest of the kids who would help make up the group of "Scoobies" as we were known throughout Shore Leave. Those were some of the tightest bonds I've ever made with people, and they are very much my chosen family.

On Ideas for Improving the Cons:

Honestly? I'd ask more *youth* what they want to see at the cons. Today's youth are children of the Internet. Online content is where it's at--web comic artists, YouTubers, online fan films--those are the next step in keeping these long-standing cons around, alive, and thriving. Guest lists that include more Netflix and HBOGo stars, too. I'm not saying get rid of everything that has built the con up, just tweak things a bit. Otherwise I see many long-standing, local events not lasting much longer, sad to say.

On Masquerade:

I've been in several group masquerade projects during my teen and adult years, but I think my favorite costume I ever did was when I was 18 and entered in the adult categories by myself. Because of all the group projects I had done, I had always been entered in the adult category. After winning three adult awards, you have to enter as a master, even if all your wins were with a group, and you later enter as an individual. I had been working on this one dress for *months*. The premise was that the Reigning Monarch from Pluto was visiting Earth in an attempt to regain Planetary Status. It was gorgeous and took ages to make. This was the first year Thomas Aktinson was running Masquerade and had also designed the trophies. When he showed STAT the prototype, I told him I was entering masquerade, and that I intended to win every single award. I, in fact, won "Most Beautiful Costume." I was thrilled. Afterwards, I ran over to Thomas screaming "Uncle Tom! Uncle Tom! Look, I told you I'd win one of your awards!" and this woman who hadn't even *entered* masquerade threw a fit about nepotism. She demanded that I be stripped of all my awards and banned from any future masquerades. Thankfully, that didn't end up happening, but I went from being on Cloud Nine to spending the next hour in absolute tears over the idea of never being able to compete again. Since then, most of my costuming energy has been spent making things for my kid.

On Raising a Child in Fandom:

Raising a child in fandom has been so amazing! Munchkin is such a great kid and is like a lot of kids raised in fandom who have always been super-advanced for their age. One of the best moments of that was during her three-year well check. We had to do a development test while in the waiting room, and I asked her, "What is a ball?" Her response killed me. "It's a big party with dancing and costumes and music and lights." Well child, you're not wrong! The downside to that is that sometimes you forget that she's still just a kid. Children like her are so smart and so mature that, when you let them out in the world, sometimes you forget they really don't have the life experiences yet.

On Future Con Involvement:

I will *definitely* be a lifelong con-goer. Conventions are such an integral part of my life that I honestly can't image cutting them out completely. In 2018, I became overwhelmed with other things in my life, and I did seriously cut back on cons, but I could never give them up completely. In fact, I have been repeatedly asked when I'm starting my own convention. I actually have a few ideas, but there have been some first-year horror stories out there recently, and I'm so afraid that would make people shy away. I'd love to have something similar to VidCon but with a Shore Leave-sized feel to it.

On Her Favorite Con Activities:

Large-group programs, like Ten Forward and karaoke, are some of my favorites, because, when I'm not staffing, I want to spend as much time as possible with all of my people. I also enjoy more niche panels, with round-table discussions to get the attendees involved. They give everyone a chance to discover something new. I've been on a few panel discussions, and my absolute favorite has been "Growing Up in Fandom." I think part of its popularity came from adults who were starting to raise their own children in fandom and wanted assurance that their kids would eventually find their feet in the community the adults loved so dearly.

On Guest Stars:

I think my favorite con guest has to be Michael Welch. In 2004, Michael came to Shore Leave, and, being a teen of the same age, he ended up spending quite a bit of time with a portion of "The Scoobies" that weekend. Well, in 2014, he came back for another Shore Leave; and, of course, we had to hang out reunion-style. We'd both spend the day hours working (he as a guest, I in the Art Show), but, during the night, we'd all hang out as a group in one area of the hotel or the other, playing games, swapping stories, and just hanging out as young adults. It was for sure a work-hard/play-hard weekend. The best part? After Mike left our Sunday night room party, he sent a friend of mine back to my room with an autograph and heartfelt note about all the great times we had between the two cons. I don't collect many autographs, but that one is among my favorites.

On Reasons for Attending Maryland Cons:

I mostly attend Maryland conventions because I can stay close to home without sacrificing content or enjoyment. I *could* spend thousands of dollars on travel and hotel for DragonCon, and while it would be a heck of an experience, and I totally plan to go someday, that, for me, is like a trip to Disney--once in a lifetime. Maryland cons I can day-trip to (if I can't get time off from work for the whole weekend), or commute from home if really necessary. They also have a more family feel to them, I've gone to AwesomeCon the last few years, and, while I *loved* it, I was nostalgic for the smaller con feel. No way you're gonna be able to sit with Michael Dorn at the bar during a con with 20,000 attendees. My best con stories are from the smaller events where the guests could relax a bit. Devon Murray at PotterVerse One had my sides splitting all weekend!

On What People May Not Know About Her:

Something that even my convention friends don't know about me? That's tough, because I'm pretty open and honest about myself and my life. Maybe how hard I get hit by Imposter Syndrome? Even doing this interview, I feel like, "Why the *heck* would Diane ask *me* to be a part of this project??" Even with the evidence in right in front of me--what I've accomplished over the years--I feel like it's been embellished by other people, and that, no, I really didn't do these things. I've been slowly working on it the last few years and a moment like this, being asked to be a part of such an amazing project with such wonderful, accomplished people, reminds me that what I've done matters. That working behind the scenes, building up these local events, has given so many people such amazing experiences! It really gives me the motivation to keep going, and hopefully one day run my own Maryland convention.

Ethan Wilson, Christian Wilson, & Jessica Headlee

On When They Realized That They Are a Part of a Fandom Family:

Ethan: I don't know that there's just a single moment for me. It's been a part of my life for as long as I can remember, so I personally didn't have much of a moment of awareness. I think I had sort of a soft realization when I started introducing my non-fandom friends to the convention scene. I recall a particular incident, exiting a movie theater with a friend. Someone from a con recognized me from across the parking lot and called out my name. It was a little bit like an episode of *Cheers*, but I never really noticed until someone else pointed it out to me.

Christian: This might seem strange, fandom being my bread and water for my whole existence, but it wasn't until just a few months ago. I had come down to the technical booth, looking for a television for the game room at Farpoint, and I was explaining what I needed; and they all stared at me wide-eyed and with jaws dropped. When I asked what the deal was, they told me, "You are so like your dad!" I have a great relationship with my dad, and I know that people around these conventions love him; so to know that people saw even a glimpse of him in me was the watershed moment, albeit later than I might've first thought.

Jessica: I don't know if there ever was "a moment." It sort of snuck up on me, I guess. Some people know me as Ethan Wilson's girlfriend, but that wasn't when I felt like I was a part of "The Fandom Family." I think it might've been when I realized that strangers knew me by my job or actions at the con. When, ten years after I started working at the cons, I had people come up to me and say that they remembered when I wasn't tall enough to be seen over the crowd in a panel, that they could only see my scrawny arms hold up the stop sign. Maybe that's when it clicked that people remembered me year after year, even if we had never officially met. Or when they would go up to my parents, who are fairly new to conventions, and tell them stories about the things I did.

On Having Parents in Fandom:

Ethan: It's given me a different perspective on con-going, I think. From an early age, I've been on the back-end of things. I don't think I just attended a con as a straight attendee until I was in my teens, and it was a rather surreal experience. I actually found myself getting a little restless and being a little lost about what to do. I just don't think I know how to enjoy a con that I'm not working.

Christian: Daunting. They say you can only remember 150 people at one time. When I see my parents interact with the regular con-goers I think "How in the world do you *do* it?" I couldn't and still can't see myself knowing these people as well as they do. But, while I may not know names and may waver with faces, being held up in front of a sea of love and called, "The new generation of fandom" makes me nothing but warm and touched. Because, for almost 20 years, I've been instantly accepted and cared for. It's like being born into a big family which, in this instance, has a couple hundred cousins.

Jessica: My parents don't actually work at conventions. Sometimes my dad helps out by doing odd little jobs for people. My mom mostly attends conventions as an author, trying to sell her books. No, the family member that I have to be like at the conventions is my Aunt Karen, and, honestly, there's no real pressure to be anything but myself. Some of you may know her as one of the "Wonder Twins" who auction off unique items for charity, or the fun-sized woman backstage who never stops going and knows how to use her cane. Sure, I want to do my best because I do work for her, but she trusts in my ability to get the job done and she's done that since I was eleven years old. So, I guess it's not so bad having a family member that's so involved in fandom, especially since I get to hear all sorts of cool stories about her from her younger days.

On the Freedom to Roam the Cons:

Ethan: For me, the hotel became a second home. I've always felt very comfortable just wandering from place to place. With that said, I think "total freedom" is sort of relative. The more familial aspect of the conventions meant I always felt a bit like someone was keeping an eye on me.

Christian: There were so many opportunities to leave the hotel and yet I never really did. With all this connectivity via social media, it's awesome to get all your friends in one place and just stay there for a couple of days and get away from your phone. That said, I always loved Friday and Saturday nights. Usually a bunch of friends find a corner and talk, roaming wherever it's quiet until we hear people sing, and then we get up and or dance like hell. I guess that's why I don't overly fancy these huge mega-cons. It's super-tough finding a quiet spot to just chill with your close con family.

Jessica: As a child I actually roamed the hotel the most after the convention was over. Sure, I ran all over the place doing my job, and a bunch of other little odd tasks for people, but I didn't really hang around anyone until I was older. But the most interesting times in the hotel were definitely during the quieter times, because I got to see a lot of the aftermath of late night shenanigans, or after the con was over. When everything was packed up and most of the people were gone, it was almost like walking through a deserted area. Everything would be so quiet compared to the cacophony of sound played by so many people in a limited space. It was eerie and almost magical, like witnessing Cinderella's carriage turn back into a pumpkin. In many ways that was what it was, my grand ball experience was the convention, and Sunday night was few moments after the stroke of midnight.

On Collecting:

Ethan: I collect action figures and comics primarily. The action figures definitely are my main focus. At last count, my collection contains over 4500 unique pieces. I've even started writing about them on a daily basis, at my site The Figure in Question.

Christian: I'm big on retro video games. I have about 50 individual systems, from Atari to Xbox, with over 500 games. On a college budget, my collecting takes a hit, but refraining from buying really helps me appreciate the culture and fandom way more when I'm not worried about the physical media.

Jessica: For the longest time I denied that I collected books. I'm an avid reader but my collection of books was rather small growing up, because the closest bookstore was over an hour away. That's what happens when you live in the boonies of Virginia. Then I moved off to college and was within 20 minutes of a bookstore--my poor wallet never knew what hit it. Now my shelves are spilling over with books from every genre. Most of them are from various big name bookstores, others are from independently owned ones, and a growing number of them actually come from the conventions that I go to and the authors that attend them. I have comics that are piling up (thank you Ethan) and entire series of Manga that I might've read online first but then bought the US-released volumes. I even started a book blog so that I can review all the books that I buy and the ones that self-published authors ask me to review!

On Becoming Future Con Chairs:

Ethan: I feel that's the natural progression of things, the way they are now. It's less a desire, I think, and more a general lifestyle. It's just what I know, and it's a role in which I'm pretty comfortable. That said, I'm not trying to push anyone out the door just yet.

Christian: I'm in a transition stage of my life. Balancing the conventions and college is stressful, and, right now, I can hardly manage being on top of my own class schedule. But I agree, it seems like these things are passed down whether you think you're ready or not. Having an "in" with my parents who have run these cons shows me that each year they aren't 100% on what they're doing either! Yet because of the fluid and flexible nature of these things, combined with their years of experience and expertise, the cons manage to go as smoothly as can be. I hope I can accomplish that someday.

Jessica: I don't think that was ever really a question for me, I've just always assumed that I would eventually step into that kind of role. Not saying that I want to push anyone out, and, if there's someone more qualified, then they can have it. However, if I was ever asked if I wanted to receive the torch, so to speak, and help carry it into the future, then I would do it to the best of my ability. Small, homey, conventions are a lot of fun, and I want to make sure that they can continue brining all sorts of people together, creating families for those who feel like they don't belong anywhere else.

On Ideas for Changing the Cons:

Ethan: I think the biggest thing I would change is just making sure we don't get too complacent and set in our ways. The cons are at their best when they're more fluid and free-form, or at least more friendly. I think there's some still some residual "Well, this is the way things are done" mentality that crops up from time to time. I think a focus on the younger generations is essential moving forward.

Christian: Mimicking my brother, I think shaking things up every so often is a great way to keep a con fresh. Like when you reorganize the furniture in your home or put up new decorations; a convention works best when it's modular and fluid. I never want to reach into an old crusty plastic bin for "the usual plans," or find myself in an episode of *Pinky and the Brain:*

"What are we doing for this year's convention?"

"Same thing we do every year."

Jessica: Is there more to add for this question? I feel like the boys have said it well enough, but I'll use a science metaphor. Okay, picture the conventions as a species. In nature, if a species lacks the ability to adapt to the changing surroundings, then natural selection eventually weeds it out, like woolly mammoths or marine sloths. Side note: you should totally check out pre-historic marine sloths because they're super cool to read about! Anyways, so if conventions are not open to the possibility for change, especially with the ever-evolving world of fandom, then eventually people will stop going and these kinds of conventions will disappear. So, conventions need to have the ability to adapt to how people enjoy their fandom, whether through video games, animation, cosplay, etc.

Also, for those who do know me, yes this was an excuse to talk about marine sloths. I freaking love sloths in general, and marine sloths are like the next level. Also, fun fact, sloths can move three times faster in the water than they do on land. And you know those big curved claws? Yeah, those were inherited from their extinct marine cousins.

On the Craziest Thing Seen at a Con:

Ethan: Klingon Stormtroopers in tutus and tiaras. Hard to top that, I think.

Christian: I played a game of hand ninja with roughly 30 people for about three hours, uninterrupted.

Jessica: So, one year I dressed up as a steampunk version of the White Rabbit, and I was roped into giving away stuffed bunnies to the Shore Leave guests of 2015. One of those guests was John Barrowman from *Doctor Who*. In the span of about five minutes, I saw my aunt Karen pose to smack him in the butt with her cane (I still have that picture too) and I was faltered by the man when he joked about taking me home. I will never forget those few moments on stage, especially since there are videos of the experience on YouTube somewhere.

On How Fandom Gives Happiness:

Ethan: The general inclusiveness. I like that it doesn't really matter who you are out in the "real world," that when we all get together, we have our common interests to unite us and keep us going. There's some great stuff that comes of that.

Jessica: Fandom isn't perfect. Sometimes it frustrates us and makes us question why we still try to be a part of it. But I think what I love most about fandom is just how passionate people can get with it. From fanart to cosplayers, I love seeing how people express their enthusiasm and passion for their fandoms. And it makes me happy to see all these people, who may be misfits, social pariahs, or the most popular kids on the block, come together because of common interests and shared enthusiasm. I can't begin to describe how happy it makes me when I see very different people talk and laugh and "geek out" about something that they all love. To see people who might be really shy in real life just glow under the ringing endorsements from other fans about their cosplays, fanfiction, fanart, etc. It really makes you feel like you're part of a community that's made from the best intentions. Sure, sometimes we lose sight of those things when politics and such get in the way; but, at the end of the day we realize that we're so much more, especially to each other.

On Being a Stage Ninja for the Masquerades:

Ethan: It's exhausting, to be sure. It can feel thankless at times, but then inevitably, there's some costumer who comes along and goes out of their way to make you feel appreciated. And once the mask goes on and you're out on the stage, it's quite exhilarating. It's a nice outlet for goofiness.

Christian: It goes by so fast it's like I was never even there!

Jessica: Even with a mask, I feel like I'm overly exposed to everyone. I'm terrible at improv and I can get terrible stage fright, even when I have no lines to speak. But the experience, in the end, is always worth it. Even if we're overlooked amidst inflated egos, people still laugh at our on-the-spot miming, and the participants always appreciate when we can add a bit of flare to their acts.

On Current Con Jobs:

Ethan: For Farpoint, I'm running the Con Suite and co-running the charity auctions. I've had the Con Suite for a decade now, so it's become second nature for me. Charity auctions, I've just taken over this year, so I'm excited to see how that goes.

Christian: I am the social media manager/webmaster for Farpoint. I also run a video game corner inside the Con suite with Ethan.

Jessica: I'm a time-keeper at both Farpoint and Shore Leave. Some of you may have seen me frantically rushing down hallways and taking stairs two at a time while carrying a laminated sign. For those who don't know, my job entails me telling program guests when they have five minutes left of their panel and when to stop talking so the next group can come in and set up. It's normally a fairly easy job that can go unappreciated by some, but there's also a small satisfaction in telling some bigwigs in the fandom (not like big name guests, but, like, authors and such) to shut up and move on--and I mean it with the utmost respect! I also help Ethan with the Con Suite when I can at Farpoint; mostly I make sure nothing blows up and kids don't hang from the ceiling like Peter Porker. And, on occasions, I act as a sounding board for possible Wonder Twins' ideas for puny charity items.

On a Person Met at a Con who Made a Lasting Impression:

Ethan: Jess. We met at a Shore Leave five years ago and started datng a few months after that. That's been pretty big for me.

Christian: Felicia Day. She gave me her chocolates and actually seemed happy to be at our small little con.

Jessica: I've met so many people that have impacted my life so much, even if it's only a few days every year, that I miss them when they don't come. But the one person who has really made an impact on my life is my future husband, Ethan. We met at just the right time. Neither of us was really looking for a serious relationship, just a friend to talk to and connect with in a way others were failing to do in our lives then. I'll never forget being introduced to him in my pajamas--him a little fueled by liquid courage--and spending the next night dancing in a corner of the dance floor like the shy, awkward people that we were.

On Favorite Movies and TV Shows:

Ethan: *Aliens* is my all-time favorite movie, hands down. After that, the list gets a little nebulous. I'm a big fan of the current crop of Marvel movies, though, as well as most of the *Star Wars* films. TV is an even more nebulous answer.

Christian: When it comes to my favorites, I'm surprisingly not as nerdy as I thought. My top three movies are *The Breakfast Club*, *Yellow Submarine*, and *Inglorious Basterds*. Obviously, I love *Star Wars* and the MCU, but I think what captures my attention most in all of my top three are their own unique cultures and time periods. So, you may not see any of those as typical sci-fi/fantasy, but I love them for the same reasons a fan loves *Star Trek*. I love their world, whether as real as *The Breakfast Club* or psychedelic like *Yellow Submarine*, and I geek out about them. They in just their being fascinate me and inspire my creativity.

Jessica: Diane, I don't think you're being paid by the word or page so I'm gonna keep the list as brief as I can. For movies, I really enjoy Studio Ghibli and Marvel films. I would watch *Ponyo* and *Howl's Moving Castle* everyday if I could, especially the dubbed version of *Ponyo*. I get a weird kind of joy from listening to Liam Neeson lose control of his children. I'm also really in love with the *Star Wars* films, and I won't even start the discussion on which ones are better. For TV shows, oh boy, that list can go on forever! Though I will say that a lot of my favorites are animated, like *Steven Universe* or *RWBY*. I'm also a huge anime fan, if you haven't guessed already.

On What Makes Maryland Cons so Popular:

Ethan: I don't know. Heart? I think the cons here are just very genuine, and not purely about cashing in on anything. We really focus on building a community.

Christian: I see only a handful of these people more than two times a year, and those two times are at the two cons I go to. Being able to have almost an equally meaningful friendship with someone I see every day to someone I see six days out of the year is hard-to-describe sweet.

Jessica: I honestly don't know because I haven't really been to many cons outside of the Baltimore, MD area. I've been to one each in West Virginia, Virginia, and New Jersey. Those cons were either just starting up or ones that have been around for a while, but I will say that they all felt kind of subdued compared to the ones I've been to in MD. I'm not talking about guest or panel-wise, it was almost as if it was treated like a quiet affair whereas the ones in Maryland have been loud and energetic by comparison. I guess the cons in Maryland, even if they have a lot of the same age demographics as other cons, are more lively because it's a larger creative outlet than other conventions in neighboring states.

On Career Interests:

Ethan: I can honestly say I don't really know. By day I'm in IT, but I can't say that's where I want to be long-term. I think I see myself running a toy store or the like, but I'm not sure that's all that much outside of fandom. I certainly do like writing about toys, though.

Christian: I'm an Acting major with two minors in Deaf Studies in Astronomy. I'm really trying to keep my bases covered. They all link back to fandom. I love to perform because I meet performers and working these cons is like doing a show. I love learning sign language and learning about deaf culture because Farpoint and the like take great strides in including deaf people in almost every panel and talk because we care that much. Astronomy is another one of my passions because, well, how many astronomers got their start because they love *Star Wars* or *Star Trek*? Fandom and science fiction inspire us to look forward and beyond for what lies in store for the human experience. I hope to find a career where I can incorporate these three things and one day give proper thanks to the family that raised me.

Jessica: I've known what I wanted to do since I was in elementary school, and I was only encouraged more by my stubbornness when I was told (by a community college representative) that I would only grow up to study people's drinking water. With the support of my family and the people closest to me, and my childhood dream, I got a degree in Marine Science with a focus in biology and conservation. I want to study coral and help to find ways to conserve the reefs so that my grandchildren will see them in the same awe-inspiring way that I did when I was a child. And, somewhere along the way, I want to help inspire other people to get interested in science too. Not everyone can be a labcoat-wearing experimenter, but even the most average person can find ways to help further the pursuit of knowledge in science.

On Final Words:

Ethan: For me, fandom's always been a way of life. I genuinely don't know where I'd be without it, and I've met some truly amazing people along the way.

Christian: I'm sure than in another 18 years, this family will make me feel like I'm a part of them in a way I'd not thought possible. Life has its ups and downs, and I'm happy fandom will always be here when I need it most.

Jessica: Sloths are pretty cool creatures and so are cuttlefish, especially flamboyant cuttlefish, which is the smallest cuttlefish species and is high poisonous—its muscles contain an unknown toxin that has no known antidote and will kill anything that consumes it. Oh, were we supposed to have last words about fandom? Oops.

I would have never gotten into conventions if it weren't for my aunt Karen, and by extension I would've never found the love of my life either. It's oddly terrifying wondering what life would've been like if I'd never decided to help out as a kid. I'm happy that I did though, even if some of the experiences were less-than-stellar and some of the people weren't the best examples found in the community; because I've been able to make so many happy memories and meet so many fantastic people. What would your life have been like without getting this involved in fandom?

www.ingramcontent.com/pod-product-compliance
Lightning Source LLC
Chambersburg PA
CBHW031427160426
43195CB00010BB/641